The Search Conference

The Search Conference

A Powerful Method for Planning Organizational Change and Community Action

Merrelyn Emery

Ronald E. Purser

Epilogue by Fred Emery

Jossey-Bass Publishers • San Francisco

Substantial discounts on bulk quantities of Jossey-Bass books are available to corporations, professional associations, and other organizations. For details and discount information, contact the special sales department at Jossey-Bass Inc., Publishers (415) 433–1740; Fax (800) 605–2665.

For sales outside the United States, please contact your local Simon & Schuster International office.

Manufactured in the United States of America on Lyons Falls Pathfinder Tradebook. This paper is acid-free and 100 percent totally chlorine-free.

Library of Congress Cataloging-in-Publication Data

Emery, Merrelyn.
  The search conference : a powerful method for planning organizational change and community action / Merrelyn Emery, Ronald E. Purser ; epilogue by Fred Emery. — 1st ed.
    p.   cm. — (The Jossey-Bass public administration series)
  Includes bibliographical references and index.
  ISBN 0-7879-0192-X (cloth : acid-free paper)
  1. Organizational change—Planning. 2. Strategic planning—Employee participation. I. Purser, Ronald E., date.
  II. Title. III. Series.
  HD58.8.E463 1996
  658.4'012—dc20   96-9960
                                                               CIP

FIRST EDITION
HB Printing   10 9 8 7 6 5 4 3 2 1

Contents

Preface

Here at the end of the twentieth century, most people recognize that the world has been undergoing rapid and discontinuous change. The social environment has become as turbulent as the weather, and traditional approaches to planning have proven ineffective for mobilizing large groups of people to take responsibility for their collective futures. Successful planning in turbulent environments requires collective learning about where we want to go, where we are now, and the strategic goals that, if implemented, seem most likely to achieve the desired future state. For this to happen, planning in organizations and communities must be done *by the people, for the people, and with the people.*

For many years, however, planning has been in the hands of an elite few—managers, technical experts, bureaucrats, social engineers. There were those who did the long-term strategic thinking for the firm, community, or agency, and then there were those who were expected to carry out and implement the plan. However, even under the best of conditions, this form of traditional planning often fell flat on its face. There are countless cases where a great deal of time, money, and energy has been wasted planning for a future that never came to pass.

We are now confronted with a dilemma of needing to plan for our future in the face of decreasing knowledge, in environments where people are drifting apart. It seems like a paradox: the more society changes, the more we need to plan, but the knowledge we need keeps receding from view. But perhaps this is because we have been looking for knowledge in the wrong places—and for the wrong sort of knowledge. Typically, we have turned to experts to do the planning for us, or an elite few have legitimized their right to impose their plans upon us without our consent or participation. In either case, we have a situation where the few have been planning the future for the many. The result has been myopic vision, alienation, and a loss of confidence in the social fabric of our institutions. If we are to resolve these dilemmas, we will have to ask whether what we call expert knowledge is the kind of knowledge required for planning in a turbulent social environment. We think there is great room for doubt.

The solution to this puzzle has never been far away—the link to creating a desirable future for any system lies in the hearts and minds of the people who live in that system. All that is needed is to democratize the planning process, that is, to develop a participative planning method where all people are experts in their own right. Search conferencing offers just such a methodology; it has been under development for over thirty-five years, and is now sufficiently polished to be used whenever there is a need for long-term planning.

As currently defined, a Search Conference brings together from twenty to thirty-five people who work together as a group to develop strategic plans for a system they share. This system can be a corporation, a geographic region, an organization or association of any kind; if the sponsors find people for the conference from all the areas needed to make the system work, the conference managers can help them develop a living community based on participative democracy. Search conferencing reliably results in action-based strategies that participants freely commit themselves to implementing, because the approach keys into human aspirations for healthy, responsive, and effective social interactions. The popularity of the Search Conference method in North America is steadily increasing in a variety of planning and policy-making contexts. Search Conferences have been used for such purposes as:

- Setting new policies for governing institutions
- Development of systemwide plans for reinventing government
- Corporate strategic planning meetings
- Organizational renewal efforts
- Mergers of companies and hospitals
- Community-based planning and development
- Planning the future of cities, regions, industries, and professional associations
- Managing conflict among contentious parties and diverse interest groups in the public sector

- Creating strategic alliances between organizations or networks
- Developing long-term partnerships with customers, suppliers, or government regulators

Why a Book on the Search Conference?

We saw several compelling reasons and emerging needs for this book. First, the field was in need of a systematic, conceptual understanding of the Search Conference methodology. Although search conferencing is a highly flexible planning tool, its application requires a secure grasp of the principles, theoretical framework, and behavioral science research that undergird the method. Designing and managing successful Search Conferences requires more than a passing familiarity with the agenda, tasks, and external features of the method. Understanding the conceptual foundations, in our opinion, is a prerequisite to becoming a competent and qualified Search Conference manager. Therefore, we wanted to provide a sound theoretical framework for educating both aspiring and experienced Search Conference practitioners.

We also felt that professionals are in need of an original sourcebook on the Search Conference. The Search Conference methodology has evolved over the years since Fred Emery and Eric Trist reported on the Barford Conference—the original Search Conference—in 1960. Merrelyn Emery's report on the field was published in Australia, and was not easily accessible to professionals on other continents. In addition, her work was directed primarily to social scientists, which made it seem less useful to practitioners wanting to learn more about the application of the Search Conference method. Fred and Merrelyn Emery have been offering training in Search Conference management to U.S. practitioners since 1993, and comments from seminar participants made it clear there was a need for a reference on the theory and practice of Search Conferences.

For these reasons, our intent was to provide an up-to-date, comprehensive, and lucid exposition of both the theory and practice of search conferencing, so that professionals in different fields could understand its deeper significance and versatility for empowering people in organizations and communities. We hope that this book will help to establish a firm foundation for conducting successful Search Conferences in North America.

Who Should Read This Book?

Because search conferencing—and the topic of participative strategic planning in general—has relevance to a variety of organizations and communities, we have written this book for a broad audience. Academic jargon is kept to a minimum, without sacrificing the depth of the original theoretical principles derived from research in the applied behavioral sciences. The theories, methods, and cases covered are important not only to academics and consultants but to all who are concerned about finding more effective ways for future planning with communities, organizations, and governmental institutions.

Public administrators, government officials, managers, employees, community leaders—in short, anyone interested in participative approaches to strategic planning and community development—should find this book a valuable resource guide for understanding how and why Search Conferences work. Many readers will use this book to acquire an in-depth understanding of the Search Conference method. Practitioners seeking to learn more about the Search Conference method should also find this to be a valuable reference and handbook. Organization development consultants will find the detailed instructions for planning, designing, and managing a Search Conference particularly useful.

If you are considering the possibility of sponsoring a Search Conference, or are in the process of organizing one, this book will be quite helpful. The numerous case studies and examples of actual conferences provide road maps for those who simply want to know more about how Search Conferences have been conducted for corporations, government institutions, and communities. In addition, researchers and socially engaged social scientists should find this book to be a useful reference on the conceptual underpinnings of the method. And any class on organization or community development should find it a valuable textbook.

Overview of the Contents

Chapter One introduces the Search Conference method, describing what happens in a conference as well as the results and outcomes that can be expected once the conference is over. The chapter explains why search conferencing is an effective approach to planning given the increasing amount of social turbulence in the world. This chapter emphasizes the importance of the Search Conference method as a process whereby communities and organizations can tap the highest aspirations of their members as they go about planning for the future. It also presents the authors' values, assumptions, and philosophy about people, underscoring the way ideal-seeking behavior helps people discover common ground.

Chapter Two highlights several examples of Search Conferences that were successfully conducted for a variety of purposes. These vignettes illustrate the utility and versatility of the method. The benefits of using the Search Conference approach are also outlined here. This chapter introduces the core theoretical principles that undergird the Search Conference method. It also provides an overview of three major phases that constitute the design of a Search Conference event.

Chapter Three explores the shift from a stable to a turbulent environment. It examines why planning methods that worked well in the past are ineffective for dealing with the type of environment that organizations and communities currently face. The dilemmas and shortcomings of expert-driven planning are reviewed in light of the challenges of planning in a turbulent environment. Search Conferences are often used an alternative to expert-driven planning, but this does not preclude experts from participating in such conferences. As a case in point, the last section of the chapter describes a Search Conference where water experts made real progress toward resolving a regional conflict over water resources on the Colorado Front Range.

Chapter Four reviews open systems theory, which provides the underlying framework for Search Conference design. This chapter also stresses the importance of defining the system properly, so that the right participants attend the Search Conference. The discussion then turns to the importance of human ideals to the planning process. Shared human ideals that emerge in the Search Conference help to provide the conditions for finding common ground. These conditions for finding common ground are compared to a modern-day equivalent of barn raising, where people with diverse backgrounds and values can find enough commonality to work creatively and collaboratively toward a shared purpose.

The first half of Chapter Five looks at the differences between bureaucratic and democratic design principles—the former being used to structure traditional conferences, and the latter to structure Search Conferences. The democratic structure of the Search Conference places responsibility for the control of planning processes squarely in the hands of participants. It is a forum for practicing and learning citizenship behaviors—those dispositions and habits necessary for ensuring the vitality of a civil society. In addition, democratic structures based on full participation are distinguished from those designed to give an appearance of participation while retaining decision-making power outside the group. The second half of this chapter discusses the educational paradigm that underlies the Search Conference method. This paradigm supports the observation that people can learn directly from their own experience and can gain legitimate knowledge of the world directly without the need for expert intermediaries.

Chapter Six covers the areas of group dynamics, psychological conditions for effective communications, and the rationalization of conflict model. It explains the relationship between design, structure, and optimum learning, showing how dysfunctional group dynamics can be minimized through conscious efforts to structure a Search Conference along the democratic design principle. This ties in with the management of the conditions for open communications and trust. Establishing these conditions is a key process design requirement. When conflicts and disagreements do arise between parties, the Search Conference uses a rationalization model for handling issue-based conflicts, rather than a consensus decision-making model.

Chapter Seven provides a detailed account of the activities involved in planning a Search Conference. These include making the initial contact with a sponsor, deciding the conference purpose, choosing participant selection methods, and selecting and inviting participants. Examples of Search Conference planning activities appear throughout the chapter.

Chapter Eight describes the steps and decisions involved in the design of a Search Conference, with details on the time allotments and design considerations for each of the phases and tasks. A corporate Search Conference for Xerox is used to illustrate a typical conference design.

Chapter Nine considers the unique role of the Search Conference manager and reviews the key knowledge and skills necessary for managing a Search Conference. The discussion then moves deeper, showing how Search Conference management makes effective and practical use of a coordinated body of theory. The chapter presents tips, instructions for managing a conference, and rules of thumb for conference managers, as well as useful guidelines for organizing activities after a Search Conference.

Chapter Ten presents an in-depth case study of a Search Conference that created a community-based economic development strategy on the West Side of Chicago, highlighting the actual issues and outcomes from beginning to end. This case provides an inside view and rich description of what actually happens at a Search Conference, from the perspective of the participants and the conference managers.

The Conclusion takes a broad look at the social forces that stand in the way of increasing cooperation in organizations, communities, and society as a whole. Radical individualism and bureaucratic organization are viewed as restraining forces, both needing reform if social institutions are to realize their cooperative potential. The Search Conference is not only a strategic planning tool, it is a communitarian force for social change. As Trist suggested, new directions of hope are to be found in change efforts at the domain level, that is, in the middle space between single organizations and the nation state. Grassroots social movements, self-managed change initiatives, and interorganizational collaboration offer a great deal of hope in resolving large-scale social problems.

The Epilogue is by Fred Emery, the coinventor of the Search Conference method. Emery sounds a siren to warn us that search conferencing could be corrupted into yet another social science and organization development fad if it is regarded merely as a technique. He urges social scientists and organization development practitioners alike to give careful consideration to the theory behind the tool so as to ensure that the critical preconditions necessary for running successful Search Conferences can be met. Emery speculates that the social demand for search conferencing is likely to increase as we head into the future, and that such social institutions as voluntary associations, local community governments, and private sector enterprises will find merit in the Search Conference method because of its potential to create genuine democratic dialogue and learning-planning communities.

At the end of the book is a selection of helpful material. The Appendix presents a historical overview of the Search Conference method, including an interview with Fred Emery on the first conference. The Resources section includes an introductory slide presentation on the Search Conference method and a listing of contact information for key educational resources.

Acknowledgments

This book represents a collaborative effort that draws upon the practical experience and intellectual energy of many people who have worked hard over the years to develop the Search Conference method. First we would like to especially thank Fred Emery and his long-time colleague, the late Eric Trist, the coinventors of the Search Conference. In our view, they were decades ahead of their time.

We have had the good fortune to collaborate with many stimulating colleagues and fellow Search Conference practitioners. Many of them have contributed ideas, suggestions, or cases that have found their way into this book. Some who have shaped our thinking and practice include Oguz Baburoglu, Steve Cabana, Nancy Cebula, Alastair Crombie, Don Deguerre, William Pasmore, and Robert Rehm. We also owe our thanks to Joel Diemer and Rossana Alvarez at New Mexico State University, who made it possible to make Search Conference training available in the Americas.

Many Loyola students and alumni also helped us make this book accessible to a practitioner audience. Participants in a graduate seminar on the Search Conference provided valuable feedback, including Paula Bartholome, Phyllis Difuccia, Kathy Grady, Frank Heckman, Judd Lawrie, Dennis Mayhew, Bob Sullivan, Greg Tanski, and Linzy Waters.

We would also like to extend our thanks to the many sponsors of Search Conferences who have allowed us to report and share their successes with a wider audience—particularly Walt Grady at Hewlett-Packard; Dan Dotin and Chet Terry at Xerox; Kevin Purcell at Microsoft; Governor Roy Romer of Colorado; and Douglas

Robotham at the Department of Natural Resources; Governor Benjamin Nelson of Nebraska; and Nancy Intermill at the Department of Public Institutions; Sue Higgins at the Macatawa Area Coordinating Council; Mary Nelson and Abu Bakr Nurruddin at the Chicago West Cluster Collaborative; and Dr. Bud DesCarpentrie at School District 21 in Wheeling, Illinois.

While writing this book, we were fortunate enough to work with two very helpful editors at Jossey-Bass: Alan Shrader and Susan Williams. Both Alan and Susan encouraged us to make our work accessible to the scholarly practitioner. At the copyediting and production stage, Hilary Powers edited the manuscript to make every word count, and Pamela Berkman stepped in to ensure that nothing fell through the cracks. The figures and illustrations were done by Ron Purser's sister, Susan Utterback of Utterback Design.

Finally, we sincerely thank Fay Purser for helping us put this book together. We often consulted with her for advice and leaned on her for support. Based on her thorough knowledge of Search Conference theory and practice, she provided fresh insights and was instrumental in helping us distill essential points. Her editorial ability to decode academic jargon into plain English was a lifesaver, resulting in significant changes in the text. Without her generous support and dedicated attention to detail, this book would never have made it into print.

Merrelyn Emery
Ronald E. Purser

Canberra, Australia
Chicago, Illinois
March 1996

The Authors

Merrelyn Emery is a lecturer in the Centre for Continuing Education at the Australian National University. She received her B.A. degree in psychology in 1960 and a B.A. Honors degree in 1964 from the University of New England. In 1986 she was awarded a Ph.D. in marketing from the University of New South Wales. Trained originally as a psychologist, she became more interested in the prevention of individual and social problems rather than attempting to cure them. This led her to educational research and then to adult and continuing education based on the open systems perspective.

She is an active researcher, conducting both empirical studies and action-research-based interventions. The focus of much of her work has been the development of methods that enable people to regain control over their own lives through learning, planning, and structural design. The best known of these are the Search Conference and the Participative Design methodologies. Emery has designed and managed hundreds of Search Conferences, experimenting with the method in communities, city and national governments, regional and national industries, large corporations, and rural aboriginal settlements. Outside of Australia, she has conducted Search Conferences in India, England, France, Holland, Norway, New Zealand, Honduras, Mexico, the United States, and Canada.

Ronald E. Purser is associate professor of organization development in the Center for Organization Development at Loyola University of Chicago. He received his B.A. (1985) degree in psychology from Sonoma State University, and his Ph.D. (1990) in organizational behavior from Case Western Reserve University. He worked for several years as an internal organization development consultant at General Electric's Lighting Business Group. Before pursuing his college studies, he worked as an industrial electrician at the now defunct Pullman-Standard plant in Chicago, Illinois.

Purser has served as a consultant on organizational change projects for such companies as Amoco Oil, Andersen Consulting, Eastman Kodak, Exxon Chemicals, Goodyear Tire, Polaroid, Procter & Gamble, Storage Technology, United Airlines, Whirlpool, and Xerox. He has also worked with a number of nonprofit community organizations, local school districts, and various agencies in the federal government. His research has been published in over twenty-five journal articles and book chapters, on such topics as the redesign of knowledge work organizations, ecologically sustainable organizations, and social creativity. He is coeditor (with Alfonso Montuori) of *Social Creativity* (1996), a three-volume series published by Hampton Press.

The Search Conference

Part One

The Power of Search Conferences

Chapter One

Learning and Planning Our Way to Desirable Futures

Think about it. Noble visions and high ideals have spurred the birth of new organizations, educational and religious institutions, progressive social movements, flourishing communities, creative epochs, even new civilizations. Visions and ideals bring out the best in people. People power. Collaborative social action. We can see it in the civil rights movement; we can see it when creative groups generate breakthrough ideas and turn them into winning products; we can see it in the solidarity of people united by a common cause. There is an unquestionable energy unleashed when people work collectively to bring their most desirable future into existence.

This ability to seek and create a more desirable future for our social organizations is a unique human capacity. We might even say that such ideal-seeking behavior is the lifeblood of healthy organizations, vital communities, and the good society. But this basic human need to create a more desirable future is often blocked, covered over, or frustrated. Unfavorable conditions can prevent groups from understanding their common ground, inhibiting their ability to work toward a shared purpose. We have all been in groups like this. Organizations and communities can suffer a similar fate.

When groups, organizations, and communities are out of touch with the ideals of their members, they go into decline. The future looks grim, and the force of routine forecloses ideas for change and transformation. But ideals can still become the group's conduit to the future. For when people can envision and imagine a more desirable future, present obstacles and past conditioning cease to bind them. The most telling advantage of the Search Conference method is the way it helps organizations and communities restore and strengthen their ability to create plans for the future that are consistent with the highest ideals of their members.

What Is a Search Conference?

In a nutshell, a Search Conference is a participative event that enables a large group to collectively create a plan that its members themselves will implement. Typically, twenty to thirty-five people from a community or organization work progressively for two to three days on planning tasks, primarily in large-group plenary sessions. They develop long-term strategic visions, achievable goals, and concrete action plans. After the conference, participants have a strong commitment to implement their plans with a great deal of energy and determination. Search conferencing offers a benchmark of strategic planning at its best. Organizations have found that it is an effective method for fast-paced, participative strategic planning in today's turbulent environment. Communities have used it for bringing diverse groups together to work on issues and areas of common concern. It is an excellent means of planning large-scale systems change in real time, and it generates excitement, energy, and purposeful behavior.

For a history of the development of the Search Conference methodology, see the Appendix.

What Does a Search Conference Accomplish?

The outcomes of a Search Conference are various: new strategies for growth, innovation, or renewal; joint visions for a more productive and humane workplace; new forums for collaborative decision making; new alliances, coalitions, and partnerships for resolving complex problems; mobilization of a community of citizens around a pressing issue of common concern. The element these outcomes all share is action; Search Conference reports don't gather dust. A Search Conference is an exciting experience that evokes the participants' untapped and often unknown creative energies. Direct participation in the creation of a plan for an organization or community generates enthusiasm, and such energy is contagious. Thus, the plans that come out of Search Conferences have the momentum of positive human energy behind them. And at the end of a Search Conference, participants—those who created the plan and who will be responsible for its implementation—are elated about their collective learning and achievements. They feel confident about themselves and their ability to make a difference.

After the Search Conference, the word spreads, people connect in new ways, forming new alliances and networks, and things get done. And as efforts expand outward and diffuse, more and more people are drawn into the process. Those who sign up to help with implementation do so because of the enthusiasm and energy of the original participants.

Learning Toward the Future

Who are the people conducting Search Conferences? Who are the participants? Why did they choose this method over others? How can groups be expected to cooperate when they are dealing with difficult issues? How does a Search Conference overcome people's resistance to change? How do groups of people reach consensus in the face of strong disagreements and conflicts? Can people really be expected to say what is really on their minds at a Search Conference with their managers in the same room? What guarantees are there that this event won't result in gridlock and frustration?

These are good questions, and we will address them in the chapters to come. One thing is certain: those who take part in Search Conferences learn a different way of knowing, a different way of relating, and a different way of working. The Search Conference process helps people learn to perceive the wider environment, share their ideals for a more desirable future, and pool their efforts toward developing plans consistent with their ideals. The great power of the method is that it allows people to learn about their system in its environment, and see how they have created the system and world that they live in today. At the same time, Search Conference participants learn about their system's unique history and cultural heritage, and begin working to preserve the best of their past and carry it forward as they plan for the future. The Search Conference also provides the opportunity for participants to learn how to deal with disagreement and conflict while respecting their differences. They can do so because the method is designed to help participants find common ground. Most important, people learn how to move forward together as a unified community, and—above all else—to accept joint responsibility for their common purpose.

The main reason why Search Conferences are successful is that every dimension of the process has been designed in human terms. Clearly, there are many other methods of planning. But rarely does a method succeed in helping people think beyond their existing frameworks. A Search Conference does this, and at the same time, it encourages people to consider the concrete realities that must be addressed if their plans are to produce tangible results. In the conference, learning and planning are conducted as a seamless process, from the conception of an idea through its development during the planning stage and all the way to its implementation in the real world.

Restoring Civic Responsibility

If we are to create a more desirable future, we must look carefully at the world we live in today. Currently there is an explosion of information but a lack of meaning; there is a great deal of frantic activity geared toward solving problems, but much of it is too single-minded to cope with the complex puzzles that we face; there is a lot of conflict and competition, but victory is often impossible or undesirable—we must learn to live with differences and disagreements. Certainly we must pay attention to tasks, immediate issues, and minute details, but we also need to dream large and learn to think systemically. Many planning decisions are based on partial understanding, fragmented and specialized knowledge, or political self-interest. Poor planning decisions not only generate more problems, they also alienate people, creating an atmosphere of gloom and doom.

There is a growing body of evidence that Americans are becoming more cynical and withdrawing from community and public life (Elshtain, 1995; Kanter and Mirvis, 1989). This trend is leading authorities at the state, community, and organization levels to try to institute more controls and to police society into good behavior. However, the greater the efforts at control and correction, the greater the citizen apathy and passive resistance to such reforms.

Unhappy, disenchanted people have neither the energy nor the will to change their communities and organizations. Many people believe that it is no longer possible for them to make a difference. Healthy organizations and communities require that this withdrawal from civic life be halted and replaced by responsible involvement. If we are to reverse the cultural slide into passivity and cynicism (Kanter and Mirvis, 1989)—or, as one Search Conference participant put it, to "lift the curse" that is eroding our capacity to ensure a desirable future for ourselves, our children, and our planet—new ways of learning and planning must be made accessible at all levels of society and quickly put into action.

A Powerful Method for Learning and Planning

This is a big undertaking because there is so much that has to be unlearned—we need to abandon our beliefs that the world is an inhospitable and scary place, that people cannot be relied upon to be responsible and trustworthy, that only the powerful can make change happen. (The latter belief maintains itself tenaciously, despite the number of high-level plans that fail.) Only a very vivid experience to the contrary will be able to convince people to change their disempowering beliefs and behavior. Moreover, this experience must demonstrate to them in a significant way that they can indeed work with others outside their immediate circle to create a more desirable future. Research has shown that when people are provided with an opportunity for learning and planning in the right environment, they will mobilize themselves to act purposefully in the interest of the whole (M. Emery, 1982, 1986).

Search conferencing provides this opportunity for creative collaboration. The Search Conference is designed and managed as a process that actualizes the highest common denominator of large groups—shared human ideals. People search trends and possibilities in the broader environment surrounding them, work toward finding common ground, and develop strategic plans for the future that are both bold and realistic. And they leave the conference having accepted responsibility for implementing the plans they helped make, so that every step in the conference and beyond becomes a living lesson that their old, cynical withdrawal from society is unnecessary and unwarranted.

Building In the Capacity for Active Adaptation

As a by-product of the planning process, a Search Conference leads to the development of a *learning-planning community*, that is, a large group of people who know how to learn and plan together. Groups that have gone through a Search Conference are more likely to be on the alert for changes in the environment that could affect their long-term directions or plans. This is active adaptation, which is quite different from simply accepting the way things are and making incremental adjustments to current trends. And because groups take responsibility for their own planning in a Search Conference, they are also more likely to make sure that implementation stays on track. The capability for learning and planning—for active adaptation—becomes just as important as the plan itself. This creative capacity provides early warning signals of environmental changes and a foundation for organizational learning that spreads throughout the system.

Search Conferencing is thus a comprehensive approach for effecting social and organizational change. Real change. A Search Conference is not a human relations exercise. A Search Conference is not a T-group, team-building session, or training event. It doesn't delve into the group unconscious, provoke chaos or confusion, or therapize people. Rather, it is a creative, task-oriented method for large-group planning. It employs sound behavioral science principles to organize a meeting where people can find and work within their common ground, deal rationally with their real differences, and take collective responsibility for action toward shared goals.

Despite the mind-set of the "me" generation, human beings have an inborn need to be part of a group, to have a sense of belonging. Within their groups, they also need to have the freedom and right to exercise individuality and autonomy. Both are absolutely necessary. However, people can grow in individuality only within a setting that gives them respect and support to be themselves and to exercise their special talents. Such an environment must be, by definition, a cooperative structure in which responsibility for outcomes is shared. The Search Conference provides such an environment for human growth and learning. It is this capacity that, once tapped, will continue to grow, leading to increased awareness and learning.

Utility of the Method

Search conferencing has been used for a wide variety of purposes. It has been used successfully for setting new directions and strategies in both public and private sectors, and for resolving heated conflicts concerning public policy issues and other types of disputes. Many Search Conferences have been used to help with efforts aimed at revitalizing communities as well as for organizational renewal. Other Search Conferences have been designed for bringing new alliances, networks, and consortia into being. More specifically, conducting a Search Conference is ideal for:

• *Communities and regions* that need to bring together people with diverse and often conflicting perspectives on complex social issues, such as the environment, education, economic development, and public safety. The Macatawa region near Holland, Michigan, for example, generated a community-based strategic plan for dealing with the region's rapid economic growth and changing population. This led to a host of grassroots initiatives in the areas of land use, environmental conservation, social services, health care, and public safety, to mention a few.

• *Organizations, private companies, or public agencies* that need to develop long-term strategic plans, or redefine their future directions. For example, at Hewlett-Packard, some fifty managers and informal leaders from throughout a division participated in a Search Conference that resulted in a thorough business plan. This group made key decisions regarding the core competencies they would develop to grow and reenergize the business.

• *Groups of organizations or formal and informal associations* that need to develop more collaborative approaches to strategies and issues of mutual concern. In Colorado, for example, water engineers from different municipalities in the Rocky Mountains Front Range area cooperated to develop a breakthrough plan that for the first time made it possible for communities in this region to share scarce water resources. The Search Conference provided an ideal forum for overcoming past conflicts over water usage, thereby avoiding future litigation between municipalities.

These are but a few brief samples of the utility of the Search Conference method. Chapter Two includes more detailed examples, and Chapter Ten presents the highlights of a full conference.

Basic Overview

The face-to-face meeting—the Search Conference itself—is actually the centerpiece or cornerstone of a three-phase process that also includes a planning and design phase and an implementation and diffusion phase. Chapters Seven, Eight, and Nine go into great detail on practical aspects of this process; here we will simply sketch in enough detail to put the discussion of underlying theory in perspective. A Search Conference is normally a two-and-a-half day event, usually held off-site in a retreatlike setting. Ideally twenty to thirty-five people are selected to participate in a Search Conference, based on such criteria as their knowledge of the system and their potential for taking responsibility for implementation. Participants are also selected to reflect a full range of perspectives on the system, but they attend in their own right, not as representatives of stakeholder groups. The governing factor is each individual's own importance to the conference task. The idea is to get the *right system* in the room—that is, to assemble those people who are critical to achieving the purpose of the Search Conference. Therefore, precise specification of the purpose of a Search Conference is crucial, for it determines how the conference system is defined—and that, in turn, shapes the criteria for participant selection. (Chapter Four goes into detail on defining the right system.)

Participants in a Search Conference work on planning tasks in a mixture of large-group plenary sessions and small groups. As a whole community, participants scan their external environment, review their history, and analyze the strengths and weaknesses of their current system. This provides a shared context for their most important task: the development of strategic goals and action plans. The entire conference community debates and discusses strategic issues relevant to a system, mapping out areas of agreement and common ground through a process of generating, analyzing, and synthesizing data into an integrated community product.

As learning and planning for the achievement of shared purposes is an integral part of an evolving process, the outcomes of the Search Conference are open-ended. They cannot be predicted in advance. "In a Search Conference you don't know where you will end up; it is an adventure," asserted one of the participants in the Nebraska state mental health system conference. The plans and strategies developed in a Search Conference reflect the unique character of each organization or community, thereby increasing the probability that effective implementation will follow. "The level of observed commitment managers had to the plan they created coming out of the Search Conference was unprecedented," recalls Walt Grady of Hewlett-Packard.

An Environment for Learning

The Search Conference is designed to provide a learning environment where all perceptions are valid regardless of source, and where participation is equal and open, regardless of hierarchical position or status. People vocalize their ideas in large and small groups, using flip-chart paper to record everyone's ideas for all to see. Everything is out in the open, aboveboard, and shared in the public domain. There are no workbooks, questionnaires, or other occasions for private writing, as the emphasis in the Search Conference is on restoring an oral culture based on mutual trust and people's confidence in their own direct perceptions. Modern culture has created a widespread tendency for people to hold private, self-contained conceptions of themselves as individuals (see, for example, Sampson, 1988, 1989); encouraging face-to-face discussion works to combat this tendency. It is through the spoken word, through dialogue and conversation, that people in a community develop a shared context for planning joint action (Ong, 1967, 1982). Other large-group planning methods—for example, Weisbord and Janoff's Future Search (1995)—do have people write in workbooks or fill out predesigned worksheets, and this type of activity can feel congenial to the participants because it reflects our cultural predilection for written media. However, it subtly draws people apart.

Marshall McLuhan (1964) suggested that different media reinforce different human capacities and thinking patterns. In his view, modern culture has altered the human sensory balance with the invention of print and type. Favoring the written word and visual modes of perception, linear lines of type and print tend to induce a linear, one-thing-follows-another view of the world. Writing is also a private medium; it promotes introspection, abstract thought, and individual self-expression, but not community building and collaboration.

Besides private writing, search conferencing also does without presenters, lecturers, and guest speakers. There are no keynote addresses, speeches, games, icebreakers, or training sessions, no theatrical skits and no guided fantasy exercises. Instead, the participants scan their own environment, analyze the current situation, generate imaginative but achievable visions, formulate strategic goals, and devise detailed action plans. This is all real work for the real world. The conference managers' job is to provide the best possible conditions for building a learning-planning community capable of this work—that is, to constantly monitor all aspects of the speed and process of the conference, adapting its structure and its design to ensure that the tasks are completed to the satisfaction of all participants.

External Structure and Conference Design

A Search Conference resembles a funnel. It begins by taking the widest possible perspective, getting the participants to step outside themselves and their immediate concerns so as to explore possibilities. Then it narrows down to specific key strategic visions and actions, pouring them out into the world as the group diffuses and implements its vision to the rest of the community. As discussed in more detail in Chapter Four, the design is essentially the translation of the concept of open systems into a learning environment.

Figure 1.1 shows the generic process of a Search Conference.

Every Search Conference is unique, requiring special planning and design. There are no standardized guidebooks or worksheets to take off the shelf and apply to every situation—those who want to learn how to manage and design Search Conferences need a solid grounding in the underlying theory, so that the innovation and experimentation inevitable in their work will follow productive lines and produce consistent results. Nonetheless, it is possible to summarize the general flow of a Search Conference.

Participants always begin with activities designed to help them learn about what is happening in their environment. Next, they explore their system's past and present as a prelude to long-range planning. Then they develop strategic goals for creating a desirable future of their system, along with realistic action plans. After the conference, groups work to ensure that others become involved in the implementation and diffusion of the strategic plan.

Figure 1.1. Search Conference Overview.

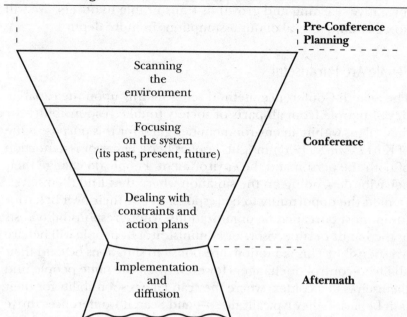

Timewise, roughly a third of the conference is focused on learning about changes and trends in the environment. Another third is spent on looking at the system—its past history, its present strengths and weaknesses, and its most desirable future. Finally, the last third of the conference shifts into high gear as future visions are reality-tested against existing constraints, and action planning groups figure out how to implement their strategic goals.

Assumptions about People

Search conferencing is based on a set of consistent assumptions and principles. First, we assume that people are purposeful creatures with the capacity to select and produce desirable outcomes. Second, we assume that people will accept responsibility for a task that is meaningful to them. Third, we assume that people can function in the ideal-seeking mode under the appropriate conditions. Thus, once people have chosen a set of purposes based on ideals and accepted responsibility for the task of planning, they can grow and contribute to the well-being of their system. This type of transformative learning and growth is transferable to others. We will now examine several of our assumptions in more depth.

People Are Purposeful

The Search Conference method relies heavily upon the capabilities of people from all parts of society to take responsibility for their plans within an environment designed for this purpose. One of Kurt Lewin's (1951) insights applies here: behavior is a function of both the person and the environment. People do change their behavior depending on the situation where they find themselves. Denied the opportunity to be responsible for their own behavior (as in most bureaucratic organizations, where responsibility rests in the hands of supervisors or administrators), people will behave irresponsibly. This is a rational response to situations beyond their ability to control or change. However, when the same people find themselves in a context where they can take responsibility for their own behavior, they typically do so—and Search Conferences thrive as a result.

People welcome genuine opportunities to make a more desirable future for themselves, and for those they share a future with. The Search Conference assumes that people are *purposeful*. By this, we mean that people display the will to live meaningful lives (Ackoff and Emery, 1972). People are not limited to adapting to the environment as given (F. Emery, 1981). Being purposeful, people will actively attempt to change their environment to suit their needs for learning, growth, support, and autonomy. People can also learn to change their goals under new conditions, creating new paths to achieve them. This perspective is at odds with the mechanistic model of many modern organizations.

The stable order within hierarchical organizations is disintegrating as people assert their purposefulness. People are more aware of opportunities where they can exercise their collective will. In some cases, people are abandoning traditional structures that have been encapsulated in the dominant hierarchies of family, workplace, church, and state. In other cases, more progressive organizations are working to reform and change in order to become more responsive to the needs of their employees, customers, and constituencies. As people reassert themselves—either by taking action outside institutional frameworks or by launching massive campaigns for reforming those frameworks—traditional institutions are experiencing ever more uncertainty and instability.

The values of self-reliance, community, and human dignity that are central to Western culture were never completely eradicated by the incursion of bureaucracy. The bureaucratic-machine age was doomed to a relatively short life. Once people became more educated and affluent, they had little tolerance for being pushed around and treated like cogs in a machine. Now we live in a new era, where people expect more from institutions and organizations. People want to exercise their rights to freedom, dignity, and community. At the moment, many of these voices inside organizations may be muted by fear of reprisal or need for job security. However, this groundswell of expectation is a powerful and untapped force. Most people, whether vocal or silent, do want to make decisions about their own lives and futures.

People Can Be Ideal-Seeking

It is true—people often disagree about the best way to manage or govern their organizations and communities. But when a shared purpose or common goal is in view, people set these conflicts aside. Such commonalities derive from a set of basic human ideals that are found in every culture and may be elicited from everyone, from the poorest and most downtrodden to the most affluent and privileged.

When people come together to plan and bring into being their most desirable future, they find they must rise above their petty differences, narrow concerns, and conflicting interests, and examine what they have in common as people. In almost every Search Conference, four higher ideals or ultimate human concerns seem to surface when people are defining the most desirable future for the world: belonging, nurturance or care for others and the environment, a sense of humanity, and a desire for beauty (which is akin to an aesthetic appreciation for balance and attractiveness).

Although these ideals are forever unreachable, when people search for their most desirable world in this ideal-seeking mode, exhilarating and inspiring—and practical—ideas are born. The quest gives rise to high levels of creative thought and energy.

Shared ideals unite a community and fuel the hard work that must be done to translate those ideals into reality. Ideals are one of the most potent sources of common ground. No matter how diverse the participants in a conference, they come to discover they are all human, and all share the same set of concerns, aspirations, and hopes for a more desirable world. They know that these ideals will never be entirely realized in practice, but they recognize them as a target for the community's aspirations.

Common Purpose Is Powerful

Search conferencing is based on the assumption that when groups share a common purpose or ideals about a more desirable future, they can learn to work together, respect each other, and cooperate toward the achievement of shared goals. It doesn't matter whether these people or groups are from different cultures, races, or religions. If diverse people and contentious parties can find common ground, it is possible for them to set aside their negative views of each other, their stereotypes, and their prejudices.

The Search Conference has been used successfully for community development in racially diverse neighborhoods, for resolving conflicts over environmental issues, and for forging new partnerships between labor and management. It works in communities and industries that are composed of a diverse mixtures of ethnicities, generations, and interest groups. The first task is to get people into the room together. Once this is achieved, the detailed design features of the Search Conference, in the hands of a trained and experienced Search Conference manager, will accomplish the rest.

In our experience, people need no remedial skills training to prepare them to participate, cooperate, and take responsibility for their own work. We have found the skills the usual human relations training programs seek to build—improving communications, listening, giving feedback, valuing differences, and so forth—appear naturally and effortlessly when people begin working on real tasks relevant to a shared purpose. The reason for the common assumption that people need human relations training is that we frequently see people not communicating, not cooperating, and not taking responsibility in institutions that have been organized along traditional bureaucratic lines. Human relations skills and behaviors lie dormant in these settings, but they are there. Repeated experience in Search Conferences proves that it is the circumstances and the context in which people find themselves that determine their behavior, and not their lack of skills.

From Conflict to Common Ground

People fear conflict when they are not sure where the area of agreement lies, or whether or not there is a mechanism for dealing with serious conflict if it should arise. People differ in the degree to which they worry about the expression and handling of overt disagreement and conflict, but it is a general source of anxiety. Search Conferences allay these fears by creating the conditions under which commonalities take precedence and human diversity is appreciated. These conditions—a structure conducive to sharing responsibility for creative work, an environment that satisfies needs for both autonomy and belonging, the conditions for effective, influential communication based on the power of the spoken word—together with the flexibility of the overall design and management, work together to create a protected site. A Search Conference becomes a sanctuary within which people can practice different ways of planning and learning together, behaviors they can continue long after the conference closes.

Our experience of conducting Search Conferences in North America suggests that people are not afraid to argue over issues when their collective futures are at stake. When people come together for the purpose of learning to plan and implement strategies for creating their own future, they do not perceive differences and arguments as necessarily negative. They respect them for what they are, indications that people care about the issues that are being discussed.

Sometimes these arguments do grow heated. People who care passionately about their future will stand up for what they believe in if they think they see a better way for achieving it. However, when people first come together, they won't really know where others are coming from. It is critical that the line between agreement and disagreement be drawn precisely and honestly. Therefore, Search Conference managers do not sweep conflicts under the rug. In Chapter Six, we describe this process as the *rationalization of conflict* and discuss ways to make it work. We have found that people are basically rational and reasonable when they are clear about their disagreements.

A Search Conference does not set itself the goal of reaching consensus on every issue. In our opinion, consensus decision making has been overrated—some issues simply cannot be reconciled. Others do not lend themselves to resolution or consensus in a span of days. Polarized viewpoints that are deeply entrenched in moral beliefs and personal value judgments will defy any effort at consensus decision making—consider pro-choice versus pro-life arguments, for example. Even less-polarized issues—those where there is simply a reasoned and substantive disagreement between parties— do not lend themselves to consensus. But how long have we spent agonizing in groups when this form of decision making was inappropriate? Most of us have spent hours in meetings where one contentious issue overtook the whole agenda. Even when real differences of opinion are clear to everyone at the table, people often spend a great deal of time and energy trying to force themselves to a consensus—which promptly shatters as the parties go their own ways after the meeting.

The structure of the Search Conference event and its process quickly establishes and enlarges the ground for agreement and cooperation, essentially eliminating any danger that conflict will get out of hand. People can speak freely and argue for their points of view, knowing that the debate takes place against a backdrop of solid common ground. The prospect of assembling a large group of strong-willed and vocal people—and turning them loose to argue—can seem daunting. But remember that people behave differently in different circumstances. It is often assumed that a person's behavior in one context—say, in a traditional business meeting—will be identical in a Search Conference. However, this assumption is incorrect. The conditions set up in the Search Conference are very different from those in a traditional, hierarchical organization. In a context that offers real influence and an equal voice in shaping the future direction of their organization or community, most people reveal a surprising range of interpersonal skills.

In Praise of Theory

Practitioners need a theory to guide their actions (Argyris, Putnam, and Smith, 1985). Lewin's famous phrase, "There is nothing so practical as a good theory," still holds true. Competition among consultants and practitioners has led to an increase in the differentiation of organization development interventions, products, and methods (Mirvis, 1988). While the concept of *equifinality* is sometimes used as a sort of professional courtesy to support the idea that any approach can get good results, the term actually refers to a property of open systems that gives them the capacity to develop from one steady state to another by a variety of means. The concept does not apply to the array of methods and interventions in the field of organization development (Cummings and Srivastva, 1977). Different methods do not magically lead to the same results, especially when they are informed by different theories.

Unfortunately, the accumulated experience of social science theory and action research on democratic forms of organization, open systems thinking, effective communications, and group dynamics sometimes seems inaccessible to practitioners with businesses to run. Therefore this book is not a cookbook or instruction manual for running people through exercises or filling out training workbooks in the hope that something good might come out at the end. We recognize that while there are a wide variety of participative events (and the Search Conference is a participative event), not all participative events are Search Conferences. As practical theorists in the Lewinian tradition, our hope is that those aspiring to design and manage Search Conferences will internalize the principles in this book, using them as a guide and compass for finding their own way in the field. Like the ocean and its rolling waves, the theory and method of search conferencing form a seamless whole. The two are simply inseparable. Attempts to separate them will inevitably lead to a distortion of the philosophy and values that are central to ensuring the efficacy and integrity of the method.

Our intention then in this book is to provide much more than a simple toolkit or laundry list for conference management. Rather, we begin by grounding the Search Conference methodology in the results of research and theoretical development. We then present as much of our practical knowledge and skills as can be compressed into one volume, to help the reader make a start toward becoming a competent Search Conference manager. We place both the theory and the practical skills in context by reporting on many examples and case studies of highly successful Search Conferences—and some unsuccessful ones, as well.

Chapter Two

Uses and Advantages of Search Conference Methods

Search conferencing has been applied in a wide variety of organizations and communities, and its versatility as a method continues to expand. Here, we present a small sample, to illustrate how search conferencing has been used as an alternative to traditional planning meetings for a variety of issues, purposes, and concerns. Next, we provide an overview of major principles and critical success factors that underlie the Search Conference method. Finally, we conclude this chapter by presenting a brief run-through of how the various phases of a conference unfold.

Search Conferences in Brief

These vignettes illustrate the versatility and benefits of the Search Conference method in action. More detailed and in-depth case studies (including some of these conferences and some others) follow in later chapters.

Strategic Planning for a State Mental Health System

The Nebraska Department of Public Institutions (DPI) sponsored three Search Conferences. The first two focused on the future of the adult and child mental health system. The third conference looked for performance improvement in the entire state mental health system. Administrators at DPI had engaged in strategic planning efforts periodically over the years, but they had never involved people from the system to the extent feasible in a Search Conference. In previous years, they had brought together mental health administrators from around the state for interagency strategic planning. DPI administrators felt that this process had not been very effective, and they wanted a method to expand the strategic planning process to a wider variety of constituents.

The experience of the three conferences was similar, and one will serve for our purpose here. With the help of external consultants, DPI convened "The Future of the Nebraska Adult Mental Health System" to bring together key people with a view to developing shared commitment to plans for building a unified and integrated adult mental health system that would be driven by consumer needs. The Search Conference included administrators and staff from both public and private sectors, as well as key department heads from various state agencies, institutions, and community-based programs. In a departure from previous practice, consumers of mental health services (formerly referred to as patients) also participated in the conference. Search Conference managers often recommend that sponsors exclude external stakeholders from the roster of participants, but in this case the consumers were part of the system that was being planned for, so they couldn't be left out. (More on defining systems in Chapter Four.) And the definition worked; consumers felt that they had a stronger voice after the conferences. They reported having a less adversarial relationship with mental health professionals, and having more influence over strategies and policies. Participants found that having people from all parts of the system in the room meant that their collective knowledge included all the information needed for strategic decision making, so they were able to proceed smoothly to develop practical plans for improvement.

A total of twenty-two high-priority action strategies emerged from the three conferences, and seventeen of them are currently in various stages of implementation. Strategies adopted at the conferences include creating a training and research institute, restructuring regional adult centers, centralizing the funding process for all mental health services, and revising system accountability and outcome measures. Presentations of strategies and action plans from each of the Search Conferences have been made to the governor, district attorney, and state legislature staff of Nebraska. Government officials who attended the closing session took back a positive message to Governor Benjamin Nelson about the powerful outcomes that these conferences achieved. Implementation teams made up from representatives of each strategy group continue to meet to follow up and coordinate their efforts.

Urban Planning and Community Development

Sudden growth in the Macatawa region in southwestern Michigan led to a number of problems. Area population grew from 45,000 in 1960 to nearly 80,000 in 1990. Besides an influx of new residents, there was also a remarkable growth in industry in the area. Such combined growth meant that traffic was becoming more congested, the demand for social services was increasing, and juvenile crime was on the rise.

In response, the Macatawa Area Coordinating Council (MACC), a local community development organization, sponsored a Search Conference for the future of the area that involved people drawn from across the community. The Search Conference was billed as a "A gathering of the diverse people of the Macatawa Area in a collaborative quest to create a common vision and develop paths to a more desirable future." Conference participants included mayors, police officers, corporate executives, local business owners, chamber of commerce representatives, school teachers, principals, parents, clergy, social service agency directors, transportation engineers, environmentalists, housewives, and students. Chapter Seven returns to this conference to describe the planning process involved.

The group developed a common vision statement and identified eight strategic areas with action plans for guiding future community development initiatives. At the close of the conference, people made public commitments to endorse the plan and help move it forward. Their conference report states: "We as a community are committed to improving the quality of life in the Greater Macatawa Area through creative, cooperative, and comprehensive work in the areas of economic development, environment, health care, land use, transportation, lifelong learning, residential life, personal safety, and social services."

Richard Vander Broek, former chairperson of the MACC, remarked, "We walked into the conference as *stakeholders,* but we walked out as a *unified community.*" Reflecting on the event, Sue Higgins, executive director of the MACC, said the Search Conference was unique in that "it brought people together that normally wouldn't come together." Vander Broek also described the Search Conference as a novel approach to planning, noting, "From my experience in corporate settings, traditional strategic planning is myopic from the start because it leapfrogs immediately to examine impediments and constraints, whereas the Search Conference reverses this sequence." The new chairperson of the MACC, Leroy Dell, found that the Search Conference allowed "time for people to dream by not having the agenda set in advance by a few people." Several newspapers covered the event (see Exhibit 2.1).

People in the community previously viewed the MACC as another layer of bureaucracy that was unresponsive to their needs. Shortly after the conference, the Macatawa Area Coordinating Council restructured its organization to support the implementation of the strategic community development initiatives. Eight strategic initiative task forces, which included both MACC members and people from the larger community, met on a monthly basis after the conference to work on implementation.

Within a matter of months, the environmental task force developed plans to purchase properties that would create a greenbelt around the area, and raised funds for dredging a harbor. The land-use/transportation task force sponsored a forum for coordinating activities among existing planning commissions, similar committees, and government offices to promote land-use planning from a regional perspective. The personal safety task force concentrated their efforts on the Macatawa Weed and Seed Program, a cooperative effort between public and private resources to reduce crime and preserve neighborhood safety in targeted areas. The goals of the program are to weed out crime within an area and then seed the area with a wide range of crime and drug prevention programs. The health care initiative group is working to forge collaborative alliances among public and private agencies, insurance companies, hospitals and long-term care providers, physicians, and recipients with the goal of developing a coordinated system of health care and medical services that meets the needs of the Macatawa community.

**Exhibit 2.1. News Coverage of
the Macatawa Search Conference.**

Editorial: **The regional view**
Cooperation becomes a necessity

Years from now the great Holland-Zeeland area may be known as Macatawa.
That may grate on some ears. Local civic pride is a strong, productive force. But it
also can inadvertently work against the kind of concerted planning needed when a region becomes an urban area—as greater Holland-Zeeland has done.

The issue:
Conference of
area leaders
addresses prob-
lems of area.

Our view:
Event should
prove to be the
first in a cooper-
ative alliance.

When the Dutch settlers came to western Michigan, they brought
with them their comforting provincial affiliations. So we still have
Vriesland, Drenthe, Graafschap and Overisel—as well as Holland and
Zeeland. Though intergovernmental cooperation has not been unknown by any means, the toughest issues demanding the most cooperation have yet to be fully addressed: an area center, a regional
library system, a regional land-use plan.

The time has come to plan regionally as a matter of course, rather
than as an exception. That was one of the points of consensus that
emerged when nearly 70 representatives of the seven municipalities
that make up the Macatawa area, joined by other community mem-
bers, gathered at Big Rapids last week for a "Future Search" conference. The conference was planned and administered by the Macatawa Area Coordinating Council,
which was an outgrowth of the 2010 report issued in 1988.

A concern for the future quality of life in this area was not only the reason for the conference, it also provided the emotional energy that sparked some honest confrontations
and revelations. That fates of Holland, Zeeland and their surrounding townships were
inextricably bound together, participants agreed. Having collectively recognized that,
conferees saw that virtually every public policy required some degree of coordination;
no small order for a set of municipalities with a proud tradition of independence.

The primary points of concern that emerged from the more than two days of planning demonstrated compassion, as well as prudence.

The need to intervene to prevent further segregation by socioeconomic class was
brought up. The demographic disparities between some municipalities were noted
aloud: Holland has the most poor people and the highest public-service demands,
while some townships have dramatically higher average incomes. That is the dubious
equation of urban blight evident in so many larger cities—Detroit, Chicago—one that
the Macatawa area must avoid at all costs.

Ethnic diversity, it was agreed, must be celebrated rather than simply tolerated or
observed. Equal access to good-quality health care and education must be a part of
the Macatawa region's vision of the future. Social services must be well-coordinated
and aimed at keeping family relationships healthy and preventing further deterioration of families.

Crime prevention and law enforcement, both aimed at leashing that most fright-
eningly destructive destroyer of communities, was a priority, the planning agreed.
Preservation of the natural environment—water, air, and soil—was another top priority that emerged from the planning sessions.

Many people are skeptical of planning, perhaps because their expectations are set
too high. Planning, such as that accomplished by the "Future Search" group last week,
is only one of the initial steps toward creating the type of community an area's residents want. Genuine progress in achieving a desirable future requires a lot of effort,
as well as time. Last week's "Future Search" conference can be a significant step toward a good future if area residents build on what was begun.

—Clay W. Stauffer

Source: Holland Sentinel, Sunday, May 29, 1994, p. A4. Reprinted by permission.

Exhibit 2.1. News Coverage of
the Macatawa Search Conference, Cont'd.

MACC conference looks to the future

By Shandra Martinez
The Grand Rapids Press

The walls of the hotel conference room were covered with butcher paper, filled with goals, illustrated with words and sometimes drawings of circles or trees.

The words and pictures were the culmination of the efforts over the past three days of the 68 people in the Future Search Conference hosted by the Macatawa Area Coordinating Council.

The conference, held at the Big Rapids Holiday Inn, cost the MACC $30,000, which paid for the food and lodging expenses of the participants and contracted Change-Works of the Rockies, a consulting firm in Boulder, Colo. to facilitate the conference.

The conference's purpose was to bring together a variety of people to design a long-term plan for the Macatawa area.

After hours of discussion, participants decided the area needs to focus on eight issues: socio-economic diversity in the community, a clean environment, social and family services, education including culture and the fine arts, the economic climate, land use and transportation, health care and a crime-free environment.

The conference began by looking at the big picture and eventually narrowing the focus to the seven-community area which includes Holland, Zeeland, Fillmore, Laketown and Park.

Then participants divided up into groups to focus on one of the eight topics. Each group was responsible for creating a mission statement for the topic.

MACC Director Sue Higgins described the conference's approach to brainstorming as innovative. Haworth Corp. used the same type of program several years ago, she said.

The participants were picked from government, businesses, social services and different ethnic groups, and ranged from a high school student to a bank president.

"The group of individuals was really a labor of trying to replicate the fabric of community with the selection of individuals presented here," said Rich Vander Broek, chair of MACC's board.

Source: Grand Rapids Press, Sunday, May 29, 1994, p. L2. Reprinted by permission.

This bottom-up planning process was able to bridge the gap between the MACC and the larger community. Six months after the Search Conference, the participants held a reunion event to update the plan and to solicit more participation from members of the community. Also, as part of their diffusion efforts to the wider Macatawa community, they produced a video program of the Search Conference and aired it over a local access cable station.

Corporate Strategic Planning

A Hewlett-Packard division facing significantly increased competition conducted a Search Conference to work out ways to manage strategic change and identify what the division needed to do to remain dominant in its markets. The division's general manager convened a Search Conference that included nearly fifty key managers and informal leaders from the workplace. The group jointly defined the division's most desirable future and created new strategic directions and plans to reenergize the business. As a group, they managed to make tough decisions on which core competencies they would emphasize. The major result of this Search Conference was securing commitment on the part of managers to a thorough strategic plan that they all agreed to carry out and support throughout the division.

New Product Development Planning

The Microsoft Corporation found the Search Conference to be a useful method for planning the future of four product lines. Kevin Purcell and Susan Voeller of Microsoft's Executive Management and Development internal consulting group joined Elizabeth Dunn of the Product Division to conduct four back-to-back conferences that culminated in a meeting for integrating ideas, strategies, and action plans. This resulted in a comprehensive strategy for each of the product lines in the division. The integration of the ideas for improvement that were generated in the four Search Conferences also led to a more efficient use of resources across product lines.

Rethinking Strategy for Global Markets

A new director of Motorola's worldwide semiconductor division used a Search Conference to map out a global business strategy for the mini-chip business. Janet Fiero managed the Search Conference in Tokyo, Japan (Cabana and Fiero, 1995). For three days, a global team of twenty-five managers from the United States, Europe, Japan, and Hong Kong worked to create six key strategies for the mini-chip business. Technology, marketing and "Centers of Excellence" task forces have been working to implement major elements of the strategic plan. Through staff meetings, strategic goals developed at the conference have been shared with the entire organization.

Assessing the outcome of the conference, the director stated, "This search process has been an excellent way to get a thorough overview of the issues facing the business and to build rapport with the regions" (Cabana and Fiero, 1995, p. 30). The director goes on to summarize the results of the Motorola action planning task forces to date:

> All three task forces are doing well:
>
> • The technology task force has built upon our strength and is beginning key programs to fill our technology voids
>
> • The marketing task force has made significant progress in expanding markets and beginning a systems solution approach to our customers
>
> • The task force on Centers of Excellence has initiated a critical shift. No longer will the design of new products be centered in the United States but instead it is dispersed into the regions.
>
> This allows us to both respond adaptively to customers' needs and avoid redundancy by having the expertise in one center available to other regions. Critical resources have been added in the regions in support of the goals developed during the Search Conference. For example, we now have a design engineer in Japan, an applications engineer in Europe, and a new product development champion in the United States. . . . We are maintaining the focus on the goals rather than just the action plans. In this way organizational members are clear about our desirable future and can align their activities accordingly (even if they are not directly involved in a task force). Commitment to the goals of our desirable future is high and we have gained a great sense of a family environment worldwide, rather than just in the United States. This will pay dividends for us over the long term. [p. 30]

A New Vision for Empowerment

Jim Heckel, production manager at Hewlett-Packard's Greeley, Colorado, facility, sponsored a Search Conference to develop a plan for empowering the workforce (Cabana, Emery, and Emery, 1995, p. 8). His personal vision was to create an organization where workers would see themselves as owners of the business. Heckel stated, "We used the Search Conference to develop a plan to build manufacturing flexibility by developing a workplace where employees are supported by management to act as if they are owners." Heckel hoped that the conference would explore strategies for a number of pressing issues:

- Center on core manufacturing competencies
- Get closer to customer needs
- Redesign and restructuring of the workplace
- Explore information technologies that can aid productivity
- Rethink compensation and recognition systems
- Promote awareness of diversity issues

Three outside consultants ran the Search Conference at a remote conference center in the Rocky Mountains. All the managers of the plant participated in the three-day session, along with workers selected through a community reference approach (see Chapter Seven). Natural work groups selected people from their areas to attend. Management took special care to ensure that the selection process was not politicized, and that people who attended did not see themselves representing the special interests of any group while at the conference.

One of the main concerns going into this Search Conference was a fear that there was not enough dissatisfaction with the status quo at the plant for change to occur. Early in the conference, the consultants guided a serious discussion focused on "changes causing us to change," which helped people voice their reasons, either from a corporate or community perspective, about why the people working in this plant needed to make change happen. In fact, it was not until well into the discussion that people realized that the real need was to create a strong and compelling statement spelling out the business case for change. Strategies and actions coming out of this conference included a decision to develop self-managing groups throughout the plant. The results of the conference produced other innovations—a blueprint for a new reward system, plans for a new marketing strategy, and process improvement objectives.

At the end of the conference, the entire group designed an inclusive process that would allow everyone back at the plant to fully understand and further contribute to the outcomes of the search. They called this process a search *Trade Fair.* The Trade Fair was used as a medium for explaining the strategies and enlisting more employees to participate in implementing the plans. Participation has rapidly diffused to employees throughout the plant. Now employees are truly behaving as though they owned the business; their feeling of ownership has increased because they were directly involved in the creation and implementation of the plan.

School Reform

"A Community Dialogue on the Future of Education in District 21" was the stated purpose of a Search Conference that was convened for developing new initiatives for school reform in Wheeling, Illinois. Frank Heckman and Ron Purser helped the district superintendent organize this conference, which brought together teachers, administrators, school board members, teachers' union officers, parents, and members from the business community. One teacher who was interviewed immediately after the conference remarked, "This was the first chance I've had to talk to the community, the board and administrators, and parents especially about what kids need in this district. Usually I only hear from parents when they have an immediate problem they want me to solve. Instead, this conference gave us the opportunity to focus on future needs, and in a relevant way. . . . we had to seriously come up with a plan for the students." Those participating in this Search Conference realized that their common ground lay in their willingness and commitment to work together to promote the quality of education in the district.

Looking back on the conference, Bill Meyers, assistant district superintendent, made these remarks: "We've been holding an internal dialogue for a long time on education. This conference was a good reality check because it caused us to look outside ourselves and get a different perspective. By bringing the community into the dialogue, we were able to overcome our myopia."

Conference participants developed several innovative initiatives for the future of education in the district. There was widespread agreement that the traditional boundaries of the classroom would change and expand to include interaction with the wider community. New partnerships between the community and the school district, and an expansion of the site-based management concept, would allow community members to become directly involved in educational projects. Their vision called for the school to become a community center that would be open in the evenings, providing constant access to learning activities. A major thrust of their plan entailed the development of a team approach to learning. District learning teams have been formed in that the teachers act more as facilitators of the learning process, and students, parents, and community members are actively involved in the educational process. The focus of education is integrative, which includes the development of critical thinking, problem solving and life skills. New technology is used as an integrated tool, which provides the ability for individualized instruction and variable, self-paced learning.

Regional Water Quality Planning

The Search Conference has been used to address regional water quality and resource management issues. Contentious groups fighting over water rights and water quality in the upper Colorado River basin traditionally resorted to lengthy and costly lawsuits. In 1991, a breakthrough in this stalemate was achieved when a regional planning agency responsible for the state Water Quality Plan decided to convene a Search Conference to seek "common ground regarding the future of water quality decision making in the upper basin of the Colorado River" (Rehm, Schweitz, and Granata, 1992, p. 221). This Search Conference brought together fifty people from different perspectives on water quality—federal and state agency officials, water experts and providers, local and municipal government officials, ranchers, and industrial, agricultural, and recreational users—from both the high mountain country and the low plains. They agreed on strategies for cooperation. Thirty of the participants were actively involved in four different action groups during the implementation phase after the conference. Specifically, these four action groups worked diligently on clarifying procedures for collaborative decision making, evaluating new technology and information management systems that could possibly support collaborative decision making, assessing educational needs, and searching for funding sources to support the activities and recommendations from the action groups.

Six months after the conference, task force members formed themselves into the Colorado River Headwaters Forum, a nonbureaucratic group that mediates water quality issues between different interest groups in the surrounding regions of the river, including environmentalists. The Headwaters Forum reports that it has implemented a new collaborative model for water quality decision making, resulting in a significant increase in cooperation and information sharing between what were formerly highly adversarial groups. Besides its direct success, the conference also provided a model and inspiration for the Front Range Forum Search Conference mentioned in Chapter One and discussed in detail in Chapter Three.

Reinventing the Juvenile Justice System

In North Dakota, the director of the juvenile courts sponsored a Search Conference for thirty state officials to develop a set of common goals for the delivery of services in the juvenile justice system. Increased numbers of unruly status offenses and violent juvenile crimes in the state required a revamping of the whole state system. Nancy Cebula and Terry Swango, the Search Conference managers, helped a group of judges, probation officers, directors of state agencies, and the attorney general to develop strategies for reinventing the entire juvenile justice system. These strategies and actions included giving the juvenile courts jurisdiction over parents, redefining the roles of State's Attorney and juvenile court officer, and clarifying the relationship between the juvenile courts and the division of juvenile services, providing a continuum of care for children. Six months after the conference, groups are continuing to work toward implementation of the plan. Another group has taken on the additional task of changing the organizational structure of the juvenile court system.

Theoretical Core of the Search Conference

Search conferencing is a theory-driven method, designed and managed through a core set of principles. The chapters in the next part of the book address each of the theoretical principles in more depth. Here, we provide a brief overview of the core principles and defining features of the Search Conference method. These are the principles whose incorporation into practice is critical to the success of any Search Conference:

- Open systems thinking
- Getting the right system in the room
- Puzzle solving and direct perception, not expert-driven problem solving
- Democratic structure
- Meeting conditions for effective communications and dialogue
- Searching for common ground by making conflicts rational

Open Systems Thinking

The Search Conference methodology integrates "open systems thinking" (F. Emery, 1969, 1981) into every step of the process. Open systems theory maintains that for any system to remain viable and healthy over time, it must maintain an open and actively adaptive relationship with its environment. We define *system* to mean any organization, community, or network that coheres around a single principle or set of shared purposes in relation to the external environment. The *environment* is whatever lies outside the boundaries of a system.

One of the defining features of a Search Conference is that the first task begins by engaging participants in a scan of their environment. Participants look outside their own system, taking the widest possible perspective. Most organizations and communities have a tendency to focus inward, and to look forward only so far in time as the next election or business quarter. A Search Conference challenges participants to think outside the box, and to expand their scope by shifting their attention to the wider global context. Search conferencing also requires participants to analyze and synthesize this data, to make sense of it in such a way that it becomes useful and relevant to their own future.

Starting the conference by taking a look at the wider environment contextualizes the immediate system in the room—the organization, community, or issue that is of concern. As participants gain a direct understanding and appreciation of the changes that have been happening around them and the underlying changes in values, they begin to see their own system and issues in a new light. A great deal of learning occurs as participants develop a shared context for the host of changes that present challenges to the future of their system.

Getting the Right System in the Room

The only people who attend a Search Conference are those who are part of the system, since they are the ones who have true responsibility for its future. It is important to get the right system in the room, that is, to assemble the people whose knowledge is essential to achieving the purpose of the Search Conference. A Search Conference should be convened only if there is a clear purpose for doing so. At minimum, there must be a felt need to plan the future of a system so as to bring into being a state of affairs that does not currently exist, and would not come into existence on its own.

The purpose, or conference task, determines the nature of the system and the criteria for participant selection—in other words, who's in and who's out. For example, if the purpose of a corporate Search Conference is to develop a strategy for organizational renewal, the system is clearly that of a cross section of managers and employees from various departments and levels. Customers, suppliers, government regulators, and the like are extraneous to that system. They are not in a position to take responsibility for the fate and survival of an organization of which they are not a part. Of course, if it is important for the system to have accurate and up-to-date information about the way its products and services are perceived by customers, then this information can be collected prior to the conference, during the preparation and planning stage. This is quite different from having outsiders involved in the actual conference event.

Does this mean that customers or suppliers never participate in a corporate Search Conference? Never say never. If the purpose of a corporate Search Conference is to forge new strategic partnerships with customers and suppliers, this purpose will result in a completely different definition of the system. In this case, the system boundary would include customers and suppliers, since their participation is critical to achieving the purpose of the Search Conference.

Puzzle Solving and Direct Perception

Because the Search Conference shifts planning from away from means (tactics, operations, and short-term goals) to ends (ideals, strategies, and long-term purposes), the learning component is different from that involved in problem solving. Rather, it requires thought processes similar to the type required when attempting to solve a jigsaw puzzle. Each situation is so complex and unpredictable that one has to learn and step through the problem in a nonlinear fashion. Previous learning or existing knowledge may not be relevant. One can determine what is required for a piece to fit, but until that piece is found, one has very little idea of what is going to be required of the next pieces. Because the path to a puzzle solution is nonlinear, it is difficult to specify routine procedures or predefined steps that one can rely upon to solve puzzle-like situations. Puzzle solving is more a function of an ability for perceptual synthesis than for analytical conceptualization, since the search for possibilities is more important than a reliance on existing conceptual knowledge. This implies that expert knowledge is not privileged. In the Search Conference, each participant attends because of potential for contributing knowledge and expertise about some piece of the overall puzzle. Thus, everyone attending a Search Conference is considered an expert.

The emphasis is on becoming more perceptive of trends and possibilities. This implies that direct perception of the environment becomes central to the purposes of active adaptation. Search conferencing is based on a theory of ecological, direct perception that maintains that human beings have an innate ability to directly perceive meaning from the environment (F. Emery, 1993; Gibson, 1979). No firm barriers can be drawn between this form of common-sense knowledge and scientific or scholarly bodies of knowledge (F. Emery, 1981, 1993; Yankelovich, 1991). A Search Conference allows people to regain confidence in their innate abilities for direct perception, searching, and puzzle solving their way through patterns, trends, and complex situations.

Democratic Structure

The Search Conference builds a democratic structure, locating responsibility for coordination and control of planning tasks with those who attend the conference. That is, the people doing the planning, the learning, and the work have the responsibility for controlling and coordinating their own affairs. Because responsibility for work and outcomes is located squarely in the hands of participants in a Search Conference, the participants coalesce naturally into a cooperative organization rather than a competitive one. This essential feature is known in theoretical terms as the *second organization design principle,* or more simply, as Design Principle 2 (DP2) (F. Emery, 1977).

This is in stark contrast to the first design principle (DP1), where responsibility for coordination and control is located a level above the one where productive activity is actually occurring. We are all familiar with this sort of bureaucratic organization and the reactions it evokes. Consider the traditional academic "talking heads" conference, where responsibility for the content is invested in a small group of speakers and the rest of the participants are in the audience, theoretically relegated to a totally passive role devoid of responsibility. How much of the productive work of such a conference gets done in its official sessions? And how much in the hotel bars?

Work Mode

Bion (1961) used the term *mode* to describe a group's approach to its operations. He pointed out that when people come together they establish a group very quickly, and that a group, like an individual, has a life of its own. A group is not just a collection of individuals, but a separate entity that has its own dynamics, behaviors, and operating assumptions. Bion observed that at any given time, a group is operating out of either *work mode* or *basic assumption mode.* The work mode occurs when a group is fully responsible for the control and coordination of its own process and output, with prior agreements established among members with regard to their goals and overall purpose. It is characterized by the display of high levels of energy, learning, and cooperation, and sustained concentration toward completing tasks on time. Through a democratic structure and clearly specified, time-bound tasks, a Search Conference establishes a work mode among its participants.

When groups feel threatened and insecure, they fall prey to basic assumptions as a means of preserving group identity. Emotions become extraordinarily intensified, while intellectual abilities become markedly reduced (Bion, 1961, p. 174). Bion identified three basic group assumptions: dependency, fight-flight, and pairing. When a group is in a dependency mode, members look to a leader to sustain the functioning of their group. As in a bureaucratic structure, individuals do not develop creative relationships with each other, but instead depend upon a supervisor to tell them what to do (Bion, 1952, p. 238). The emotional tone of a group is negative when any of the basic assumptions are operating, and energy and learning are particularly low in a dependent group. In the grip of dependency, the learning process appears quite similar to the process of television viewing—people are passive, uncritical, and mentally lazy. In fight-flight, group members will often look to a leader or person to mobilize the group for action against a real or imagined threat that is seen to reside outside the group. When group members are in a fight mode, their concern is with winning their arguments and making telling points, not with enhancing their understanding. In flight, a group may unconsciously ignore directives and appear impatient, edgy, and distracted. By contrast, a group in the pairing mode seems happy and high-spirited. Bion observed pairing when animated discussions, usually between two members at a time, take precedence in a group, diverting attention toward some new and hopeful idea. Pairing can actually be a prelude to the work mode. In this case, the pair is attempting to give birth to a new idea, yet, for the group to remain in the pairing state, the new idea must remain unborn. So there is often a lot of hopeful talk, but no real committed action.

The Search Conference is designed to minimize outbreaks of Bion's three group assumptions. The Search Conference manager needs the skills to manage these dynamics should they occur by redirecting the conference back into work mode before emotional group assumptions become entrenched.

Meeting Conditions for Effective Communications

A Search Conference seeks to realize the rich potential of face-to-face human interaction. This potential goes beyond the ordinary goal of improving information exchange. Rather, the Search Conference is intent on establishing the conditions for effective and influential communications, of creating a shared context for collaborative group work.

Communication has come to be equated with the transmission and acknowledgment of message packets between a sender and receiver. But this digitized conception of communication—now expressed in such words as interact, connect, interface, and network—conveys a completely different tone from the richness of real face-to-face conversation or dialogue. Interestingly, the word communication derives from the Latin root verb *communicare*—meaning "to share" as a general term, going far beyond words or even ideas.

Solomon Asch (1952) outlined four conditions essential for effective and influential communications: openness, shared field, psychological similarity, and trust. These four conditions should be an integral part of any Search Conference design.

The first condition—openness—is critical to all facets of Search Conference design and management. In operational terms, openness means ensuring that things are what they appear to be, with no hidden agendas lurking behind the scenes. Joint action is more likely to emerge from communication among participants who can perceive that their surroundings are open and accessible to them all equally. For this reason, all information in a Search Conference is public and out in open view for inspection by all. Individual note taking or filling out of worksheets is discouraged in favor of recording perceptions on flip charts, while managers of the process refrain from becoming involved in the content of group discussions. Indeed, all group work is self-managing. Any hint of manipulation will violate the condition of openness, and inhibit the development of trust.

Search conferencing is also designed to lead to the emergence of what Asch called a mutually shared field. In the first phase of a Search Conference, participants focus on their environment, thereby establishing the presence of a field that has features they all perceive. With the emergence of this shared context, people validate their perception that they all live in the same world. The third condition, basic psychological similarity, is established primarily through the sharing of human ideals that are elicited when people articulate and decide on a desirable future. As these conditions are established, so the fourth condition of trust develops and evolves.

Searching for Common Ground by Rationalizing Conflict

The Search Conference is unlike other team-building interventions, which tend to force groups to reach consensus on just about every issue. Rather than striving for consensus, a Search Conference focuses on identifying common ground, that is, areas in which people do agree spontaneously or after brief discussion. However, finding common ground is not an end in itself. At least not in the Search Conference, since to pursue common ground as an ultimate goal shifts the purpose away from task-oriented strategic planning. Rather, finding common ground is a means to an end, the end being serious commitment to action plans focused on achieving a more desirable future for the system.

The Search Conference builds common ground so that groups can also safely and rationally discuss their differences. Argument to sort out differences is essential when everybody's future is at stake. We don't try to put conflict on hold or facilitate it away. Instead, we deal with conflict directly by making it rational, objective, and discussable.

The rationalization of conflict is an essential feature of the Search Conference. Rationalizing conflict means taking it seriously, clarifying the thin line between agreement and disagreement. This process seeks to differentiate the points where participants agree— the area of common ground (which is normally much larger than expected)—from the points that evoke clear disagreement or irreconcilable difference. This cannot be done if task groups produce shopping lists of items, reporting them out without the benefit of serious debate in the larger community. What is found then is not so much common ground as an undifferentiated array of opinions and data. In contrast, the Search Conference method involves a highly intensive process of integration aimed at generating plans that are owned as a final community product. This means that all group reports in the Search Conference are integrated into a binding piece of community property.

Phases of a Search Conference

Regardless of details of design, each Search Conference has three discrete and irreducible phases. Because each phase consists of specially designed tasks that elicit a special set of learnings, none of these phases should be omitted, mixed up, merged, or compressed. Figure 2.1 illustrates how these three phases follow the logic of the open system, focusing first on the environment, then on the system itself, and ending with an integration between the two.

Phase One: Environmental Appreciation

The Search Conference community together begins by looking outside their system in the first phase, searching for relevant changes and trends in the environment. It is in this first phase that recent changes in the environment, along with a search for the most desirable and probable future for the world, are put into perspective in the present. The global scan of the environment also serves the purpose of community building. As a community or organization that is coming together to search for a more desirable future, people quickly realize that, as participants and as a system, they share the same ideals and aspirations. This is how common ground is established at the outset of the Search Conference.

Figure 2.1. Three Phases of the Search Conference.

Environment

System

Learning Planning

Phase One
Environmental
Appreciation

Changes in the
world around us

Desirable and
probable futures

Phase Two
System Analysis

History of the system

Analysis of present system

Desirable future for
the system

Phase Three
Integration of system
and environment

Dealing with
constraints

Strategies and
action plans

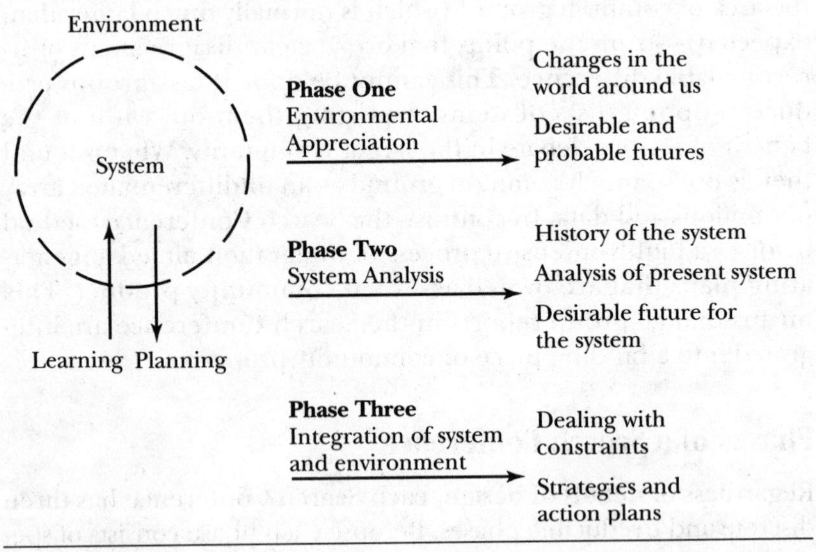

Phase Two: System Analysis

In the second phase, participants explore the unique character of their system and where it has come from.

Examining the Past

There can be no viable future that does not have its roots somewhere in the past. New futures will not spring into being without sharing some of the continuities that people value in their lives and their previous work. The past of the system is examined in a history session, which serves to appreciate those continuities in the present, providing a platform from which participants may then proceed to evaluate the current system. Participants reflect on such questions as What is unique about our culture? What historical events have shaped our identity? and What aspects of our character do we need to preserve and value as we plan for the future? The history of a system is as much a part of the context as is the environment. Strategy development cannot be detached from a system's culture and history.

Analyzing the Present

Participants then are primed to examine the workings of their current system. They analyze as broadly as possible the system as it exists in the present, and begin a discussion of what they wish to keep and what they need to change, given the continuities inherited from their past. They also begin to foreshadow their desirable future by including discussion of gaps in the present system, identifying system features that do not currently exist but that need to be created or developed. As both the history of the organization and the probable future of the environment have been examined within the present, along with a critical look at the current operating system, these data sets provide plenty of creative stimulation.

Dreaming of the Future

By the time participants have worked their way through learning about the environment and about their system, they are literally buzzing with new ideas and possibilities. Here, participants envision the most desirable future for their system and a set of strategic goals for making this desirable future a reality. They are encouraged to dream of their desirable future, that is, what their system will actually look like five or ten years out (or some other suitable time frame). "Dream prepares the way for action; man must first dream the possible before he can do it" (Caudwell, 1937, p. 82). Search Conferences have been conducted successfully across many cultures and with many age groups, demonstrating the universal truth of Caudwell's insight. The learning environment within the Search Conference encourages a great deal of social creativity, stretching the imaginations of all participants.

Phase Three: Integration of System and Environment

By the time the community has worked on strategic goals and is ready to develop action plans, it has done its dreaming. The Search Conference—like a lot of other methods—provides the conditions for dreaming, but it also ensures the conditions for planning the action. Throughout its design and process, the Search Conference focuses on the possible, not merely the probable, the feasible, or the conventional. In this third phase, the Search community has to bring its dreams to earth. Because the Search Conference is a task-oriented event, time is also spent identifying the major constraints likely to be encountered during implementation. Constraints to achieving strategic goals are often associated with time, money, resources, internal politics, and so forth. Here, participants not only identify constraints, but they devise strategies for bypassing or overcoming them. Participants review all the data they gathered in previous phases, selecting the points that provide the best guidance for their plans. These plans specify steps to be taken by the participants themselves, who thus—as part of the planning process—make detailed public commitments to making their desirable futures happen.

Phase Three is where the solid action planning takes place. This involves making specific, detailed operational plans that specify how the desirable future will be brought into being. During this phase, participants decide how they are going to begin implementing their strategies. This involves specifying who is going to take responsibility for each action item, by when, and how such activities will be monitored and evaluated. Another major task of this phase is directed toward deciding who else needs to be involved in the implementation effort. This phase creates the active adaptive relationship between the system and the environment, drawing together the key dimensions of all previous work.

Time for a New Way

Corporations, school systems, government agencies, and nonprofit community organizations are all feeling the pinch of change and uncertainty. Many of these organizations have discovered that it is self-defeating to separate thinking from doing, planning from implementation, head from heart. Further, many organizations are discovering that expert-driven planning processes take too long, are costly, and inspire little commitment on the part of those who have to take responsibility for implementation. This should come as no surprise: conventional planning fractionates the planning process into bits and pieces, with some of the intelligence gathering assigned to staff specialists, and other assessment tasks delegated to consultants, while an elite group remains the centralized brain of the firm. The Search Conference is an alternative planning method by which a large group of people can collectively search for new directions, in new ways, for new times. In the next chapter we will learn that effective planning in a turbulent environment must necessarily be a synthetic activity of seeing wholes and gestalts, which is exactly what the Search Conference was designed to accomplish.

Part Two

Understanding Search Conference Principles

Chapter Three

Planning in Stable and Turbulent Environments

Learning to plan in a world characterized by uncertainty is a major challenge for every modern government, community, and organizational leader. Popular metaphors reflect a widespread effort to make sense of the world's sudden shift into an age of uncertainty. Such phrases as "change is the only constant," "thriving on chaos," and "managing in permanent whitewater" (Peters, 1988; Vaill, 1982) permeate the management consulting literature. Although coined in the hope of awakening leaders to the challenges their organizations face today, such phrases often evoke a defeated, doom-is-inevitable response instead.

Yet this environmental uncertainty has certainly jolted organizations and communities. Massive layoffs, downsizings, and budget reductions are frequent. The speed and extent of change in the world has been a popular topic since Alvin Toffler's *Future Shock* (1970), which now stands as a harbinger of the sweeping changes that ushered in the postindustrial age. Search conferencing as a strategic planning tool can help organizations and communities develop an internal capacity to respond actively and adaptively to environmental uncertainty.

Accustomed to methods of planning that worked well in the past, many organizations and communities have become complacent. If natural selection is operating on the level of the social environment, the degree to which societal institutions appear to be failing to heed signals and perturbations calling for new approaches to planning evokes a chilling prospect of institutional extinction. Many organizations and communities seem to be unaware of how radically their environment has changed. To meet the challenges of planning in an uncertain world, it is necessary to understand the evolution of the social environment.

Evolution in Social Environments

Emery and Trist (1965) described a concept they called the "extended social field" or "contextual environment"—that is, literally everything external to an organization that influences its operations. This extended social field contains a web of interdependencies and social forces that can have an indirect influence an any organization or system, none the less intense for being regarded as outside the range of its planning processes. For example, consider the operations of a paper mill that relies upon a certain lumber company as its preferred supplier of pulp. If the paper mill's favorite lumber company finds itself besieged by environmentalists, sued by government regulators, or boycotted by consumer groups, the paper mill is likely to find that its costs for raw materials have increased overnight. Many groups, organizations, and social forces in the contextual environment can have an indirect yet significant impact on an organization, while being far removed from the scene of action.

The contextual environment is a quasi-independent domain distinct from any particular system in the social field itself. This is, however, only half of the story; the implications go much deeper than this. One such implication is that the environment is subject to laws and dynamics of its own that are often incommensurate with the processes governing the exchanges and behaviors that define the internal dynamics of organizations. Translation: the strategies, mind-set, and behavior of managers who guide organizational decision making can be completely at odds with the rules of the game set by the type of environment the organization is operating in.

Task Environment

Within the contextual environment, a more immediate, local set of external forces can be identified. This is called the *task environment* (see Figure 3.1). The task environment is a subset of the contextual environment that consists of groups and organizations that interact directly with the system. It has also been called the transactional environment. For example, the task environment of an electronics firm would consist of raw material suppliers, sources of labor and talent, regulatory bodies, competitors (domestic and foreign), and customers (wholesalers and retailers). It is through these direct relationships that systems and environments mutually influence one another.

Because the task environment has more direct and highly visible links to the system, it is often assumed to be more powerful and important than the broader contextual environment. Indeed, the contextual environment is often ignored entirely. However, while the task environment is closer in proximity, the contextual environment can exert its influence indirectly on both the task environment and the system in ways that are often irreversible. Changes occurring in the contextual environment are beyond the direct control of any single organization. If changes in the contextual environment are not monitored, they can take a system or even a whole industry by surprise. Pasmore (1988, p. 7) cites such

Figure 3.1. Task and Contextual Environments.

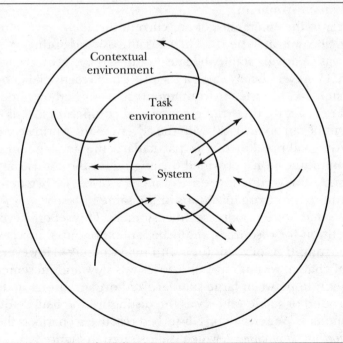

classic examples as Penn Central Railroad's refusal to acknowledge changes in the transportation industry and the U.S. automakers' dismissal of early Japanese competition. Therefore, organizations and communities must be highly aware of changing conditions occurring in the contextual environment when developing long-term plans and strategies.

The Stable-Competitive Environment

Emery and Trist (1965) went on to discuss the relevance of different environmental textures to organizational planning and design. The term *texture* is used by analogy with the surface of a body of land or water, whose quality has a major impact on those who travel on it. As conditions evolve and shift over time, the texture of the environment changes, resulting in fundamentally different types of environments that require fundamentally different survival behavior from systems within them (thus, the phrase "causal texture"). Emery and Trist (1965) describe four causal textures: Type I— placid, randomized environment; Type II—placid, clustered environment; Type III—disturbed-reactive environment; and Type IV— turbulent environment.

Prior to the emergence of our current turbulent environment, U.S. society was in Type III. The causal texturing of this environment was relatively stable, because values in society were widely shared. However, society earned the disturbed-reactive label by the way systems within the environment were disturbed by, and compelled to react to, the strategic moves of competitors. This environment began about 1790, with the advent of the world economy. Technological breakthroughs, particularly in energy generation and communications, provided the engine for the Industrial Revolution. As this competitive environment evolved, we began to see two or more large organizations in the same industry competing for the same finite resources and customers. This set off a cycle of competition for resources, requiring an exponential increase in the consumption of fossil fuels and heavy metals. However, the pace of change within most industries was slow and incremental. Competition between large standardized organizations against a background of stable values was the distinguishing feature of this environment. We refer to this disturbed-reactive scenario as the *stable-competitive environment,* which is illustrated in Figure 3.2.

Figure 3.2. Stable-Competitive Environment.

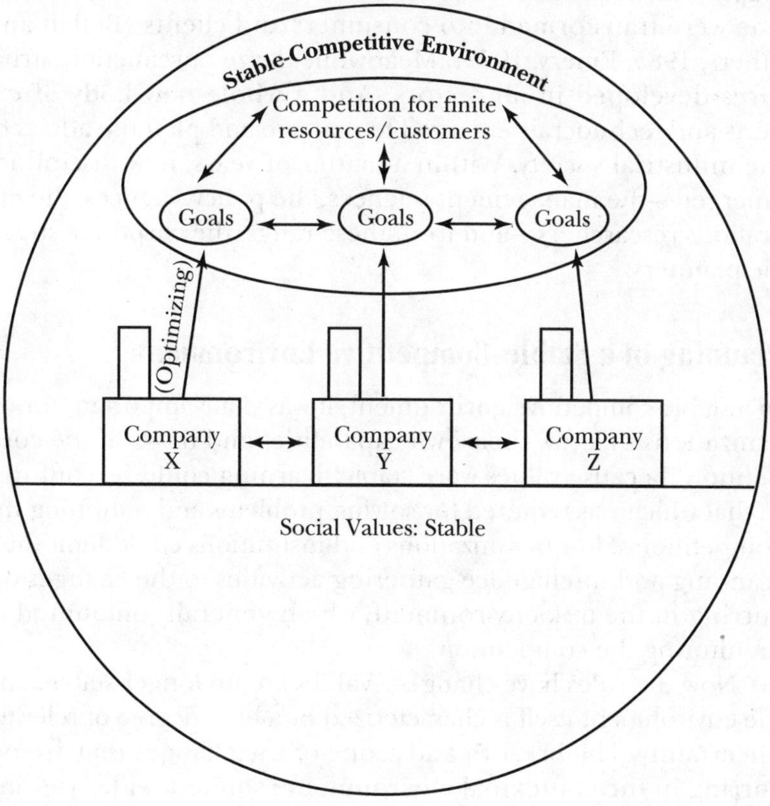

Rise of Bureaucracy

Coincident with the emergence of the stable-competitive environment, people flocked from the countryside to work in urban industrial centers. Industrial managers regarded these people for the most part as unreliable. To produce standardized, foolproof organizations out of supposedly unreliable human raw material, scientific management (Taylorism) was introduced on a wide scale, using a design principle called "redundancy of parts," which treated people as dispensable, replaceable parts—cogs in the industrial machine (Taylor, 1911). (Chapter Five discusses the effect of this view on the development of democracy.) Responsibility was removed from workers and given to supervisors who themselves were supervised, and so on, up the organizational pyramid. While employees on the inside were treated as cogs, citizens on the outside were transformed into consumers and clients (Bellah and others, 1985; Emery, 1977). Meanwhile, large bureaucratic structures developed in all sectors. And a whole new body of experts and technocrats emerged to manage and plan the affairs of the industrial society. Within a matter of years, new disciplines emerged—the management sciences, the policy sciences, the operations researchers—and from these ranks, the corporate strategic planners.

Planning in a Stable-Competitive Environment

In a stable-competitive environment, it was vitally important for organizations to know their own capabilities and those of the competition. Because values were stable, learning could be confined to that which was required for solving problems and outwitting the competition. Most organizations and institutions could limit their scanning and intelligence-gathering activities to the changes occurring in the task environment, which generally amounted to monitoring the competition.

Now the rules have changed. Values are no longer stable, and the environment itself is characterized by a high degree of relevant uncertainty. The breadth and scope of the changes that are occurring in the contextual environment require a wider viewing angle. Managers, leaders, and officials have been blindsided by unexpected events that could have been avoided if their antennas were attuned to changing trends in the contextual environment (Emery and Trist, 1973).

Outmoded Planning Assumptions

The fundamental reason why many organizations lost their dominance was that their managers and administrators believed the world had not changed. Had they still lived in a stable-competitive environment, their use of operational planning to devise short-term tactics and strategies for outmaneuvering the competition would have succeeded. Such outmoded assumptions about the environment eventually led to a crisis and failure in many industries.

In the early seventies, for example, executives at the Big Three U.S. automakers assumed that Japanese imports did not pose any major threat to their dominance of the market. The U.S. consumer electronics industry maintained the view that the Japanese could only produce and export cheap and shoddy goods.

The uncertainties of market forces that existed during this period of stability were also cyclic in nature. Thus, prediction based on linear planning and operations management methods were still effective. The purpose of planning was straightforward: compete for a higher budget, attain more resources, increase return on investment. Strategic planning was a relatively simple matter of reviewing the past performance of the enterprise and trying to second-guess the potential moves of competitors. Given this environmental context, strategic planning was approached as a high-level problem-solving exercise. The goal of planning was to increase efficiency and optimize the use of technical and financial resources.

Power Concentrated at the Top

Environmental stability also made it feasible to rely on standard but specialized planning procedures. Bureaucratic organizations universally concentrated power at the top of the pyramid. Those at higher levels were responsible for the thinking, and those at the bottom were held responsible for the doing. Consequently, the task of planning was considered the sovereignty of an elite few—a senior executive team, a city council, a school board—who then communicated their plans to employees and the public, expecting the masses to obey and efficiently implement the directives. There was no objective reason or seeming need to involve more constituents in the planning process. A handful of knowledgeable people entrusted with the task of planning could manage to plot a feasible course in an environment that was basically predictable. During the period of stability, this method worked.

Closed Systems Thinking

One of the major assumptions of expert-driven planning is that complex issues or problems can be broken into component parts and studied in isolation from their context. In other words, expert planners attempt to understand problems by abstracting and removing them from the environment in which they are embedded. This mechanistic approach reduces apparent uncertainty, but only at the cost of narrowing the scope of the problem. This amounts to a form of tunnel vision. In turbulent fields, problems are not discrete events or objective entities that can be studied or treated independently of their context.

Russell Ackoff (1994, p. 211) refers to these complex problems as *messes*. In our view, the word—and the instant sympathy it evokes—is symptomatic of a general failure to come to grips with the new environment. When so-called messes are placed in context and analyzed holistically, they may well cease to look messy; indeed, they often allow themselves to be dealt with. In a turbulent environment, the fact that the environment exists and is a partner in all problems and issues requires an entirely different approach, one that includes an analysis of the environment. If the environment is ignored, then of course the problem will look like a mess and remain insoluble.

Expert Problem Solving

Another major assumption of expert-driven planning is that scientific and technological knowledge will provide sufficient information upon which to base planning decisions. However, the use of such criteria assumes that the future endpoints or goals for a plan can be precisely defined. Expert planners use economic and technical criteria to gauge the trade-offs or evaluate the costs versus the benefits of various planning decisions. The propensity of experts to focus on means rather than on ends presumes not only that the desired future state of affairs is already known, but also that consensus around goals is widely shared. This is a big presumption to make in a turbulent environment.

It turns out that one of the main features of a turbulent environment is the virtual impossibility of completely defining future endpoints and strategic goals, or of extrapolating them from rational criteria. If they were definable, then expert problem solving would suffice—but what is needed in real life is adaptive puzzle solving instead. Despite its shortcomings and limitations, however, many managers and policy makers still hold to the myth of rational planning (Mintzberg, 1994).

Elitism of Experts

The scientific approach uses facts, hard data, and statistical analyses without inquiring about how the results will be received by those whose lives are affected by them. Under this view, firm barriers are drawn between experts and the general public. The experts assume that their knowledge is more legitimate and reliable than public opinion, dismissing common-sense knowledge born of first-hand perceptions and experience as unscientific. As a result, public judgment is devalued and marginalized (Yankelovich, 1991). Of course, rational problem solving and the knowledge of experts do have their place, and their ongoing usefulness to society is not in question. We all use doctors if we are seriously ill. It is *expertism* and not expertise that we challenge; the idea that power resides in a special class of professionals who maintain their status, authority, and privilege by marginalizing and alienating those outside their expert domains. As Bellah and his colleagues point out, "Democracy is not the rule of experts" (Bellah and others, 1985, p. 272).

Value-Free Planning

Expert planning also accepts the assumption that scientific and technical knowledge is value-free and objective, even though the claim of value neutrality and objectivity is the subject of heated debate and controversy in the natural and social sciences. Meanwhile, the stature of science and public confidence in expert-technocratic solutions has steadily eroded. The public is less willing to pour billions of tax dollars into megascience research and large-scale social engineering projects. Big, bureaucratically managed programs are the targets of growing public suspicion and skepticism.

Even if the claims of value neutrality were accepted, there is still the sticky question of whose interests and value criteria will determine the strategic agenda and ultimate ends to be served by such programs. Policy makers are no longer able to simply specify a set of objectives for projects and assume that expert planners will crunch out the optimum set of feasible alternatives. In a pluralistic society, there are no longer clear-cut agreements about what constitutes the good life or desired ends.

The Dilemma of Expert-Driven Planning

It often appears as though an inverse relationship exists between the amount and complexity of knowledge accumulated by the expert and the willingness of the people who would be affected to trust the expert enough to support and implement the expert's plan. As Emery (1977) observed:

> The hard won agreements that the optimizer has for the initial, hard-nosed definitions of objectives are no guarantee of active support when it comes to implementation. On the contrary, I think that these agreements carry with them the needs of subsequent subversion. . . . Nor can the optimizer carry the day with his array of facts, statistical forecasts and impartial, objective calculations of the cost-effectiveness of alternative paths. These things do carry weight, but, when there is a feeling that justice is not being done facts will not convince otherwise. . . . The apparent dilemma in "modern" planning is "how does the expert make his contribution to planning without alienating people?" [p. 124].

This is followed by a second, related dilemma: the turbulent environment demands totally different methods of planning that use a much wider base of information, while the knowledge available to planners becomes increasingly less relevant and trustworthy (M. Emery and Emery, 1978). These two dilemmas underscore the ineffectiveness of expert-driven planning today and show that expert knowledge on its own is inappropriate as the base for planning in an uncertain environment.

Expert Planning Backfires

Planning that only takes into account technical and economic criteria will often produce outcomes that trigger unexpected problems and that have unintended consequences. Such outcomes are *quasi solutions* (Schwartz, 1971). Quasi solutions result from closed systems thinking. When planners shut out and ignore environmental influences, they are apt to generate quasi solutions that leave a residue of new problems. These new problems proliferate faster than solutions can be found to meet them, and each successive set of residue problems is more difficult to solve than its predecessor. Public policy decisions have often been driven by the sort of rational but short-term logic that results in quasi solutions. For example, DDT appeared to be an effective pesticide until its ill effects on the food chain were discovered. Although DDT was banned from use in the United States, the government still allows it to be exported to foreign countries. Unregulated on foreign markets, DDT and other hazardous chemicals have had a severe impact on farmers in Third World countries. Further, traces of DDT have been detected in vegetables and other produce that have been imported to the United States. Recently, the U.S. Food and Drug Administration prevented a shipment of thirty million pounds of Australian beef from entering the country because of illegally high residues of DDT and dieldrin (Global Tomorrow Coalition, 1990). As quasi solutions proliferate, more remedial measures are needed that require more and more expenditures.

What is going on here? Expert-driven planning focuses on solving aspects of problems that can be defined in terms of economic or technical criteria, allowing rational predictions to be made with respect to the probability of success for various alternative solutions. However, because the planning situation cannot be precisely defined in turbulent environments, the probability of failure for a solution alternative depends a totally different set of criteria than the probability of success (Simmonds, 1972). For example, the planning that led to the design and production of the supersonic transport plane was successful in meeting engineering criteria, but underestimated the general public's reaction to noise effects. The nuclear power industry was immobilized by public outcry when consumer action groups questioned the safety and standards of this form of energy. Expert criteria are value-based judgments that reside in the broader social environment.

Effects of Turbulence on Expert Planning

As stated earlier, leaders and managers are discovering today that expert-based approaches to planning are becoming increasingly unreliable. Such approaches usually fail to take into account changes happening in the wider social environment, especially those changes that can have a significant impact on the future. The failures and shortcomings of top-down strategic planning are now evident. While the upper echelons of an organization or community are involved and highly committed to the strategic plan, the rest of the membership and citizenry, having been excluded and distanced from the planning process, feel disenfranchised and alienated. Plans that disregard the distinct character of an organization or community usually result in lack of commitment, resistance, or even outright sabotage. As a result, when the plan reaches the rank-and-file or grassroots community level, implementation or completion of a project usually founders.

The Two Forks dam project in Colorado provides a case in point. In the late 1980s, water experts responded to an impending shortage in the Denver area by proposing to build yet another dam—following the standard expert response to water scarcity in the semiarid West. However, the proposal failed to take into account significant changes in the contextual environment. This time, the public exploded. Conservation groups protested the destruction of another canyon and watershed. Tourists and sporting industries decried the impact on fishing and camping. Taxpayers rebelled against another perceived government pork barrel project when they could not see the need. Finally, the federal government killed the project because of environmental impact the expert planners had not foreseen.

Old Paradigms Die Hard

Why then, one might ask, are outmoded planning approaches still widely used in our institutions? Upon first glance, simple answers come to mind: force of habit, lack of knowledge of alternative methods, or resistance to change (Michael, 1973). Despite the way leaders and managers habitually speak of their organizations, communities, and institutions being embedded in a complex, dynamic, and uncertain environment, they still use planning processes suited to a type of environment now long gone.

While they may well be aware that environmental uncertainty has increased, the realization has not led to a commensurate shift in planning methods. Many managers and leaders seem to be caught in a double bind; they realize that the old practices and techniques of planning and organizing are not working, but feel compelled to try harder in applying the old paradigm. Even many of the so-called participative planning methods are really remnants of the old paradigm in disguise. As the saying goes, "Old paradigms die hard." One thing is clear, though: expert, top-down approaches to planning are now obsolete. Their continued use will surely lead to more planning disasters and missed opportunities (Goodman, 1971), not to mention to yet more alienated employees and apathetic citizens. Those responsible for charting the course of their organizations and communities need to appreciate more fully the role of the social environment in the planning process.

These problems and limitations emerge when planning methods more suitable for a stable environment are used in a turbulent one. In the face of complex interdependencies, high degrees of relevant uncertainty, and rapid change, simple linear projections by expert planners focused upon optimizing technical and economic goals are doomed to fail. These closed system methods cannot be applied successfully in a turbulent environment.

The Turbulent and Uncertain Environment

Emery and Trist (1965) observed a new type of environment emerging, characterized by a condition that looked like the social equivalent of having the ground in motion. They classified this new type of environment as a "turbulent field," noting that the environmental contexts for organizations were becoming increasingly complex. The complexity they observed came not only from the interactions between competing organizations, but from interactions among other components in the field itself (see Figure 3.3).

The texture of the new type of environment is described as turbulent because of the myriad of unpredictable interactions and enmeshed connections between different facets and groups in society. The long-term effects of organizational actions in turbulent fields are also difficult to predict and trace. Because of closely linked interdependencies, small errors can be amplified beyond all expectations. Turbulence also describes the condition where dramatic and unpredictable shifts in social values produce high relevant uncertainty and institutional instability.

Up through the late 1960s and early 1970s, it was possible for planners to ignore the environmental context. But as sweeping social changes took hold and dramatic discontinuities emerged, relevant

Figure 3.3. Turbulent Environment.

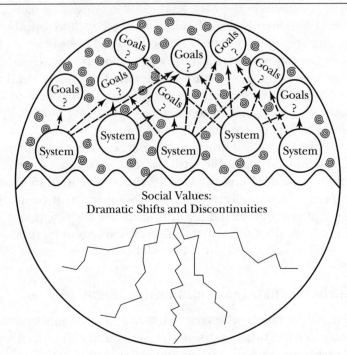

uncertainty increased. Consider these examples, adapted and enlarged from a list generated by Steve Cabana, that represent dramatic value shifts and discontinuities in the environment over the last several decades:

- The resurrection of European and Japanese manufacturing from the mid 1960s to the present
- The oil crisis and rise of the OPEC cartel from the mid 1970s to the late 1980s
- The flooding of the U.S. market with Japanese consumer electronics and automobiles from the late 1960s to the present
- The recent explosion of personal computers and the information superhighway
- The increase in crime, drugs, and violence across the United States
- The end of the cold war

- The increase in the number of single-parent families
- The emergence of a permanent underclass, and a growing gap between the rich and poor
- The rise of the environmental movement and of public concern with environmental degradation
- An increase in school drop-out rates in the inner cities

Flexibility Alone Is Not Enough

Further discontinuities and social changes like those mentioned here are not only possible or even probable, they are virtual certainties. Organizations and communities are increasingly affected by changes in spheres far removed from their direct control. Many popular management consultants have exhorted that in order to deal with turbulence, people and organizations need to become fast and flexible (Meyer, 1993; Peters, 1988; Stalk and Hout, 1990). However, flexibility and speed will not necessarily reduce turbulence. Taking a flexible stance toward rapid change often amounts to nothing more than passively adapting to every changing condition that demands our attention.

Some of the conditions we are now being asked to adapt to are in fact pathological, noxious influences that have arisen because of our prolonged passive adaptation to turbulence. The dual-career family, for example, is now expected to adapt to the demands of bureaucratic workplaces by securing outside child care. Teenagers are expected to adapt to the absence of their parents by filling their time as they see fit—which often amounts to MTV. Citizens in Los Angeles are expected to adapt to high ozone levels by restricting their outdoor activities to certain times of the day. The high-powered sales executive is expected to adapt to the growing demand for instantaneous communications by installing a car fax. School administrators are expected to adapt to gangs by installing metal detectors at the entrances of school buildings.

Unfortunately, adapting to change has been misinterpreted as meaning acceptance of change. Ackoff (1994, p. 31) elaborates:

> When most of us speak of adaptation we mean passive response to an environmental or internal change that reduces a system's effectiveness. The passive adaptive response restores the original effectiveness or increases it. Thus, when an enterprise responds to the

introduction of a new product by a competitor by bringing out a similar product, it adapts passively. . . . In contrast, to adapt actively is to produce a change that is not a response to a decrease in effectiveness, but to a perceived opportunity to improve. It is adaptive behavior that is self-initiated, not externally stimulated . . . Passive adaptation is seldom creative or innovative; active adaptation often is.

Management metaphors like the ones discussed at the beginning of the chapter ("permanent whitewater" and so on) promote the idea of passive adaptation. By interpreting turbulence as natural and perpetual, they stop people from inquiring into the societal currents that have contributed to the production of a turbulent field. However, people and organizations do not need to adapt to turbulence passively. They can and must reduce turbulence by actively changing and improving the conditions that surround them. In theoretical terms, this means that systems and environments must evolve together. People in organizations and communities can reduce environmental turbulence by planning and implementing their own collective future directions.

Strategy of the Indirect Approach

In a turbulent environment, the action of any one system is nested within, and affected by, the constellation of interdependencies among all other systems. The complexity inherent in this social field is the source of a great deal of relevant uncertainty. For these reasons, dynamic changes occurring in the turbulent environment trigger the need for dynamic changes in organizations and systems. The implication here is that for any planning system to be effective, it must become actively adaptive to the changes and discontinuities that are brought about by turbulence. In turbulent environments, value shifts and sharp discontinuities create a minefield for traditional planners accustomed to linear logic. Organizations and communities can no longer assume stable endpoints and fixed goals. Rather, endpoints and goals need to change frequently to ensure an effective and creative response to changing conditions. This means the pathway to a desirable future in this type of environment is not a linear course or a straight line, but rather a nonlinear, zig-zag pattern.

Strategic planning based on active adaptation assumes the possibility of discontinuities and the necessity for nonlinear maneuvering. Interestingly, *strategy* is a term taken from the art of war. Today, in this context, strategic planning is equivalent to the art and science of maneuvering. The Search Conference is a unique planning method because it addresses the contextual environment and its dynamics of interdependence and change. To artfully maneuver through turbulence, strategies need to be based on a broad approach. Such an approach to strategic maneuvering must anticipate likely constraints and obstacles, and devise pathways that can maximize gains while minimizing losses. This is known as the strategy of the indirect approach.

Figure 3.4 illustrates several means for enacting indirect strategies. These scenarios resemble moves on a Go board. Go is a Japanese game that requires the successful player to view the board as an integrated whole rather than as a series of independent situations with only vague or coincidental influence on one another.

One of the first tenets of an indirect approach is to avoid concentrating resources and efforts in one area. In Go, territory is captured and power concentrated by placing the stones over a widely dispersed area of the board such that the stones command areas of influence over previously unoccupied territory. This entails the strategic notion of concentration as the product of diversity. Often the strongest forces for change (or resistance) are found in coalitions within the informal system. The Search Conference employs this indirect approach: each individual who participates in the conference becomes a potential diffuser of the strategy. This is why broad-based participation is necessary; those immediately affected by strategic change need to be involved in designing the change. In a turbulent field, there is little point in rushing forward with a direct approach or concentrating your resources at one point; you could lose entirely the first time around. This principle also applies to action plans coming out of a Search Conference. Multiple action plans focused on different parallel initiatives stand a better chance of diffusion than those that concentrate all their resources on one big hit.

A second means of enacting an indirect approach is to apply effort in those sectors where there is likely to be the least resistance to change. It is in these areas where diffusion is likely to be

Figure 3.4. Strategy of the Indirect Approach.

Purpose: To control maximum territory with a minimum of resistance

Means:

1. Concentration as product of diversity
     • broad-front approach
     • not putting all your eggs in one basket

2. Effort directed towards points of least resistance and most future potential (multiplier effect). Capture the weakest link.

3. When attacked, pull out. Learning doesn't disappear.

4. Go around or encapsulate sources of resistance.

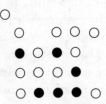

5. Encircle from within.

6. Victory and defeat are relative, depending upon the context.
    Field needs constant reevaluation while one moves within it.
    May have to shift or sacrifice some efforts and reassess priorities.

successful, thus creating a multiplier effect. Indeed, the most effective strategy will be that which positively diminishes the resistance to innovation and thereby increases the ratio of success to effort. Capturing the weakest links often amounts to infecting people in positions of power and decision making with the new ideas for strategic direction that are generated in the Search Conference. Those known to be guardians of the previous order are converted to champions and advocates for the revolution.

Since active adaptive planning involves continuous learning, it is far better to pull out of the battle scene when attacked than to be attacked twice in the same place, for the learning acquired doesn't disappear. This is based on the proposition verified by military experience: "The cumulative effect of partial success, or even a mere threat, at a number of points may be better than the effect of complete success at one point" (Hart, 1946, p. 169). Even the best-planned strategies can encounter an unexpected show of strength by competitors or resisters. Rather than expending all resources in areas that are fortified and impenetrable, it is better to concentrate attention on capturing new ground or seeking out areas of less resistance.

While it is prudent to focus strategic initiatives on points of least resistance, it is even wiser either to go around difficult areas or to encapsulate sources of resistance. Where there are key points of resistance in the system, these parties can be invited to participate in the Search Conference planning process. As potential sources of resistance are brought into the process and encouraged to become active participants in the search for puzzle solutions, obstacles to implementation can be preempted. Barriers to strategic change are circumvented by inducing shared ownership of plans in the wider system.

Another example of the indirect approach is that of encirclement from within. This is a strategy by which the attacker succeeds in gaining territory because he or she has infiltrated territory of the enemy and therefore can advance simultaneously from both within and without. In terms of the Search Conference, this infiltration is accomplished by creating conditions and tasks that evoke ideal-seeking behavior, and thus the excitement and joy that leads to psychological ownership. Those inside the system who have been so infiltrated may then join forces with those on the outside, together putting pressure on points of resistance.

Go is a protracted game—a war of patterns, in which victory and defeat are relative phenomena. The same is true of indirect strategies. Indirect strategies assume that discontinuities will change the rules of the game, requiring a constant reevaluation of the situation and the search for puzzle solutions. An active adaptive strategy is one that stays abreast of the whole situation, searching the external environment as a means of gauging where to make the next move, make the next change, commit necessary resources.

As in the game of Go, one cannot make assumptions about the stability of any of the positions on the field, including the assumption that one has a well-defended and safe base of operations. In other words, with indirect strategies, one must continually sense the field while moving within it. This is illustrated in Go by the fact that dead stones can come to life as the strategic situation changes. This often requires a temporary sacrifice of stones or areas of influence. As there can be no fixed front line, so there can only be total fluidity across the board.

How Search Conferencing Deals with Turbulence

The Search Conference is a method of planning that has the power to move people from passive to active adaptation to turbulence. By awakening and revitalizing the human capacity for seeking higher ideals, and by engaging people in a process of creative collaboration, it can initiate community development and social change. Moreover, in the Search Conference, people come to learn and appreciate that in a turbulent environment they cannot predict discontinuities in advance, but need to be in a constant learning mode in anticipation of them (Mintzberg, 1994; Purser and Pasmore, 1992). Search conferencing highlights the importance of constant vigilance (Cabana, Emery, and Emery, 1995; Pasmore, 1988) while introducing a wider viewing angle for scanning changing trends in the contextual environment.

We discussed how a narrow and myopic view of the environment leaves a system vulnerable to surprise and unexpected change. Here is where the Search Conference expands the scope of expert-driven planning. Search conferencing generates an information base beyond the range of any small group of experts by exploring multiple perspectives of the environment through the direct perceptions of many individuals—all experts in something, whether it be marketing research or shop floor operations. No one individual, party, or department can claim that their view of the environment is exclusive or privileged. Perception of the environment is in fact highly colored by the viewer's position, disciplinary background, past organizational experience, tenure in the company, and so forth (Purser and Pasmore, 1992). The Search Conference provides a structured forum where these multifarious perceptions of the system and environment can be appreciated, explored, and analyzed (Vickers, 1965). Going beyond rational methods of planning, the Search Conference validates the perceptual diversity of human experience. Indeed, it is this search process that allows a whole view of the planning situation to come into focus.

Those with technical expertise attend the Search Conference as full participants, not as guests or special resources. However, the Search Conference does not just result in more information and data about the environment. Rather, the Search Conference process also yields a *shared view* of the environment as conflicts or perceptual disagreements are made rational, data and information are integrated, and common ground is discovered.

Further, by exploring and remaining open to possibilities, the Search Conference also challenges people to question the status quo. Strategies that were successful in the past are no longer viewed as sacred. Assumptions that were previously taken for granted, especially those that pertained to definitions of success and organizational effectiveness, are reevaluated and opened to question. Since clear endpoints cannot be precisely specified in an uncertain environment, the Search Conference instills a new mindset: effective strategic planning comes from sensing trends and initiating change through the exploration of possibilities. Changing environmental conditions are understood in advance so systems can actively adapt to such changes. As an organizational system enacts plans for a more desirable future and utilizes the strategy of the indirect approach for getting around existing constraints, the system is also acting upon its environment, transforming it into a more favorable environment to maneuver in. Active adaptation to turbulent conditions entails learning how to adjust and redefine the path to desirable futures in *real time*. Direct participation and involvement in planning and implementation is how systems and the people in them learn how to become actively adaptive. This form of proactive planning is a social innovation that empowers people to take action and implement strategies that can have a turbulence-reducing effect.

Experts Use the Search Conference

To deal with an imminent crisis over regional water resources, Colorado Governor Roy Romer challenged water experts to develop a strategic plan for water usage that would satisfy the needs of the Front Range region well into the next century, without having to build new dams. After some frustrating and unsuccessful efforts, the water experts held the Search Conference mentioned briefly in Chapter One. They found it to be a practical alternative planning method. It is useful to consider this public-sector case in more detail here, as it illustrates the way search conferencing can help resolve conflicts by fostering collaboration across agency boundaries. Much of this information was adapted from an unpublished report by Rita Scwheitz.

BACKGROUND ON THE FRONT RANGE FORUM

In response to an executive order issued by the governor of Colorado, the Front Range Forum was established to enhance cooperation in the planning and development of future water supplies for the Denver Metropolitan area. The Front Range Forum is an amalgamation of political and community leaders interested in water resource management along a 150-mile stretch of cities, suburbs, farms, open space, and small towns on the eastern side of the Rocky Mountains.

The initial formation of the Front Range Forum was met with hope, distrust, and skepticism. Communities with scarce water supplies hoped that the state would play a major role in helping them find solutions to their water needs, while communities with adequate supplies of water feared that state involvement might disrupt their current and future access to water. Additionally, all involved were concerned with federal water policy, such as that mandated by the Threatened and Endangered Species Act.

Despite these reservations, the mayors of many of the Front Range communities, representatives from water interests and conservancy districts, legislators, and state officials agreed to support the Forum's mission for furthering multijurisdictional interagency cooperation. Further, the state legislature appropriated $450,000 to conduct the Metro Water Supply Investigation, a study of cooperative water options for the Front Range. Engineers representing different interest groups were appointed to a Technical Advisory Committee (TAC) to examine possible engineering solutions to water planning in the area. Technical consultants were also hired to help conduct the study.

Although initial information exchange meetings of the TAC were useful, the group could not reach any substantive agreement on its mission or ground rules. The TAC also was unable to develop a protocol that everyone could agree to for conducting future water studies associated with the Metro Water Supply Investigation. The work of the TAC stalled, with no clear end in sight. The study failed to move forward. Acknowledging this stalemate, several TAC members who had previously participated in the successful Water Quality Search Conference described in Chapter Two (Rehm, Schweitz, and Granata, 1992) proposed that the TAC convene its own Search Conference.

Rationale for the Conference

The TAC chose to sponsor a Search Conference because it offered the opportunity to focus on the future rather than the contentious past. They hired conference managers to work with a small planning group of TAC members. The planning group defined the purpose of the Search Conference as to:

- Enhance working relationships among TAC members
- Develop a mission and ground rules for guiding the work of the TAC
- Determine an organizational structure that would promote the timely completion of the scoping phase of the Forum's technical investigation

More specifically, the TAC Search Conference was convened for the purpose of bringing the group together to develop a common vision and action plan for the Metro Water Supply Investigation. The planning group decided to invite all current members of the TAC, plus a number of technical consultants who were under contract to work on the study, and also some specialists from other cities, agricultural organizations, public interest groups, and appropriate federal agencies.

Conference Design

Following the funnel approach, the Front Range Water Forum Search Conference started at the broadest possible level, examining recent changes in the world, and narrowing to consider specific actions necessary to implement a shared plan. The design for the conference is shown in Figure 3.5.

**Figure 3.5. Front Range Water
Forum Search Conference Design**

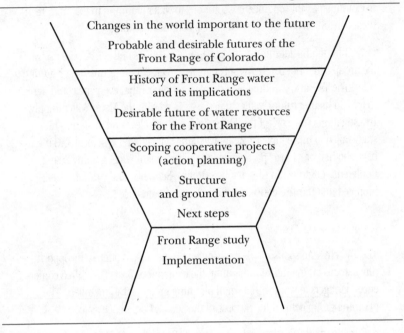

Changes in the world important to the future

Probable and desirable futures of the
Front Range of Colorado

History of Front Range water
and its implications

Desirable future of water resources
for the Front Range

Scoping cooperative projects
(action planning)

Structure
and ground rules

Next steps

Front Range study

Implementation

CONFERENCE HIGHLIGHTS

Over forty people attended the conference, which was held at a retreat center in the foothills of the Rocky Mountains. During the expectations session, participants grappled with the impact of meeting former adversaries and antagonists in an isolated setting for three continuous days. "I don't know what's going to happen here but it should be interesting. The last time I was in the same room with him was in state water court," one apprehensive participant said of another, adding "And we were on opposite sides."

The first task served to place water planning issues within a wider context of the turbulent environment. Because the brainstorming session focused on the wider external environment, this previously contentious group was quickly sharing perceptions, hopes, and fears about the world.

Next, the group explored the desirable and probable future of the Front Range of Colorado. In small, randomly assigned mixed groups, participants explored their hopes, visions, concerns, and disagreements on what the Front

Range would look like if nothing changed and trends in the environment continued on their present course (the probable future). Other small groups explored what they hoped the future could become if they had their way (desirable future). The conference managers instructed each of the small groups to agree upon five scenarios descriptive of their assigned type of future (probable or desirable) for the Front Range area. The first evening ended with animated discussions of values, hopes, and disappointments.

THE MORNING AFTER

In the morning, the TAC continued its exploration of the desirable future of the Front Range, and came to an agreement on the following vision concepts:

- Efficient and well-managed resource development
- Cooperation and coordination of planning and services
- High quality of life
- Sustainability of ecosystems (including humans)

    These shared ideals displayed that emergence of common ground among the diverse factions and competing interests in the room. Discovering this area of common ground would provide the backdrop for the more controversial topics that were to follow. One item didn't make it onto the list. Some groups argued for the "conservation of agriculture land areas" as a desirable future concept for the Front Range area. Other groups strongly contested this concept. After much heated discussion, it was apparent that there was a clear disagreement surrounding this issue, so it was placed on the "disagree list."

LOOKING BACK ON WATER PLANNING

For the history session, conference managers asked participants to talk about the key events and milestones in the history of water planning. Conference managers captured historical data on large pieces of flip-chart paper in front of the room. People were engaged as they talked about key turning points, milestones, controversies, disappointments, failures, and successes. It was clear to everyone that increasing public concern for the environment meant that cooperative and collaborative approaches to water planning would become increasingly necessary.

DESIRABLE FUTURE FOR WATER MANAGEMENT

Participants generated a list of forty items describing the desirable future for water management along the Front Range. To prioritize these forty items into a workable list, the group used a very involving cut-and-paste process to cluster items on the wall. With scissors in hand, each small group cut its list of items into strips, posting the strips on the wall. The entire large group, after long discussions and debates, arranged the items into thirteen logical clusters. Each small group defined three key criteria for prioritizing items, then evaluated each of the thirteen clusters against their criteria. This process allowed them to narrow down the list to five key cluster themes, which the TAC incorporated as guidelines for conducting the Water Investigation study. Toward evening, the entire community had selected and agreed upon four fast-track project areas to be defined in the cooperative water options study:

- Conjunctive use of ground and surface water
- Effluent management
- Interruptible supplies
- Integrated water systems

By the end of the evening the group was quite relieved that it had developed a common list of guidelines and potential project study areas.

THE FINAL CHALLENGE: DEVELOPING COMMON PROTOCOLS

On the last day of the conference, people self-selected the area they were most interested in, spending most of the remaining day organizing the work of their task forces. Each task force spent considerable time and energy defining its purpose, options, scope, outcomes, areas of concerns, and future actions that would guide the Metro Water Supply Investigation. Each task force shared its findings in plenary sessions, entertaining questions and modifying its plans based on the feedback from the large group.

The conference concluded with a session that designed a new organizational structure for the TAC and developed common work protocols and ground rules for future deliberations. Everyone agreed that a steering group composed of one person from each of the four task forces, plus two technical consultants and the Department of Natural Resources' Assistant Director, would meet monthly to coordinate activities, network, and handle any issues that needed to be addressed.

RESULTS AND ACCOMPLISHMENTS

At the conclusion of the conference, everyone was amazed about what they accomplished: they established solid relationships and developed a common mission and ground rules, and they had designed a structure and created task forces and action plans based on the tacit agreement that working cooperatively was in their best interest. In celebration of these accomplishments, a photographer took a picture of the whole group—they were all smiling, surprised and pleased with their joint products.

In the ten months following the Search Conference, the TAC has continued to meet and make progress. The Metro Water Investigation Study is now on track. The technical consultants—who before the Search Conference had feared that they would never be able to conduct the study at all—are now confident that the study will be completed on schedule.

Scoping plans and cost estimates for various cooperative water projects have already been completed. In the area of conjunctive water use, for example, the technical consultants have developed a computer model that graphically demonstrates the concept of conjunctive use and its effects. The what-if model has served as a discussion tool for all involved parties to further explore the ramifications of cooperation. More recently, some people who had been bystanders before the conference have reconnected with the process. Agricultural interests are now back on the table. As one participant from this sector remarked, "We had no reason to talk to each other a year ago, but now it makes sense to hold dialogues."

Reflecting back on the significance of the conference, some of the participants made these comments: "The Search Conference provided a structure for participants to get acquainted and hang out together in a relaxed atmosphere," and "The Search Conference was a time-out for participants to understand the Forum concept, put their stamp on the study, readdress issues of concern, and get more comfortable with people in the TAC." Another said, "I had wanted to talk about the mistrust and suspicion but we didn't do that. But that is OK now. We all understand what's going on," and "The activities moved so quickly and were so enjoyable that we didn't realize what was really happening—that we were building trust and agreement on very basic issues."

Chapter Four

Open Systems Thinking and the Power of Human Ideals

A Search Conference allows people to put open systems thinking into practice. Broadly conceived, the task of Search Conference participants is to engage in puzzle solving, a form of learning and planning that is actively adaptive to changes and demands of a turbulent environment. Active adaptation involves learning, improvising, and inventing new paths to the future. Developing this organizational learning capability requires that the Search Conference itself be designed and managed as an open system. Although they look both forward into the future and inward to identify what is most important to them, the task of participants in the Search Conference is neither to create a static vision for the future nor to discuss core values. Rather, the participants must become ideal-seeking. There are a myriad of changes in the task environment alone that require their attention: customer needs, relationships with suppliers, new technologies, market shifts, possible mergers, downturns in the economy, new budgetary policies, consumer action groups, pending legislation, new regulations, and so on. On top of this, the social forces in the contextual environment lurk in the background—unpredictable political events, changing demographics, public opinion and cultural value shifts, and other major discontinuities—require an active and adaptive response if systems are to remain viable over time.

Open Systems Thinking

A basic understanding of open systems thinking is necessary for anyone who attempts to design and manage a Search Conference.

Open systems theory is concerned with how wholes are related to their environments. With systems, the whole is often greater than the sum of its parts—which means that we cannot understand a system simply as the aggregate of its parts. Something more fundamental is going on than simple interactions among individual parts. Fred Emery offers some points of clarification (personal communication, 1995):

- A system is a *unitas multiplex*. Only if we can identify the system principle that explains this unity can we demarcate the system. If we identify more than one system principle, then we have the entanglement of more than one system. This requirement already raises our concern to the transactional level. A system principle is not to be found in any part or its relations (Angyal, 1941). A common-sense statement of this requirement is Drucker's (1980) idea that commercial organizations must first ask themselves what business they are in. When this question is raised, many existing elements may be found redundant, despite their interactions, and others sorely lacking. This begins to answer the question of what defines the set that constitutes a system. An aggregate can be defined by the summation of the present elements and their interrelations, but not a system.

- In a system, parts are not related directly according to their individual attributes, but indirectly via their relation to the system principle. The "more" that the whole presents is not the addition of some nonphysically measurable quality like soul or élan vital, but a measurable degree of organization. Measurable, however, only within the parameters of that organization.

- A statement of system principle (mission or goals) is a shorthand way of referring to the special forms of interdependence that exist between the system and its environment. Without this statement, the system principle is open to interpretation as a God-given entelechy, *sui generis* to the system. With social systems, the system principle is not some mysterious, hidden essence; rather, it is a concept that explains why particular elements enter into particular system-environment relations.

- Thus a system can only be characterized if we characterize its environment—and, conversely, an environment can only be characterized by characterizing the kinds of systems it supports. This requires description of each set of transactions, transactions within the system, between the system and its environment, between the environment and the system, and in the environment itself.

- A system can thus be defined as a set of entities that are interdependent with respect to the principle governing the set, that is, the system principle. The system principle is not *sui generis* to the set but defines a special relation of interdependence between the set and its environment.

Organizations are considered to be living systems, and as such, they must remain open and responsive to their environment if they are to maintain their integrity and coherence.

Closed Versus Open Systems Thinking

Closed systems thinking regards the enterprise as sufficiently independent to allow it to focus most of its attention on its internal operations without reference to its external environment. In contrast, open systems thinking works from the premise that no living system can be understood separate from its context. The shift from closed to open systems thinking entails a shift in focus from context-free parts to interdependent systems and environments. The open systems perspective amounts to a transformation in worldview, from a "world hypothesis of mechanism" to a "world hypothesis of contextualism" (Pepper, 1942). Rather than viewing the world as a mechanical universe consisting of isolated ensembles of closed systems, open systems thinking views the world as consisting of a complex set of interwoven relations between wholes and their parts—a universe of organized living systems that can only be understood in their context.

The closed system concept was derived from the realm of the physical sciences and revolved around the idea of equilibrium (Emery and Trist, 1965). However, when biologists began studying the behavior of organisms, closed system concepts could not describe the findings. Organisms operated as open systems, which must exchange energy and matter with their environments to survive (von Bertalanffy, 1950). Von Bertalanffy made a theoretical contribution in advancing the view of adaptation as a function of organism-environment transactions. However, von Bertalanffy's conceptualization of organisms as open systems was still deterministic in its orientation. Biological organisms (unlike human systems) do not display the ability to be purposeful. An amoeba, for example, can only react to environmental perturbations. This antiquated cell formulation and its organismic metaphors (Morgan, 1986) are still sometimes equated with the open systems concept of organization. Although it recognized the importance of organism-environment exchanges as necessary for maintaining internal equilibrium and survival, however, von Bertalanffy's explanatory formulation was not completely adequate for making open systems theory applicable to purposeful human systems. As Pasmore says, "The challenges for the manager in the open systems perspective were [seen as] the same [as] for a cell—to seek a hospitable environment in which to do business and then to engage in activities conducive to the exchange of resources. This view of the manager's role has proven to be overly simplistic" (1988, p. 13).

Von Bertalanffy also left a vacuum concerning the nature of the environment itself, and it was this vacuum that Emery and Trist filled with their concept of causal textures (1965), discussed in Chapter Three. Until then, organizational theorists did not have a theory of active adaptation because the nature of the social environment that was emerging had not been recognized to be of a type that required active adaptation, that is, turbulent.

Purposeful System Definition

Human beings are purposeful in that they display the capacity and freedom to make conscious choices. Organismic metaphors do not take purposeful behavior fully into account. Organizations need to be conceptualized as open systems, which consist of people who have purposes of their own, and which are nested within a turbulent environment that has its own dynamics and properties. And because organizations are *human systems*, they have the ability to do more than merely react or passively adapt to environmental conditions. Nonetheless, organizations that are designed and managed as closed systems tend to ignore their employees' and members' capacity for purposeful behavior; instead, they view and treat their people as redundant parts of the operation.

An open system should be organized so as to maximize the probability that human actors can make the best choices regarding ends and means relevant to the survival of the enterprise. As Ackoff (1994, p. 32) points out, "If parts of a system are to be treated as purposeful, they must be given the freedom to choose, to act." An open system—whether it be a corporation, university, public agency, or community—is defined by a shared purpose, mission, core process, or primary task. System definition requires specification of those defining functions that are bound together by a shared purpose, and of the boundaries that demarcate the limits of the system. As noted earlier, by defining a system, one also thereby defines the external environment.

Figure 4.1 illustrates that the open systems framework includes three major sets of adaptive relations: between people and their immediate or organizational task environments; between organizations and the social field; and between people and the extended social field or contextual environment itself. All sets must be in *directive correlation* with each other, that is, congruent, if true and long-term adaptation is to occur (Emery, 1981). Another way of looking at these adaptive relations is to consider them as representing three different levels of purpose: the purposes of the enterprise, the purposes of an enterprise within the larger society, and the purposes of people within a larger society. Organizations often ignore or pay little attention to the latter two sets of adaptive relations, concentrating on improving the first set—between employees and the immediate task or business environment. In particular, the set of relations between individuals and the extended social field are often forgotten. However, the adaptability of all three relationships is important to the long-term success of any enterprise.

Increasingly, the environment or social field beyond the formal boundary of the organization intrudes by way of the attitudes and values of various members, which were formed by experiences in families, schools, and community settings, as well as by media influences. Thus, people obviously bring values and expectations derived from the whole of their lives with them to any system or organization. For example, Generation X employees have very different values and expectations toward work life from those held by baby-boomers. Faced with an increasingly diverse set of expectations and values among people, organizations can no longer ignore the adaptive set of relations between people and the extended social field. Despite its recent popularity (Senge, 1990), systems thinking, as well as the idea of conceiving of organization-environment rela-

Figure 4.1. Three Sets of Adaptive Relations.

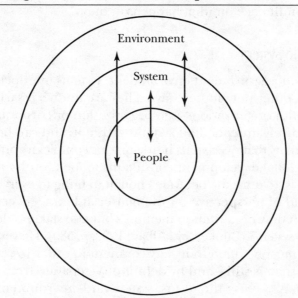

tions in systems terms, has been around since the sixties and seventies (F. Emery, 1969; F. Emery and Trist, 1973; F. Emery, 1981). Improving whole systems requires a shift away from piecemeal attempts to improve different parts of an organization, to a focus on improving system-environment transactions. Such improvement strategies require new ways of learning and planning.

Getting the Right System in the Room

A Search Conference needs a very precise system definition if it is to have any realistic hope of success. Although the traditional trappings of expertise do not matter, all the participants must have responsibility for some aspect of the job at hand. If a chemical company sponsors a Search Conference to improve safety at its plants, for example, it needs plant management and safety personnel, engineers, operators, and probably maintenance and other staff members as well; it does not need mayors of adjacent communities. Despite their profound and urgent interest in the success of the conference, local residents who don't work at the plants have no personal influence on what happens in them.

The Whole System

In the modern, turbulent environment, systems interlock and affect each other in complex ways. They are not necessarily coterminous with organizations—an organization or corporation can have relatively independent systems within it, and can be part of other systems that overlap its borders. This complexity often leads organizational development consultants to look for the *whole* system, that is, to draw the net wide enough to bring in everyone with some kind of perspective on the matter at hand. "Everyone includes not only organization members but also stakeholders from the wider system" (Bunker and Alban, 1992, p. 580). However, while a system must be open to its environment in order to remain viable, a system is still—and by definition—separate from its environment. As we use the terms, system and environment define each other; the only way to combine them is to postulate a larger environment that includes them both—which ultimately requires the ability to step outside the universe we live in.

It can be very attractive to make the attempt. Weisbord and Janoff (1995) say, "We want the 'the whole system' in the room, meaning a larger system than usual" (p. 38). They continue, "Of course we never do get the whole system in the room. Taken literally, that could mean every organism in the cosmos" (p. 48). A system, however, is part of a larger whole, not the whole itself. As Morin points out, "*system* is not a master-word for totality; rather, it is a root word for complexity. . . . The problem is not to create a general theory covering everything from atoms, molecules, and stars to cells, organisms, artifacts, and society. Rather, the problem is to consider atoms, stars, cells, artifacts, and society—that is to say, all aspects of reality, including, and in particular, our own—in a richer way in the light of the complexity of system and organization" (1992, pp. 382–383; emphasis added).

The Right System

As Bunker and Alban (1992) noted, the quest for the whole system often leads conference organizers to recommend including external stakeholders as participants. However, we have found that the only time it is really desirable to bring in people from outside the sponsoring organization is when those outsiders are part of the system under consideration. For example, if the purpose of a Search Conference is to plan a new partnership between an organization and its supplier, then the system boundary includes both organization and supplier. Both will have responsibility for future action, so people from both should be invited to take part in the Search Conference. They may be external stakeholders in each other's success in the normal run of business, but they are all directly involved here.

On the other hand, when the purpose of a conference is internal to an organization, it is best to recruit participants only from that organization. For example, if a corporation wants to improve coordination among R&D, production, and sales, parties outside the corporation—such as customers, suppliers, regulators, and so forth, all of whom do have an interest in what the corporation sells or buys—are not in a position to take responsibility for the future of the system that is the focus of the conference. While such outsiders can offer diverse perspectives on the sponsoring organization, they won't implement its action plans. And why should they? They don't work inside that system—they are part of the *environment*. Their presence at a conference dilutes the discussion: They tend to grow bored and withdrawn, reducing the energy level in the room, or else they raise issues relevant to systems other than the one the conference is supposed to work on, consuming valuable time on matters far from the purpose at hand. Therefore, if information from outside the system is required for a conference, it is preferable to gather it during the preparation phase—and if external parties need to know the results, the sponsor will serve both outside and inside interests best by sending them relevant portions of the report.

There is another reason to exclude outside stakeholders. Insiders are usually very apprehensive about the possibility that proprietary information may leak out. Few companies are willing to risk exposing strategic information that could make them vulnerable to their competitors. The inclusion of external stakeholders can inhibit members of a system from openly discussing internal issues or departmental problems. The truth is, most organizations are extremely reluctant to share their strategic intentions, hang out their dirty laundry, or discuss proprietary information when customers, suppliers, environmentalists, or government regulators are in the same room. The necessary condition of openness (discussed in Chapter Two) can be destroyed as surely by the participants choosing to keep their mouths shut as by the conference managers constricting the process.

The importance of drawing boundaries narrowly enough is supported by practice as well as theory. Here is a vivid example of what can go wrong with the quest for the whole system:

A Recipe for Failure

A group of consultants designed and convened a Search Conference to plan the future of a professional network and to look at how they could promote their services in the Chicago metropolitan area. This group was interested in developing a network for increasing the knowledge and use of participative methods in workplaces and communities. The purpose of the conference was defined as "The Future of Participative Democracy in the Chicago Area." Twenty-four people were invited to the conference. However, the conference design called for inviting external stakeholders—six community activists from various nonprofit agencies—who would be expected to join in the activities with the eight external and ten internal organization development consultants from the network. These external stakeholders were mainly potential clients or end-users with little vested interest in the future of this professional consulting network. They also were completely lacking knowledge of the consultation methods that were discussed among the consultants throughout the conference. Toward the end of the first evening, several of the external stakeholders became irritated and annoyed at the consultants in the room for using sophisticated language, jargon, and technical terms that were unfamiliar to them. One community activist spoke up: "We feel left out of this discussion because we don't know what you people are talking about." Another external stakeholder tried to shift the discussion from the diffusion of participative methods to dealing with issues of urban poverty and the homeless—important topics, certainly, but issues that were far removed from the implicit purpose of the conference. Failing in this attempt, the external stakeholder left the conference and didn't return. The next morning, another external stakeholder called attention to the absence of the community activist whose issues were ignored the previous evening, and conference managers tried to appease this person by spending a great deal of time analyzing why the disgruntled activist had left. At this point, many of the people who were less interested in this long, drawn-out discussion between the conference managers and the external stakeholder began having side conversations, reading newspapers, and making frequent trips to the coffee table.

Building a conference on the right system involves including people with every type of responsibility for the outcome, as well as excluding people with no responsibility for it. Restricting the system too far can be as dangerous as defining it too broadly. Excessive restriction can occur when the practitioner and sponsor define the purpose of a Search Conference in a way that excludes relevant aspects of the system, when they invite too few people from the chosen system, or both. What follows from such restriction is not a Search Conference; it is a problem-solving group—and one that may not be working on the right problem.

Conventional strategic planning efforts are often conducted in excessively restricted groups. For example, behind closed doors at a large Midwestern university, the president and some administrative department heads crafted a well-thought-out strategic plan. They then revealed the new plan to faculty and staff, and held a series of informational meetings in an attempt to get people to buy into the plan after it was already a done deal. Much to the administration's surprise, faculty reactions ranged from indifference to outright anger. But these are natural reactions: most people resent sales pitches designed to inform them on matters after the fact, especially when such matters can directly affect their livelihood.

Learning-Planning Functions

Open systems theory is explicitly concerned with understanding the interdependent, mutually determining relation between a system and its environment. Any open system must develop and maintain a capacity for adaptability, which can be understood in terms of four sets of exchanges: internal transactions in the system, transactional interdependencies between the system and its environment, transactional interdependencies between the environment and the system, and environmental interactions occurring in the environment itself. Figure 4.2 illustrates how transactions inside the system, or internal organizational dynamics, are usually thought of in terms of an organization's culture, history, and current set of assets and core competencies. Transactions occurring between the system and the environment consist of a learning or input function, where members of a system are open and aware of relevant changes happening in the environment, and a planning or output function, where members of a system seek to actively influence the environment to their advantage. Open systems engage in an ongoing, interactive learning-planning process.

In contrast to passive adaptation, expert-driven techniques, and closed system approaches, search conferencing enables both experts and laypersons together to learn how to learn about these system-environment transactions. When learning occurs, the system is being changed by the environment. When planning occurs, the system is acting strategically to change its environment. And the environment itself has its own set of dynamics, which must be known and monitored.

As Figure 4.3 illustrates, the elegance of the Search Conference design is that it is a direct translation of open systems thinking. Systemic change requires a systemic perspective. Because every system is embedded in a larger system, the contextual reality of a system's functioning is emphasized in the design and external structure of the Search Conference.

Figure 4.2. Open Systems Planning.

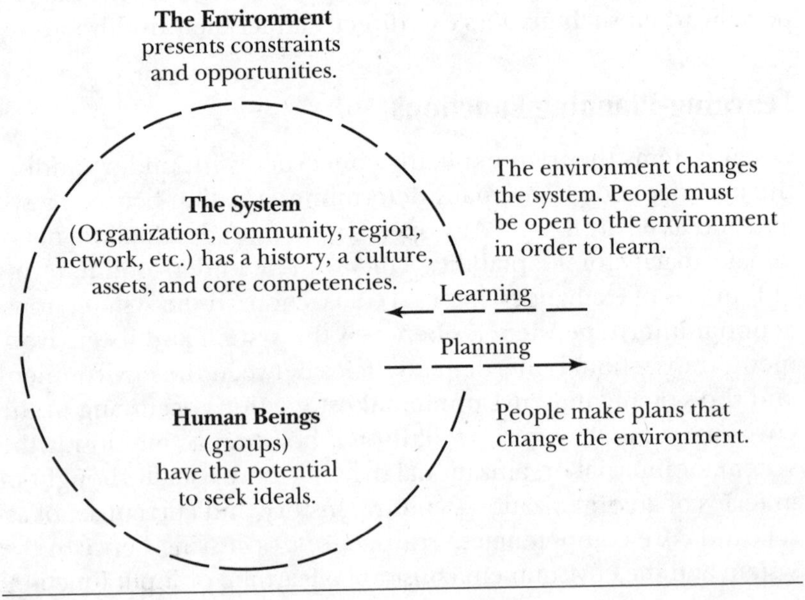

The Environment
presents constraints
and opportunities.

The System
(Organization, community, region,
network, etc.) has a history, a culture,
assets, and core competencies.

The environment changes
the system. People must
be open to the environment
in order to learn.

Learning

Planning

Human Beings
(groups)
have the potential
to seek ideals.

People make plans that
change the environment.

Figure 4.3. Open Systems and Search Conferences.

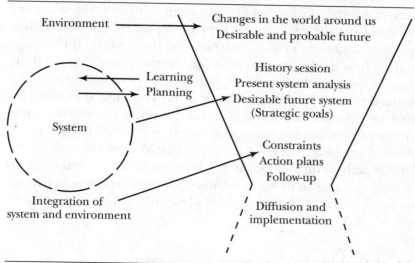

The entire search process involves learning from the environment and learning about the system for the purpose of planning and bringing into being a more desirable future. This is the essence of active adaptation. It simply means that people within a system are engaged in learning to make change happen in relation to a changing environment. The changes they seek to make happen, however, are meant to bring about a more desirable future for their system *and* its environment. Active adaptation may be defined then as the ability to continuously search the environment as a means for making purposeful choices that result in the most effective learning-planning strategies for the system within its changing environment. Conversely, maladaptive responses are characterized by a failure to adequately search the environment that leads to the choice of ineffective learning-planning strategies that are inappropriate for achieving desired purposes.

The dynamic nature of a Search Conference session can be attributed to the way it expands individual and group perceptions from both a spatial and temporal sense. Participants learn how to flex and stretch their perceptual muscles. From a spatial perspective, participants are led to look at the big picture, opening their perceptual scope to the wide world, and then converging inward to examine more local sets of concerns. Similarly, participants search through the field of time—reconnecting with the values and lessons from their past, concentrating on salient features of their present, and then taking the long view, they extend their imagination into the future to search for creative possibilities and untapped potentials. To search is to conduct planning within a human frame of reference. Because our cognitive structure is so vast, we need frameworks that can assign order to establish a minimum of continuity, to prioritize our needs, to build enduring relationships, and to develop a context in which we can make sense of our actions through reflective learning. Such a contextual ordering allows us to perceive relations between experiences that appear separate, and thus enables planning and learning toward purposeful choices.

Ideal-Seeking in the Search Conference

The task of planning in a turbulent environment now requires a search for ideals that can be a source of hope and long-term guidance for people in organizations and communities who are trying to cope with uncertainty. We need social organizations with explicit philosophies designed to produce more healthy and creative behaviors and a more stable environment. As discussed in Chapter Three, the need for this effort is barely a generation old—but it is none the less urgent for that. The massive social changes that have occurred over the last few decades have eroded our basic sense of common ideals, and the nation is searching for some semblance of commonality in values and ideals that could lead to a more sane and civil society. Amitai Etzioni hits the mark when he notes, "Our society is suffering from a severe case of deficient we-ness" (1993, p. 26).

Importance of Ideals to Planning

What does all this talk of morality, social change, and ideals have to do with the concrete task of planning for a modern corporation, organization, or government agency? A great deal. Organizations are created by people who are guided by ideals. Once created, these organizations affect the people who work within them. However, with increasing social turbulence, the erosion of ideals in society makes it more difficult for people to sustain their cooperative energies and positive motivation.

When uncertainty is high, ends or purposes cannot be assumed. Planning must involve the search for ends, ideals, and long-term purposes. These must be consciously chosen by those responsible for the future of a system. This is not equivalent to making a choice between alternative goals. Rather, it amounts to consciously searching and deliberately choosing between alternative purposes (F. Emery, 1981, p. 444).

The rapidly changing nature of turbulent environments tends to make information and knowledge regarding specific tactics very unreliable. And, to complicate the task of planning almost unbearably, policy makers also tend to distort information to fit their own agendas when competing interests are at stake and when highly contested issues are subject to debate. Even in less politicized situations, critical information for making decisions that can affect the long-term future is often ambiguous or even indeterminate. For example, consider the conflicting scientific reports on the issue of global warming. In official hearings, scientists present contradictory facts and reports, which usually lead to a decision to postpone significant regulatory action and to continue collecting more information—in other words, to do nothing, and let present trends (whatever they may be) continue unchecked.

When human systems confront issues involving a high degree of relevant uncertainty, we must be able to look beyond the accumulation of conflicting interpretations of information and scientific reports to normative ideals of what quality of life *ought* to be and what should happen to ensure a desirable future. Ideals serve then as a vehicle for melding judgments of value with judgments of fact (Trist, 1985).

Representing ultimate human aspirations as they do, ideals have a longevity that is not likely to change while planning and implementation proceeds. Similarly, only ideals seem to have the breadth of influence to encompass a range of competing interests that usually can be found in complex planning situations. Ideals thus provide the impetus for cooperative pursuits based on common interests. This is why a shared sense of long-term direction must first be established. Later, the choice of means and pathways to the desired future state can follow.

The Search Conference process is rooted in the assumption—borne out repeatedly in practice—that people all have the capacity to seek ideals. Each conference is designed to encourage participants to become ideal-seeking as they plan for their future. During the early phases of the Search Conference, participants engage in deliberations that involve decisions regarding their choice of long-term purposes, ends, and desirable futures for their world and their system. We have invariably found that whether or not they have sophisticated knowledge or the ability to provide expert judgments on specific issues, people have an innate capacity to see whether a planning process is or is not serving their ideals.

Ideals in the Search Conference

Human ideals are implicit in people's statements about their desirable future. Fred Emery (1977) found a core set of human ideals that were appropriate to curbing social turbulence in the postindustrial society. The set of four basic ideals involved a need for belonging, nurturance, humanity, and beauty. These ideals transcend any specific setting or culture.

Belonging

The ideal of belonging means that people want to be with other people, to associate with one another. Despite the familiar Groucho Marx quip that he would never belong to a group that would have someone like him for a member, humans need to belong and identify with others (Angyal, 1965, p. 114). People wish to belong to a unit they regard as extending beyond their individual self; this might be a group of co-workers, a church, or a bowling league. However, the pursuit of this ideal also means that people wish to be deeply connected with others. Communities in Third World countries may be poor, but they are rarely impoverished. The richest treasure that a person can have is friends and family. This ideal also reflects the intuitive knowledge that real assets are to be found in human and not material resources. The opposite of belonging is selfishness and alienation.

Despite the highly individualistic culture prevalent in the United States, this ideal has emerged strongly during every Search Conference we have run, often couched in such statements as "We need a strong community with individual rights respected." It is only within group life that ideals can emerge and be sustained. In the face of a turbulent environment, we have seen that the temptation, the maladaptive response, is to retreat from social interaction. In the West, the myth of the self-contained individual reigns (Sampson, 1989), but it is impossible to be a "rootless flower" (Barron, 1995). The pursuit of social ideals cannot proceed in isolation. In a turbulent environment, only the cultivation of group life can provide the fertile soil for the sustained pursuit of human ideals.

Nurturance

As with all four ideals, belonging cannot stand alone. Without the complementary ideals of humanity, nurturance, and beauty, the need for belonging could lead to overzealous nationalism, similar to what occurred with the rise of Nazi Germany. In a turbulent environment, social systems require a great deal of nurturance. And we must nurture others. The loss of this ideal can have a devastating effect on the quality of life in society. We see widespread signs of the erosion of this ideal in the diminution of the family and rising child abuse and divorce rates. People require nurturance if they are to choose those purposes that contribute most to the cultivation and growth of their own competence, while supporting the competence of others to better pursue their ends. The pursuit of this ideal also extends to our relationship with the natural environment. The opposite of nurturance is exploitation. Ideals emerge in a community as people generate images of their desirable future. In a Search Conference held for creating an economic development plan for the West Cluster Empowerment Zone (discussed in detail in Chapter Ten), participants implicitly expressed nurturance as an ideal worth seeking in several of their desirable future statements: "A holistic community where families flourish, that fosters spirituality" and "An economy in harmony with the environment."

Humanity

The third ideal, humanity, is a derivative of the first two. The pursuit of a more humane existence refers to choosing what is most appropriate and fitting to people. For example, the notion of a *human scale* community embodies this ideal. According to a community-based strategic planning guidebook distributed by the federal government for creating "Empowerment Zones" in impoverished neighborhoods (U.S. Department of Housing and Urban Development, 1994), "Human scale is the stoop of a rowhouse rather than a stairwell of a high-rise; it is a police officer walking a beat rather than a helicopter overhead." When people seek humanity as an ideal at the community level, they want a strong neighborhood focus; human-scale housing that means creating homes with detail, identity, and a sense of place—not the anonymity of public housing that separates people from their surroundings. This ideal came through strongly in the desirable future statements for the future of the West Cluster Empowerment Zone community in Chicago. For example, one group's statement expressed their ideal-seeking for humanity in that they desired a community where there was "True participative democracy, where people plan and manage the development of their neighborhoods."

This ideal also regards people as superordinate to institutions. Humanity means putting human well-being and development, both spiritual and physical, above bureaucratic and material criteria of progress. The opposite of humanity is impersonality and inhumanity. West Cluster Search Conference participants, for example, envisioned in their desirable future, "Neighborhoods are free of fear. Public safety apparatus focuses on human well-being and the protection of the same."

Beauty

The search for beauty pulls people toward choosing and creating more desirable possibilities for their future. The pursuit of beauty entails a conscious striving to choose those purposes that express people's desire for outcomes that are intrinsically appealing and aesthetically attractive. The pursuit of beauty provides a common stimulus to visions of a balanced and harmonious environment that affords a high quality of life. The ideal of beauty is what drives the desire to repair neighborhood facilities, restore historic landmarks in the community, and preserve the natural environment. People intrinsically want an environment that provides them with a high quality of life. A young architect who was a participant in the West Cluster Empowerment Zone Search Conference strongly advocated the ideal of beauty; indeed, he made a plea that the final plans for neighborhood development have "poetic beauty." The desirable future for the economic revitalization of the West Side explicitly incorporated beauty as an ideal worth striving for, as can be seen in one of the statements that was generated: "We desire a community. . . . that provides economic sustainability and safe, beautiful, spiritually fulfilling environments."

Obviously, most people do not consciously choose to create pollution and noise, or to build an ugly industrial landscape for its own sake. Most people, if given the power to choose, would tend to reject the pursuit of purposes that are likely to be ugly, deforming, degrading, or divisive. The ideal state of aesthetic beauty captures the image of a system where all individuals would have the opportunity to become ideal-seeking.

Differences Between Ideals, Values, and Visions

A Search Conference results in a vision of a desirable future based on shared ideals that tends to embody the values of the participants. At first glance, this description may seem like a fuzzy tripartite reference to the same thing, but there are useful differences among the concepts. Understanding those differences is crucial to understanding how search conferencing moves beyond warm feelings and high hopes to generate practical action in the present.

Ideals Versus Values

People often think of ideals and values as if they were the same, but they are not. Ideals refer to people's ultimate strivings for perfection. Values, on the other hand, do not involve striving on the part of people. A value of fairness, for instance, is not a source of inspiration; rather, fairness is a behavior guide. In other words, values are statements of belief that we use to guide our present behavior. Values are also more personal and individualistic in nature than ideals.

Our obsession with values is an outgrowth of our extreme individualism. During the late sixties and early seventies (Goodman, 1976), value clarification exercises were popular in schools and organizations as a means of sensitizing people to their individual differences and needs for personal growth. The implicit message in the values approach was loud and clear: if we change ourselves internally, we will change the world. Robert Gottlieb (1987) characterizes this approach to change, which was an outgrowth of the 1960s, as a form of "magical thinking." According to Gottlieb, the decade "gave us time to deepen the changes in ourselves, but deluded us about the ease of changing the world" (p. 308). The 1960s were a major experiment that proved unequivocally that it is not enough to express values and dream dreams.

In comparison to values, ideals are collective images that people are willing to strive for. Therefore, ideals are intrinsically communal properties—products of evolutionary learning—evocative of the social wisdom and community practices necessary for human survival (MacIntyre, 1984). While ideals are ever approachable, they are never fully attainable. Ideals command a longer time span of attention, often having relevance and meaning across multiple generations and different cultures. Values, by comparison, are more time bound and culturally determined. We do not seek to pursue our values, but strive to behave in congruence with them (Williams, 1982). In this sense, values both guide and limit our present behavior.

Ideals Versus Visions

Visions often turn into lofty and ethereal dreams, so abstract that they are difficult to pin down. Visions do not necessarily lead to time-bound plans. When divorced from ideals (that is, from concrete and desirable qualities that people can strive for) and from action plans, visions become vague generalities—mother and apple pie statements—that nobody would have a problem agreeing with, and nobody could picture bringing into being.

It is a form of magical thinking to believe that all an organization needs is a good vision and the rest will follow. This is the problem with pure visioning exercises. When people perform theatrical skits or go through guided fantasy activities designed to stimulate right-brain creativity for the task of imagining an ideal future, they miss out on essential elements. It is necessary to put both halves of the brain to work, tapping the rational as well as the creative sides of our human capabilities, to plan successfully in a turbulent environment.

We have spoken with frustrated managers and community leaders a year after they went through these types of exercises. Their frustration stems from the realization that they spent their energy and resources building castles in the air. Although they had created visions that initially excited them, the outcomes of these events failed to mobilize people to take action. Their lofty visions were not developed into concrete action plans. The bottom line: they implemented none of the plans they had envisioned. Not surprisingly, these people have become very cynical toward these types of participative exercises.

The truth is that the task of producing a desirable future is hard work that requires hammering out agreements with people around strategies for action-based change. In the search for more desirable futures, ideals come into play because active adaptation to turbulence requires us to learn how to create new types of direct, democratic social organizations. This is not simply a matter of providing training for individual growth or personal transformation, and then hoping for the best. The health and vitality of a community depends upon thriving businesses, good schools, active and moral citizens, decent health care, and safe streets. Active adaptive planning facilitates social creativity (Purser and Montuori, 1996), unleashes human energy, and rekindles the hope in groups of people that they can create and implement plans consistent with their ideals. Furthermore, ideals are not esoteric concepts, restricted to the province of technical experts or academics. Given the right environment (like the one created in a well-run Search Conference), all people can articulate and express their ideals in a form that lets them get real work done.

Barn Raising for Modern Times

People have an innate ability to rise to the occasion and pursue the common good when they see the need to do so. This power to achieve the highest common denominator arises when groups find and work within their common ground. Unfortunately, we can only discover common ground if the necessary conditions are present. There are three primary conditions that can foster common ground: a shared physical space, shared ideals, and the rationalization of conflict. In this chapter we will focus primarily on the first two conditions; the third—rationalization of conflict—is discussed in Chapter Six.

The first condition of common ground reflects the literal sense of the term: shared physical space (ground, land area). The two elements that draw people in shared space together are their mutual subjection to whatever physical conditions apply there, and their universal desire to ensure their personal survival. For example, consider the way pioneers reacted to conditions on the Western frontier. Kemmis (1990) relates the activity of barn raising on the high plains of western Montana as an illustration of the way people, despite their differences, found it in their common interest to help each other. It didn't matter much whether you liked your neighbors there or not; you still needed them if you wanted to survive the winter. No homesteader could build a barn single-handed, and without a good barn, livestock and stored grain would perish—and the homesteader would perish soon afterward, meaning one less mind and pair of hands in the community. People shared the harsh reality of Montana winters, and so they found the time and energy to build each others' barns together, building a web of social ties at the same time.

The second condition that can lead to the discovery of common ground is an environment conducive to ideal-seeking. When people convene in a Search Conference to plan their own future, they learn quickly—through their direct appreciation of what is happening in the environment—that their system survival is at stake. People begin to awaken to the reality that they are dealing with a very unforgiving and turbulent environment that threatens their socioeconomic survival and quality of life. They begin to realize that they are metaphorically each in need of a barn, and so they see themselves as barn raisers—that is, as co-producers of the ends they seek.

Returning to organization development terms, when participants in the Search Conference wake up to the way their system is being invaded by turbulence, they begin to discover that working more collaboratively toward mutually desirable goals has survival value. People perceive directly why it is in their best interest to forge collaborative partnerships with others, even if those others do not share their values. This realization is a critical turning point in a Search Conference. By seeking and developing shared ideals, participants are able to find common ground, rising above individual differences or even irreconcilable value conflicts.

Thus, we can see the analogy to the first condition for finding common ground. Only in this case, the natural conditions of the Montana plains are replaced by the specially designed conditions of the Search Conference. Essentially, these conditions result in:

- A wider appreciation of the contextual environment with a mutual recognition of its turbulent nature
- A stronger recognition of interdependence, giving rise to a shared sense of mutual fate and awareness that system survival is contingent upon greater collaboration in meaningful ways
- The creation of shared practices that promote the mobilization of ideals toward a form of active, adaptive planning that utilizes the power of diffusion to involve people in the search for solutions to puzzles and messes

Puzzle Learning

Puzzle solving differs considerably from problem solving. As discussed in Chapter Two, until each piece of a puzzle is individually located and placed, it is not possible to determine the position of the next piece. This is a nonlinear process that lacks a sequential, stepwise set of procedures. Puzzle learning is dependent on human perception because all possibilities must be searched simultaneously. In contrast, problem solving accepts the conceptual probabilities as perceived during the initial problem identification stage, and maintains that there is a specific series of steps that, if followed, would solve the problem as it was defined at the starting point.

Puzzle solving requires a perceptual ability that experts may be uncomfortable with or unaccustomed to using. While an expert provides specialized knowledge for one piece of the puzzle, his or her scope is apt to be too narrow to make sense of the complexity of the whole. In a Search Conference, everyone has expertise, and every participant contributes some relevant knowledge required for understanding different pieces of the puzzle.

In a turbulent environment, we are dealing with messes and not discrete problem sets; one cannot simply specify all the pieces of the puzzle in advance, let alone predetermine how they should fit together. As with a jigsaw puzzle that has lost its box, we do not know how to proceed until we learn how one piece of the puzzle fits with another piece, then another piece, and so on. We make adjustments, moving different pieces around until we acquire a sense of the puzzle's gestalt. Experts are often trained to view planning as a problem-solving process. They expect to gather existing information, specify a range of options and evaluate them against a set of criteria, and then choose the optimum solution or course of action. This rational planning method is ill-suited to issues that look and behave more like puzzles than like problems with clearcut solutions. In sum, planning in puzzle-like environments requires continuous learning and adaptation, where the value and utility of different courses of action can be reassessed on an ongoing basis.

As we have illustrated, search conferencing provides an environment for people with shared purposes to participate in the creation of strategic plans for actively adapting to a turbulent environment. The ideals people share provide a background for agreement on important future directions for their system, whether the system is a mental health agency, a community development organization, or a Fortune 500 corporation. After a Search Conference, groups not only move ahead to implement their plans, they reassess their system on a continuing basis, and make midcourse corrections in response to unpredictable environmental changes. They have learned through direct experience how to actively adapt to their environment.

As a society, we are at a critical juncture that requires a radical change in the methods we use to plan for our individual and collective futures. If we are to create a desirable, livable, and sustainable future for ourselves and generations to come, we must unleash our innate ability to search collectively for the common good. For this to take place, planning must occur in the active adaptive mode. As we have emphasized, planning in the active adaptive mode within the texture of turbulence involves a shift from research on means to searching for ends, from operating in closed to open systems.

Chapter Five

The Strength of Democratic Learning

When it comes to democracy, we pay a lot of lip service to the word but make little effort to implement the reality. Democracy is not simply a form of government and not what politicians do, nor is it simply the right to vote. Democracy is a structure, an outlook, and a way of life that must be nurtured, developed, and diffused if it is to survive the trials and tribulations of a turbulent environment. James Dewey, a prolific and influential philosopher and educator, argued that "the foundation of democracy is faith in the capacities of human nature; faith in human intelligence, and in the power of pooled and cooperative experience" (quoted in Fott, 1991, p. 33).

The theoretical premises and managerial assumptions of the Search Conference method take these capacities to be self-evident. We strongly believe that people in general possess the virtues, intelligence, and motivation to work toward the common good. The largely undemocratic nature of organizations in our society has prevented people from exercising self-management.

However, it is becoming apparent that organizations and communities that hope to survive must shift responsibility for planning to the people. But people by and large have been taught that they can not plan. To overcome this misconception, they need a democratic learning environment in which to learn how to make changes for themselves, in directions that they themselves determine. As Kurt Lewin, a social scientist who spearheaded the study of group dynamics and participation, pointed out, "Democracy cannot be taught, it can only be learned."

Search conferencing is a simple yet innovative methodology for learning democracy. Its simplicity is due to its assumption that people can always manage and govern themselves, given the right structural conditions. Its innovation stems from its use of democratic structure to promote full participation and open dialogue and debate in areas that have become the province of elite expertise.

This chapter explores the nexus between democracy and learning by examining how democratic structures combined with a new educational paradigm create environments where maximum learning can be achieved. The Search Conference is a practical tool for strategic planning, but it has implications for society as a whole as well as for the organizations that employ it. Search conferencing challenges the traditional view that planning is something the elite few do while the majority wait passively on the sidelines. It is a social practice in direct democracy that shakes people out of their passivity and civic withdrawal. Search Conferences offer an opportunity for rediscovering and actualizing the Jeffersonian ideal of civic education. A Search Conference event is a public thing that provides a forum for an intensive politics of engagement, where citizens can learn how to perceive the public interest and act on its behalf (Kemmis, 1990).

When Search Conferences are used more widely and frequently as a method for planning with communities and organizations, they have the potential for introducing second-order ripple effects in society. Their diffusive function is the revitalization of participative democracy in the broadest possible context.

Participative Democracy

Early theorists of participative democracy, such as Jean-Jaques Rousseau, argued that a democracy requires an educated citizenry. This meant more than simply ensuring that people could read and write; people also needed to learn how to become public citizens. Education into citizenship could only be achieved through a practical form of education, that is, by participating directly in local affairs. This form of education, particularly for adults who are trying to understand and behave responsibly in an environment characterized by rapidly growing uncertainty, must use every available potential. While education has traditionally been conceived as putting things into people's heads, there is now a desperate need for people to understand what their heads (and the rest of them, incidentally) are into. That is, people need to share with others their perceptions of what is going on in the environment, what they make of it, and how they can work with others to bring the environment under control. In this connection, the intensity of a Search Conference provides people with a practical experience, anchor, and benchmark in participative democracy. As one energetic participant from the Macatawa Search Conference remarked, "We walked out of the Search Conference knowing we could make a difference in our community."

Historical and Cultural Roadblocks

The diffusion of participative democracy through Search Conferences is sure to face a number of cultural barriers or roadblocks. For one, participative democracy has not fared well from a historical point of view. Two of the key architects of the U.S. Constitution, James Madison and Alexander Hamilton, were ambivalent and even fearful about the more participatory proposals for democratic governance. The notion that the citizenry could participate directly in working out solutions and governing their own affairs was dismissed as impractical and even dangerous in a large country where people were widely dispersed. Madison feared that "[allowing] ordinary men and women to gain a political voice would court the passions of the masses." In contrast, the Anti-Federalists envisioned a more direct form of democratic government where people could potentially be educated into citizenship and progressively learn to take responsibility for their own affairs. This scheme depended upon the cultivation of civic virtues and an educated citizenry in order to ensure a civil, just, and democratic society.

Madison was pessimistic; he thought granting such autonomy to the unpropertied masses would certainly lead to anarchy and a revolt against wealthy landowners. In Madison's mind, no amount of civic virtue could be expected to tame the selfish and irrational forces arising from a majority faction. Madison's view was expressed in *Federalist Paper No. 10,* a document that heavily influenced the debates in the Constitutional Convention (Hamilton, Madison, and Jay, [1787–1788] 1982). In this document, the language of civic virtue—that is, the notion that democracy requires public participation in public tasks and the ideal that requires citizens to develop the moral disposition, habits, and active character necessary for a healthy civic culture—is nowhere to be found (Kemmis, 1990; Wolin, 1989).

The Federalist vision instead led to the framing of government in terms of representative democracy. For all practical purposes, the machinery of government put in place by the Federalists abolished the emerging faith that citizens could learn how to search for and act upon the common good. With its elaborate and ingenious mechanisms of checks and balances, separation of powers, and electoral colleges—and lately the addition of term limits—democracy has been reduced to the obligatory act of voting. While this is somewhat of a simplification, in essence, the Federalists wanted to ensure that individuals were free to pursue private ends, and that the function or role of government was to balance competing interests while protecting private property rights and individual liberties.

Representative democracy has preserved individual rights and allowed citizens to choose their rulers, but we have paid a heavy price for its services. That price can be calculated in the degradation of public life, and the loss that is derived from widespread citizen apathy and nonparticipation in all things public. In the last national election, only 27 percent of the electorate turned up at the polls—yet the Democrats lost their control of Congress and the Republicans crowed about their mandate from the public. And this apathy is not new; Hannah Arendt (1958) described the shortcomings of a representative system where the powerful few rule and the alienated many are ruled. Even in the early nineteenth century, Alexis de Tocqueville ([1840] 1969) feared that this form of governance would eventually result in mass conformity and a despotic, administered society.

That masses of people might learn how to plan, control, and manage their own affairs has been denigrated as impractical and utopian. Along with these apprehensions goes the catastrophic belief that more participatory forms of democracy would lead to anarchy, social rebellion, and mob rule. Even our representative democracy has exhibited nothing but dread toward the majority. Abolition of slavery for blacks didn't occur until 1870, and suffrage for women didn't occur until 1920. The United States regards itself as the beacon of democracy for the rest of the world—which by and large agrees with that assessment—but in reality, few of our institutions embody truly democratic forms of governance.

It is probably fair to say that the average person does not participate directly in determining the direction of the institutions to which he or she belongs. In the majority of organizations, employees rarely have the opportunity to participate in determining their own goals, and it is almost unthinkable that they would play a significant role in framing the overarching purposes or strategic direction of their companies. Even in more mundane matters, people rarely have a strong voice in the management of their day-to-day affairs. Such matters are usually decided for them.

Fears of Direct Democracy

Despite the amount of praise the concept has received over the years, education into citizenship has rarely been the focus of practical implementation for administrators, politicians, or even social scientists. Instead, the attempt to create the good society steered by the idea that responsibility for matters of governance should be placed exclusively in the hands of elected officials, managers, technical experts, social service professionals, or other representatives far removed from local concerns. The right decisions, policies, and courses of action could be determined by consulting high-paid management consultants, urban planners, and a vast assortment of other professionally trained social and technical engineers. In any event, the fears associated with participative democracy have been carried forward from the past, for they still dominate our collective consciousness. This is most evident in the way we have structured and managed our major institutions. We erect tall, dominant hierarchies and manage them by principles of command and control, because we see the bulk of humanity as lacking the intelligence, capability, and motivation to manage their own work.

The assumption that people are neither capable nor qualified to govern themselves is the standard claim of guardianship and justification for the few ruling over the many. Guardianship has taken many forms throughout recorded history—theocracy, monarchy, feudalism, totalitarianism, military dictatorship. In the modern

Western world, the role of professional manager, foreman, supervisor, and administrator is that of a guardian over employees and clients.

In the following sections, we will examine two basic design principles that serve as blueprints for the structure of an organization (or a conference), one resulting in bureaucracy and the other in democracy. In addition, we will clarify some confusion regarding what full participation really means within the context of democratic structures and the Search Conference. Following this, we discuss how barriers to democratization are rooted in an educational paradigm that destroys people's confidence in their own perceptions and learning ability. We conclude this chapter by arguing for an alternative educational paradigm based on direct perception, which, when combined with the democratic design principle, can produce all the necessary elements for a full-scale learning experience of democracy.

Design Principles

It is imperative for Search Conference designers to understand there are two basic design principles, called for convenience Design Principle 1 (the traditional, hierarchical structure) and its democratic alternative, Design Principle 2. One or the other of these principles underlies virtually every organizational or conference design. (A conference, after all, is only a temporary organization.) The choice of design principle (whether conscious or unconscious) determines the operational structure of a conference or organization. Search Conference designers must be aware of the consequences organizational structures have upon themselves and participants.

Design Principle 1 and Bureaucratic Structure

Dominant hierarchies in which coordination, control, and commands come from above grow out of a design principle that institutionalizes guardianship. In theoretical terms, this is known as *Design Principle 1 (DP1)*, and it is based on a machine view of organizations.

To remain viable, any organization or system depends on redundancy to provide flexibility. Design Principle 1 builds redundancy into a system by creating a multiplicity of identical and replaceable parts. Designing organizations according to DP1 makes each part redundant and interchangeable. Large armies, for example, derive flexibility by building in more parts than required at any given moment. No one part is indispensable. Organizations built with a redundancy of parts protect themselves from damage due to the failure of any given part; if one part fails (soldier, tank, battalion), another can easily take over.

Useful as this protection is, however, it comes at a high price. Complex parts are difficult to replace, so if parts must be easily replaceable, they must be simple. Thus, redundancy is achieved at the expense of fractionating work and disempowering people. As Figure 5.1 shows, responsibility for control and coordination lies not with those performing the task but with the level above. This design principle of organization requires an elaborate control body of guardians, supervisors or some other specialized group of people, whose only task is to control, coordinate, and check on the work of those below them.

Figure 5.1. Design Principle 1 (DP1).

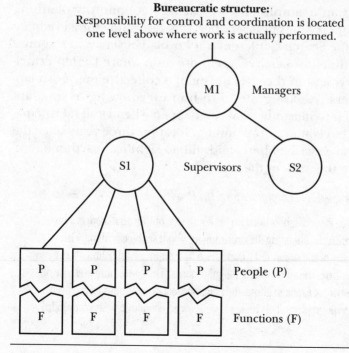

Bureaucratic structure:
Responsibility for control and coordination is located
one level above where work is actually performed.

M1   Managers

S1   Supervisors   S2

P   P   P   P   People (P)

F   F   F   F   Functions (F)

In terms of a conference, under Design Principle 1 the audience has no say over what they receive or what the conference produces, as such items are the responsibility of the organizers and speakers. Such traditional conferences usually have chairpeople who are equivalent to first-line supervisors. In a traditional conference, speakers and their topics are predetermined. Information is broadcast to the participants, or, more accurately, the audience, and the participant role is reduced to that of passive recipient.

Effects of Design Principle 1

DP1 structures disempower people, robbing them of their chance to participate as responsible citizens in the world. People are not likely to learn how to behave and act democratically if they constantly live and work within autocratic DP1 organizations or attend DP1 conferences, which are by design undemocratic. By taking responsibility away from people to plan and control their own affairs—whether on the shop floor or in the village hall or the business meeting—the DP1 principle weakens our capacities for democratic assembly, and like unused muscles, our democratic skills atrophy as a result.

Here is an example of a typical DP1 community planning process. Robert Sullivan developed this case study for a graduate course on the Search Conference at Loyola University in response to an assignment to analyze a real situation where Design Principle 1 was evident in the structuring of a collective event or planning process. We are grateful to him for allowing us to adapt portions of it to illustrate what can happen when Design Principle 1 is applied to community planning. It is now three years since the intervention described here, and still no significant action has resulted from the work of the task force.

Hyde Park "Ad Hoc Committee for 53rd Street"

In the Hyde Park neighborhood on the south side of Chicago, there is a historic commercial shopping area running for about six blocks along 53rd Street. Many of the stores, restaurants, and hair cutting establishments cater to customers from the surrounding neighborhoods. The continuing presence of the University of Chicago allows the neighborhood to maintain its relatively upscale demographics. This makes Hyde Park an economic oasis surrounded by some of Chicago's worst urban poverty and deterioration. Indeed, various forces have emerged that have pushed the disparate members of this small community into an uneasy alliance. These forces include:

- *Crime:* Everything from shoplifting by local high school students to armed robbery in broad daylight
- *Gangs:* Drive-by shootings have occurred as the street has become a cruising ground for rival gangs
- *Homelessness:* Panhandling has become a way of life in the area, clearly deterring some potential customers from shopping there
- *General economic decline:* Times are tough; there are few, if any, incentives to start new businesses here; financing is scarce; many new enterprises fail

A group calling itself the "Ad Hoc Committee for 53rd Street" has been trying to address, from a community perspective, the future of this area, which is suffering from many of the woes common to city neighborhoods. In a controversial move, the committee hired a consultant, formerly a "Downtown Coordinator" for another state, to work with them on developing the neighborhood's future direction.

What Went Wrong?

The consultant the Ad Hoc Committee hired had experience with small rural cities whose decaying downtowns were struggling against the likes of Wal-Mart. The problems of 53rd Street were quite different. Worse, the person they hired was more than just a consultant to the process, he was a zealot, a visionary with fixed ideas and sophisticated theories of urban planning which he preached like an evangelist. He was full of criticism, recommendations, and advice.

In the middle of his six-month-long consulting engagement (typical of his projects), he ran a day-long off-site "retreat" for about a hundred of 53rd Street's merchants and community leaders. During the course of the day, he lectured, instructed, and directed participants in ways and means to solve their problems. He assigned specialized roles, formed task forces and committees, and defined their projects. Three months later, having finished the terms of his contract, he went on to other projects in another state. Not surprisingly, the committees and task forces have fizzled out without producing any significant results (despite the thousands of dollars spent on this project).

Authoritarian Learning for Learning Authoritarianism

From an early age we are socialized by the hidden curriculum of traditional educational settings. The public school system is a classic DP1 design, with mass education as its product. In a traditional DP1 classroom, education is to a large extent nonparticipatory in nature. Students (and even teachers) have little control or influence over the curriculum that has been designed and decided for them. The teacher is the supreme guardian, assuming most of the responsibility for controlling and coordinating the activities of individual students. Ironically, students are introduced to the history and ideals of democracy in social studies textbooks while they are simultaneously forced to accept the unspoken reality that authoritarian management is the normal practice for ensuring control and order in social systems. Traditional education offers few opportunities for students to practice democratic habits. During their most impressionable and formative years, young people are held captive by a system that forces them into a passive role.

From school, we go on to get jobs in organizations where we are also told what to do and how to do it by someone else in a position of higher authority. It seems as though we have spent the majority of our lives in institutions where responsibility for the control and coordination of our learning or work has always been located one level above us, in someone else's hands. The point here is that the majority of people in society have very little experience of what it means to participate and work in systems geared toward direct democracy. Dewey likened this state of affairs to slavery, where people are expected to carry out the intentions of others and prevented from articulating, voicing, or framing their own intentions (Dewey, 1966).

Ambivalence Toward Democratic Methods

With so much socialization geared toward accepting the necessity of authoritarianism, and given that the only experience most people have is that of top-down, hierarchical organizational control, it is understandable why there is so much ambivalence about participative democracy. It also explains why some sponsors and managers are initially uncomfortable with the Search Conference method. When we begin to explain to potential sponsors that the Search Conference is a temporary organization that does away with traditional bureaucratic structures and managerial authority, that more people need to be directly involved in the planning process, and that the outcomes of the planning process cannot be engineered or manipulated in advance, managers often get nervous. Their fear and ambivalence is based on an erroneous belief that organizational order and predictability can only be guaranteed through tight managerial control structures, and that without these, their people would be lost, or even run amok. The catastrophic belief is that relinquishing tight managerial control over the structure and process of planning will result in disorder, chaos, and anarchy—especially if the process involves handing such responsibility over to the people whose lives are being planned.

Given that managers have never been exposed to a meaningful and practical alternative to bureaucracy, this reaction should come as no surprise. We have become so used to bureaucratic structures for managing human affairs that any alternative seems beyond our grasp. We tend to think that anything other than a DP1 organization will be unstructured, out of control, and unmanageable. These terms do describe a laissez-faire situation, but we are not forced to choose between DP1 and laissez-faire. We mistakenly assume that organizations are either structured, that is, organized under Design Principle 1, or unstructured, that is, not organized at all. But a democratically organized, self-managing group is something else entirely. Unfortunately, laissez-faire structures have been erroneously equated and confused with democratic structures.

Since there are no designated guardians issuing instructions every step of the way on what people should do and how they should do it, some people in a Search Conference may feel uneasy or uncomfortable at first. Others may question whether the Search Conference is just another management ploy or whether it is for real. However, these initial hesitations and suspicions are usually put to rest in the first couple of hours, as people come to experience first-hand what it really means to work within the democratic structure of a Search Conference, where an evolving community progressively learns to assume responsibility for its own work.

Design Principle 2 and Democratic Structure

Human affairs can be guided and managed productively without resorting to traditional command and control structures. The heart and core of the Search Conference provides participants with a genuine experience of self-management without resorting to conventional authoritarian structures. It is based on a direct form of democracy that is derived from an alternative structural design principle: Design Principle 2 (DP2), where *responsibility for the control and coordination of work is relocated with those who are actually doing the work.* This is the essence of a democratic structure, and it gives people the conditions for meaningful, full participation. Figure 5.2 illustrates the way Design Principle 2 (DP2) helps groups accept responsibility for the control and coordination of their individual contributions, as well as the outcomes of their collective efforts.

As an embodiment of Design Principle 2, the Search Conference allows a group of twenty to thirty-five people to take collective responsibility for all the content work and conference outcomes. This means participants are responsible for learning about their system and environment, articulating strategic goals, identifying constraints, and carrying out their own action plans. In other words, within a DP2 democratic structure, responsibility rests with

Figure 5.2. Design Principle 2 (DP2).

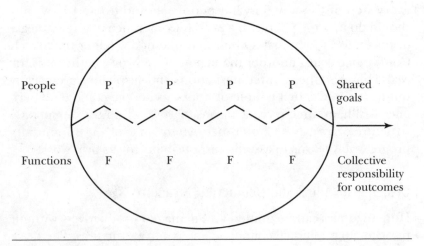

Democratic structure:
Responsibility for control and coordination is located
at the level where work is actually performed.

People   P   P   P   P   Shared
                                                   goals

Functions   F   F   F   F   Collective
                                                   responsibility
                                                   for outcomes

those doing the Search Conference work, that is, learning and planning. Of course, the Search Conference has managers whose role is to ensure that at every moment the participants have the best structure and process for their task, the best possible learning environment. Managers are responsible for juggling time, choosing between small or large work groups, ensuring that tasks are clear and manageable, and so on. But they do not intervene in or attempt to control the content.

Unlike conferences organized under Design Principle 1, DP2 structures result in the elimination of hierarchical dominance of one person over another. In other words, within democratic structures, there are no guardians constantly watching over people. This does not mean people are free to do whatever they please, however; we are not talking about a laissez-faire structure. The formation of the resulting democratic structure is very difficult to describe in abstract terms, but it will readily become apparent in the analysis of Search Conference design in Chapter Eight and the detailed description of an actual conference in Chapter Ten.

Because DP2 relies on giving participants the responsibility for the control, coordination, and outcome of the planning process, it becomes doubly essential for the people who participate in a Search Conference to be members of the system—no one else is in a position to implement the plan that they create. What is unique about the Search Conference is that participants take on multifunctional roles and wear multiple hats. All participants in a Search Conference learn how to function as analysts, historians, strategic planners, and change agents.

Mixing the Modes

There is a great deal of difference between a pure DP2 Search Conference and other types of participative event. Most large-group interventions are at best *mixed-mode* events (Emery, 1982). The mixed mode results from an alternation between the two basic design principles. For example, a typical mixed-mode conference may consist of formal chaired presentations followed by discussion groups, or participative events interspersed with short talks by experts. Mixed-mode and DP1 conferences are especially vulnerable to dysfunctional group dynamics, which will be discussed in more detail in Chapter Six.

Democratic Structure and Political Efficacy

There is a strong relationship between authority structures and the psychological orientation of individuals (Pateman, 1970). Democratic structures evoke constructive responses. Thus participants walk away from the Search Conference with a solid benchmark experience that they can function well in self-managed groups. They also develop confidence in their ability to participate responsibly and effectively in matters of collective importance. The attitudes people acquire as a result of learning from each other by pooling their perceptions are key to triggering collective action. In other words, the Search Conference increases the participants' sense of political efficacy. This is no small feat in today's bureaucratic society.

Organizations and communities need to restore to people the confidence to take responsibility for the governance and management of their own affairs. More specifically, the formation of a democratic character requires that organizations adopt democratic structures that provide opportunities for full participation.

Dispelling Myths about Participation

It is often unclear what managers and administrators mean when they claim that their people just aren't ready to participate in an event like a Search Conference. Their belief is more often than not the result of a self-fulfilling prophecy. Managers and administrators have fallen prey to a blame-the-victim mentality. Employee and citizen apathy is often taken as proof of lack of intelligence or motivation. Managers complain, "My people simply don't want more responsibility." Or administrators conclude, "People just don't want to be bothered having to learn new skills." This is simply not the case. Rather, people may *act as though they are not ready to participate* because they haven't been allowed to fully and genuinely participate in controlling and coordinating their own efforts in the past. People may have been enticed to participate in previous efforts described as empowerment programs where they did not find the conditions and democratic authority structures for full participation. Instead, they were subtly manipulated, co-opted, persuaded, or even coerced to accept a plan or decision that was already made by higher authorities. Based on such experiences with pseudoparticipation schemes, employees have good reason to be skeptical, cynical, and resistant to another management invitation to participate.

Buying into the Myths

Even when management makes a genuine attempt to move toward a participative work system, employees may still balk. Jeanne Neumann (1989) studied in depth one company's failed attempt to introduce direct participation on the shop floor. She found a host of system factors that explained why employees declined the invitation to participate. Supervisors pointed the finger at employees, all their suspicions that "These people just don't like to participate" confirmed. However, her findings told a different story: structural factors like hierarchical control, a culture that traditionally valued rank and status above knowledge or expertise, and prior socialization experiences militated against efforts to engage employees in a new participative work system. People are ready to participate, but because they have historically been led to believe that they are not, their hesitation, skepticism, and doubt seem quite justifiable.

One cannot but notice that some managers and administrators often refer to "my people," "my employees," or "my constituents." This language reflects the hierarchical relationship under Design Principle 1. In the private sector, this relationship is even more pronounced with the use of such terms as supervisor and subordinates. In a traditional DP1 hierarchy, the superordinate has the right to order and the subordinate must obey. This arrangement has the dynamics of a parent-child relationship. And a system designed to treat adults like children requires sophisticated control mechanisms for continually monitoring employee behavior (Boje and Dennehy, 1993)—adults are even more ingenious than children when it comes to bypassing or subverting rules imposed upon them.

The question then is, Can people who have worked in such systems all their lives not be expected to be passive and subordinate? How can people have faith in the validity of their own perceptions when authority and knowledge has always been seen to reside outside themselves? It's difficult. But does this mean this situation cannot be changed? Many managers and administrators would like to believe that the time isn't right for change. Yet if their logic is accepted, then it is likely that people would probably never be ready to participate.

Doubts about people's readiness to participate may have more to do with the assumptions managers and administrators hold about people than with actual conditions. Douglas McGregor's

(1960) classic proposition that "Theory X" managers assume people are basically lazy and incapable of being responsible at work apparently still holds water after all these years. A manager or administrator who holds Theory X assumptions about people is not about to let them participate in major organizational decisions. Holding to such Theory X assumptions becomes a self-fulfilling prophecy; managerial behavior communicates to employees that they are inept and untrustworthy, and employees respond accordingly, acting out the roles and scripts assigned to them.

In other cases, the unwillingness of managers, supervisors, and administrators to provide genuine opportunities for participation can be traced to fear. Jan Klein (1984) found that supervisors who resisted efforts to involve employees shared a concern that they might lose their prestige and status. Such "status seekers" were unwilling to let go of behavior associated with control (Klein, 1984, p. 89).

Our basic assumption is that people learn how to participate by participating. Participation is like learning how to ride a bicycle or how to swim, people will never be ready until they actually start doing it—and virtually everybody is ready when they do start. It is the choice of design principle that determines whether people have the opportunity and conditions for genuine participation.

Participative Management

We believe there is serious confusion with regard to the definition of the design principles and conference structure. In a journal issue devoted to large-group interventions, Barbara Bunker and Billie Alban (1992) describe "structure" on a low-to-high continuum with regard to participation. But we see the two design principles as mutually exclusive forms of structure; people either have responsibility for the control and coordination of their own affairs or they do not. If they do not, then someone else does—usually their boss, supervisor, or some other group that is in a position of higher authority.

Bunker and Alban subscribe to Renis Likert's concept of participation. Likert (1967) was one of the early theorists and advocates of participative management. Likert conceived of participation in terms of a continuum, ranging from having a little participation to a lot. Indeed, many practitioners now use what are still called Likertscales in employee opinion and attitude surveys. But participation is not a psychological attitude or feeling that one can gauge in relative degrees of strength. One can never have too much participation. Again, individuals either have the authority, right, and power to participate or they do not. Participation is always a meaningful act in something. And this something usually involves decisions that are of practical significance to the individual.

The truth of the matter is that participative management programs never provided the conditions for genuine participation. Just the term itself suggests who is really in control. It is not hard to understand why Likert didn't call his program "participative employeeship." Participative management was devised primarily as a technique of persuasion. It had enormous appeal as a technique since it could be used to persuade employees to accept decisions that had already been made by management. By exhibiting a so-called participative style of management, managers could encourage employees to question decisions, creating the feeling and illusion of participation while clarifying their understanding and improving the quality of their obedience. Participative managers would be coached to solicit input from employees, while the final authority for making decisions would still rest squarely with management. Employees might also be invited to meetings to hear and react to the decisions already made by management. In the vernacular, this is known as a way of getting people to buy into the decision, or to sign up for the program, or enroll in the vision. These schemes amount to subtle forms of coercion and manipulation. People know a con when they see it.

The pseudoparticipation schemes described here can be summarized in terms of what genuine participation is not. Genuine participation is not:

- Merely taking part in, or being present at, a large or small group activity
- Merely receiving information on a decision before it is executed
- Merely providing input on decisions that have already been made

While these schemes allow people some degree of influence through soliciting their input, seeking their endorsement, and getting them to buy in, the final say rests with an external authority.

The democratic structure that is operative in the Search Conference is based on *full* rather than partial participation. This democratic structure has nothing to do with creating the right climate, establishing a participatory style of management, or forming a new culture. By full participation, we mean each person has equal power to participate in making decisions and determining outcomes. As in a Greek *polis,* every Search Conference participant has political equality to determine ends and purposes, and to make decisions regarding the means to achieve them. The democratic structure of the conference ensures that every participant has a voice, the power, and the final say with regard to setting priorities, making decisions, and formulating action plans. Thus, the Search Conference is a sovereign assembly, for it is the *demos,* the people, that make decisions for the good of the collective, and not the traditional guardians. Once again, this is difficult to picture in the abstract, but it does work in practice; skip ahead to Chapter Ten to see it in action.

Robert Dahl (1989) claims that the measure of a real democracy is whether or not the people have the final say. Certainly, in the Search Conference, it is the voice of the participants that has the final say over their long-range purposes, strategies, and plans for action. It is because of the above conditions, based on Design Principle 2, that the Search Conference is a real democracy.

Learning Democracy: A New Educational Paradigm

The revitalization of a democratic society requires new methods of learning that draw out the creativity and intelligence of people. This is the true meaning of the word education. In Latin, *educare* means to bring up, nurture, and draw out. Search conferencing, though born out of commercial necessity (as described in the Appendix), has developed into a method of learning that empowers people to think critically and creatively, that facilitates constructive dialogue, and that directs people to plan for their common good. It works. Yet the projected accomplishments are so dramatic that skeptics might well wonder if the claim is inflated—if search conferencing is truly so effective, after all, why hasn't it become the universal method for conducting strategic planning?

This is a valid question. While a fundamental change toward democratic structure is a main component and a necessary feature of the Search Conference method, the movement toward democratization must first overcome an even more deeply rooted set of assumptions related to how human beings acquire knowledge of their world. In fact, the arguments in favor of guardianship and against democratization are directly related to this deeply entrenched educational paradigm. Barriers to the democratization of organizations in society can be traced to the assumptions underlying this educational paradigm.

Epistemology of Education

The core of this conventional educational paradigm, as Fred Emery points out, "lies in epistemology, not in educational practice" (1993, p. 43). *Epistemology* is a philosophical term for theories about how it is possible (or not possible) for people to gain knowledge about the world. We believe that the basic assumptions of a traditional educational epistemology are at the root of the widespread and deep resistance to participative democracy, and in the present case, specifically to the Search Conference method.

The movement toward more participative forms of democracy (such as the Search Conference) has been stymied by a common but generally unspoken belief that people are basically incompetent to learn from their own experience (F. Emery, 1980, 1982, 1989). Those who harbor this belief reason in the following manner: *People need to be told about the world; they can't learn anything important from their own experience. If they cannot acquire sound knowledge directly from the world, how can they possibly be expected to be capable of governing and managing their own affairs?* These fears lurk in the minds of every skeptical and conservative manager. For them, people by nature suffer from an irremediable handicap that must be compensated for by the help and wisdom of more knowledgeable guardians. This paternalistic attitude represents a limited view of human learning. It also does a very good job of preserving social hierarchies, to the great advantage of those on the higher rungs.

The distrust of people's competency to learn from their own experience is also tied to a basic assumption of what constitutes true knowledge of the world. According to this epistemology, true knowledge can only be obtained by eliminating that which is idiosyncratic. The vagaries of individual perceptions are automatically deemed unreliable until they can stand the acid test of replicability. This model proclaims that sound knowledge of the world is derived from the rigor of the scientific method, repeated observations, and an accretive process that leads to a well-structured edifice, body of knowledge, or discipline.

Given these core assumptions, the primary task of education has been that of a mass distributor of accumulated knowledge. Distribution of knowledge occurs through a long sequential process consisting of proper schooling and mastery of the canons of an academic discipline. Established truths of any field must first be learned by rote memorization of facts and figures, learning the rules of classification and logic, and demonstrating competence through tests of memory and analytical problem solving. Systematically, the pupil is trained to distrust personal and idiosyncratic perceptions. Creativity gives way to conformity. This educational paradigm channels the capacities of human intelligence into one dominant way of knowing, sharpening the powers of analytical abstraction and logical inference. Indeed, the hallmarks of an educated person within this paradigm are the ability to recall facts and figures, to think abstractly about problems, and to display strict adherence to the rules of disciplinary purity.

This educational paradigm also views the mind as a *tabula rasa,* a clean, blank slate. Accordingly, educational practice is equated with methods of teaching or instructing rather than facilitating learning in its broadest sense. Schooling is a task of imparting information and training in formalized methods of observation and analysis. This form of education resembles a mechanical process that pours information into the mind as if it were an empty vessel.

These educational practices are inherently alienating. The majority of people love to learn, but hate to be instructed. Nevertheless, the bulk of the educational system is dominated by expert-led lectures by instructors—including high school teachers, college professors, or corporate trainers—in a traditional classroom setting. This one-way, unilateral transfer of information silences the learner and breeds contempt toward education, resulting in "hatred of learning" (Bion, 1961). It is this form of education that, for all practical purposes, has contributed to the "lack of faith among people in the validity of their own perceptions" (F. Emery, 1982, p. 1114).

Ecological Learning and the Search Conference

The Search Conference method overturns the root assumption of the conventional educational paradigm. In place, it assumes that people are basically capable of learning from their own experience. The Search Conference uses a learning modality that is based on the notion of direct perception, or *ecological learning*, which offers a direct challenge to the conventional educational paradigm. This learning theory is based on the research of Fritz Heider (1959) and James Gibson (1966, 1979), who were both psychologists interested in understanding how the human senses, perception, cognition, and creation of meaning were linked. Their research demonstrated that the environment has an informational structure and that the perceptual systems of human beings have a long evolutionary history that has adapted them to recognize and extract information directly from the environment. While the environment is always in flux, people can directly perceive meaningful invariances and patterns relevant to their survival. However, a point of clarification is in order here: information is neither inside the brain nor out there in the environment, waiting to be picked up; rather, information resides in the active relationship between person and environment, as the former strives to survive in an ever-changing environment, to adapt, and to flourish (Gibson, 1979).

This way of knowing the world is similar to the epistemology of native peoples. According to David Suzuki and Peter Knudtson, the epistemology of the native mind is "firmly rooted in reality, in keen observation, interaction, and thought, sharpened by the daily rigors of survival. Its validity rests largely upon hard-won personal experience—upon concrete encounters with game animals and arduous treks across the physical contours of the local landscapes. . . . The junction between knowledge and experience is tight, continuous, and dynamic, giving rise to 'truths' that are likely to be correspondingly intelligent, fluid, and vibrantly 'alive'" (1994, pp. 20–21).

British empiricists such as Locke, Berkeley, and Hume, as well as later philosophers such as Kant, believed that human beings can never really know for sure whether their perceptions represent actual reality. This is consonant with many modern psychophysical theories, which hold that because our brain interprets external data in the form of electromagnetic energy, sound waves, and other physical phenomena by converting them into electrochemical impulses, we can never really be sure whether these interpretations are valid or true. An epistemology based on ecological learning implies a new perspective on perception.

The environment contains an abundance of richly textured information, and any person with an intact perceptual system can directly access this information. Access to information in the environment is only restricted by habit, lack of confidence, or psychological isolation, not because of any real deficiency. Thus Heider and Gibson unequivocally demonstrated that people have the natural and innate ability to directly perceive meaning from their environment. Children, for example, are born learners, naturally curious, actively experimental, playful, and open to the world. However, this instinctual drive to learn, to question, to remake the world through playful rearrangement is suppressed once the demands and rigidities of an authoritarian pedagogy take over. After many years of passive schooling and thousands of hours of taking in lectures, following rules, and engaging in teacher-pleaser behaviors, individuals gradually unlearn and forget their natural ability to learn from their own experience.

The damage inflicted by this kind of education goes even beyond this. Passive learning severely limits the development of people as democratic and active citizens. Instead of fostering their civic development or forming the democratic habits that are crucial to sustaining a democratic society, nonparticipatory education conditions people to accept authoritarian structures as normal in society, and believe that they shouldn't expect to participate in matters that concern the public trust, health, or strategic directions of their organizations and communities.

As people learn their proper place in an authoritarian classroom, they eventually come to learn and passively accept the unilateral authority of those above them, with an indignant resignation that this is the normal way organizations are structured in our society. Over time, people internalize this structural oppression. Their sense of political efficacy diminishes, fostering self-doubts about their own intelligence and civic abilities (Pateman, 1970). The end result is that people are reluctant and hesitant to embrace self-management, fearful of participation, and distrustful of anything that requires them to learn in public. Yet it is these dispositions and skills that are essential elements of citizenship in a democratic society. Individuals in a position of power point to the weaknesses of those below them, saying, "See, I told you so," and the structural oppression continues in a vicious self-sealing circle.

The findings that have been discussed form the basis of a new educational paradigm that refutes the claim that people in general lack the capacity to learn directly from their environment. The mind has never been a blank slate or empty vessel waiting to be filled up. Human beings are not machines in a mechanical universe (as is implicitly claimed by the traditional educational paradigm). That many of our school systems are in shambles should come as no surprise. No one can be expected to be excited or motivated while being force-fed information, especially when that information has little bearing on the context of the learner or to the practical affairs of society. We also cannot expect to educate adults in this manner. Education conceived and practiced in this manner is bound to be a futile exercise.

Direct Perception in the Search Conference

We have illustrated the differences between the epistemology that guides the design and operation of our formal education system with its emphasis on *teaching,* and the Search Conference, which takes as its basic unit people *learning* in an environment. As planning becomes learning, people themselves—through the process of the Search Conference—become their own educators and accept the responsibility that this entails. In this new educational paradigm, *learning to learn* means participants are learning to learn from their own perceptions, and learning to accept their own perceptions as a legitimate form of knowledge.

The first phase of every Search Conference puts people into the mode of learning from the environment. Certainly, every human being with an intact perceptual system can perform this task. Contrary to traditional beliefs about discrete bits of sensory information impinging on the central nervous system and requiring integration before meaningful knowledge is available, the perceptual system acts as a unit absorbing meaningful knowledge directly from the environment. During the first session of the Search Conference, participants draw on their perceptions of the environment, synthesize these into scenarios, and report their collective interpretations. They produce sophisticated but realistic local theories of their situation. They gain confidence in their abilities to self-manage and see the true value of their perceptions and experience.

All Education Is Political

All forms of education, as Dewey noted, are political in nature. An epistemology based on direct perception provides the educational foundation for participative democracy. It was no coincidence that highly evolved systems of democratic governance were once operative among Native Americans (before white settlers invaded their lands), as their dominant way of knowing the world was also based on an epistemology of direct perception. Direct forms of participative democracy were a way of life for tribes that were part of the Iroquois nation. Some scholars even point to historical evidence that many features of the "Great Binding Law of Iroquois Confederacy" were used as a primary model for the ideas that shaped the U.S. Articles of Confederation and the Constitution (Grinde, 1977; Mander, 1991; Weatherford, 1988; Wolin, 1989). Many of our founding fathers—James Madison, Benjamin Franklin, Thomas Jefferson, and John Adams—were deeply influenced by the Iroquois. During the Albany convention in 1754, forty-two members of the Iroquois Grand Council were solicited to serve as advisers on confederate structures (Mander, 1991). The resemblance of the U.S. Constitution to the Great Law is striking. The Great Law had such features as a federation with a separation of powers between the central councils and Indian states; a common defense system; elected representatives from each tribe at the federal and local levels; different legislative branches that debated and enacted Iroquois policies and laws; checks and balances, along with the rights of popular recall of chiefs and representatives; and universal suffrage (Fenton, 1968; Mander, 1991).

The built-in capacity of the human perceptual system makes people by nature purposeful. Every individual has the right and potential to construct purposes and meanings. That the environment offers information for direct understanding, combined with the perceptual ability of human beings to extract this information, is unique to human cultures. This culture is not limited to corporate culture or organizational culture, rather, the word is used here in an anthropological sense. Given that individuals have the ability to perceive and make meaning out of their environment, they also have the power to participate in the process of making and remaking culture. In this sense, culture is a democratic concept because all people, regardless of their socioeconomic status or educational background, have the power to shape culture. Even those who are passive and withdrawn from society have an impact, albeit an adverse one, on culture. If culture making wasn't a democratic concept, the Search Conference could be used as a manipulative and repressive tool for maintaining the power of elites.

This new educational paradigm, which the Search Conference is founded on, requires us to think of knowledge not as a hard-to-acquire possession but as an inborn and widely distributed human capacity. Viewing *knowledge-ability* as an innate human capacity democratizes knowledge acquisition; hence, the capacity to be knowledgeable no longer needs to be restricted to the chosen few. Because the Search Conference creates a democratic learning environment, participants can extract information and construct meaning out of such information without the need for formal training in abstract logic. In fact, many Search Conferences with illiterate participants have produced extremely successful results. For example, Search Conferences have been conducted for over twenty years with various groups of Australia's original people, who retain many if not all of the characteristics of an oral culture. The Search Conference contains the same assumptions and educational paradigm as their ancient cultural ways. A series of Search Conferences on Torres Strait in 1993–1994 were conducted to establish island community plans. These conferences proved successful in demonstrating the power and congruence of ecological perception. The communities on this island possess an immense amount of detailed local knowledge based on careful observation by many people over many generations. Those who have participated in these conferences rapidly assessed the meaning of this wealth of knowledge for their future. They observe their social environments and changes as astutely as they do their physical ecology. This perceptual knowledge provided them with a solid base from which to ascertain the future of various social phenomena.

Because the new educational paradigm elevates and honors the innate capacity of human beings to learn, it involves a greatly reduced need for intermediaries, trainers, facilitators, instructors, or a scholarly priesthood to force-feed abstract information to the masses. Despite these findings, the current social stratification of organizations would tend to have us believe otherwise. Having been thoroughly conditioned to think that valid knowledge always lies outside themselves, people have lost confidence in the validity of their own perceptions. This social conditioning dictates that we can only learn from qualified outsiders, that we must depend upon experts to solve every social and organizational ill, and that we must look up to someone else for information. The major differences between this traditional education and our new educational paradigm are summarized in Table 5.1.

In contrast, the Search Conference is a clear alternative that consists of integrating ecological perception with the second design principle. This combination democratizes learning and knowledge acquisition processes. All participants in a Search Conference are thus considered experts.

From the very outset of a Search Conference, people are immediately engaged in directly making sense out of the world they live in. They learn by doing that they are capable human beings who can take the task of learning into their own hands. Within the first few hours of a Search Conference, people are immersed in deciphering and analyzing the meaning of data they themselves have generated. They are immediately called upon to exercise their critical thinking skills, engage in discussion with their peers, and deliver reports of their collective perceptions by speaking out and addressing the whole Search Conference community.

This is what invigorates the life of a democracy—ordinary people taking control and responsibility for their own future—whether in communities, organizations, schools, social service agencies, parishes, or anywhere with a need for groups of people to work cooperatively toward some shared goal.

Table 5.1. Comparison of Educational Paradigms.

Old Educational Paradigm	New Educational Paradigm
Passive, abstract learning	Participatory, direct learning
Factory model of education	Discovery model of education
Imposes inert information, reproducing facts divorced from the immediate context	Extracts meaning and grasps particulars from the situation
Information storage and memorization	Reflective understanding and creative assimilation
One-way, unilateral transfer of accumulated knowledge	Collaborative inquiry, systematic acquisition of relevant experience
Specialized language and jargon of experts	Everyday conversational language of participants
Forced discipline	Self-directed learning
Encourages elitism, one-upmanship and towers of babel	Encourages dialogue and the collective pooling of perceptions
Abstract knowledge derived from scientific method and logical inference	Generative themes extracted from direct experience of the wider environment and system
Affirms only those with high IQs	Gives voice to anyone who has an intact perceptual system
Socialized dependence on authority	Autonomous, critical questioning of the status quo

Chapter Six

Conditions for Creative Collaboration

The area of group dynamics and structure serves as a bridge between the creative and productive task orientation of groups in the Search Conference. The conference manager can create the structural and process conditions that foster self-management, creativity, open communications, and the development of trust. The present chapter begins by providing a working knowledge of group dynamics and then examines how conference structure influences the course and outcomes of group work.

Establishing the conditions for open and effective communications is crucial to the success of any Search Conference. Indeed, one of the key roles of the Search Conference manager is to ensure that these conditions for effective communications are established and maintained. Working with large groups on any issue of real significance, however, is bound to lead to disagreement and conflict. We conclude by discussing the way conflicts and disagreements are handled in the Search Conference through the rationalization of conflict, showing how this model differs from conventional approaches to consensus decision making.

Bion's Theory of Group Level Functioning

As discussed briefly in Chapter Two, Wilfred Bion's classic studies on group dynamics have helped us learn why people have difficulties in establishing fully functioning self-managing groups. Bion was a veteran of World War I tank battles in France. He later trained as a psychiatrist, and his major theoretical insights came out of his work with traumatized British soldiers at a military hospital during World War II. Bion continued his work with therapeutic groups at the Tavistock Institute in London, where he developed the theories that were reported in a series of research articles and collected works (1952). His writings were eventually complied into *Experiences in Groups* (1961). Since then, numerous researchers have elaborated on his original work (Cytrynbaum, 1992; Hirschhorn, 1990; Kernberg, 1978; Miller, 1976; Pines, 1985; Rioch, 1975; Sullivan, 1995).

Work and Basic Assumption Groups

From his observations, Bion postulated that groups can operate in two modes, displaying a dual system of mental functioning. In the first mode, Bion observed that a mature group is capable of performing its task, working together in a way that is cooperative, rational, and resourceful. Such mature group functioning is task oriented; the resources and talents of individual members are marshaled in support of the group task. When a group is functioning in this mode, it is what Bion referred to as "the work group" (1961, p. 28). The work group characterizes a mode of mental activity that is conscious, rational, cooperative. In a fully functioning work group, members actively seek information, learn from their experience, and are creative in devising more effective ways to achieve their task (Cytrynbaum, 1992, p. 12).

Bion also maintained that strong unconscious forces can be operating at the level of a group. When a group gets together to perform a task, members may unconsciously experience anxiety associated with the nature of the task, and with the very nature of joining a group. Later writers confirm this observation (Cytrynbaum, 1992, p. 13). Bion argued that a group is more than just an aggregation of individuals. As Sullivan (1995, p. 10) points out, "There is posited by all members the existence of a 'group level' of feeling and behavior that is more than the sum of its parts. This assumed group level of activity is what an individual finds so unknowable and overwhelming, and it is the cause of the regressive behavior that ensues." This notion of group level functioning is most clearly illustrated in Bion's theory of group assumptions. In contrast to the work group, this mode of mental functioning is unconscious, as the basic assumption group succumbs to a shared set of social defenses that interferes with achievement of the group task (Hirschhorn, 1990). Rather than engaging in conscious coopera- tive behavior, groups are taken over by unconscious assumptions that have to do with fantasized threats to their security or uncon- trollable anxieties over their ability to maintain their identity. Fur- ther, this mode of group level functioning involves unconscious assumptions and fantasies about the leader's role and motives. In this sense, the basic assumption group is neither work oriented nor reality based. Regressing to the realm of unconscious impulses and infantile fantasies, the basic assumption group is reactive and emotional, and seeks instant gratification. There is little tolerance on the part of a basic assumption group for reflection or rational analysis.

Bion argued that both the work and basic assumption modes are operative in every group. According to Bion, the work group can be obstructed, diverted, or assisted by the emotional forces that are characteristic of the basic assumptions. However, a mature work group has the capacity to manage or make use of these powerful unconscious and emotional forces. In other words, basic assump- tion activity can help as well as hinder the work group's ability to accomplish its task. We contend that the choice of design princi- ple influences the ability of the work group to mobilize basic as- sumption energy in the service of its task. As we discussed in Chapter Five, the hierarchical Design Principle 1 structure does not authorize groups to take responsibility for their own tasks. As a result, this structure keeps groups in an immature mode of func- tioning, with all the negative and dysfunctional emotional dynam- ics that are characteristically found in bureaucratic settings. Groups in such settings lack the sophistication of managing their basic as- sumptions. Instead, such group functioning is crippled by the presence of one of three unconscious assumptions or defense mechanisms: dependency, fight-flight, or pairing.

Dependency

When the group assumption of dependency is operating, members look for a leader to provide nurturance and protection. In the de- pendent mode, the group behaves as if their task is to secure this form of nurturance and protection through an omniscient and powerful leader who can ensure the security of the group. Group members forfeit their autonomy when they assume that the leader will take care of them and tell them what to do. However, this childlike state of dependency is totally irresponsible, because while the group is asking for this leader (be it teacher or expert) to look after them, the members show little inclination to learn from the leader. They presume they do not have to learn because they have placed themselves in the leader's hands. This group acts as if the leader's knowledge will make them self-sufficient. Further, because of this infantile state of group dependency, they act as if they must be spoon-fed simple instructions for everything they do. Thus, energy and learning are low in the dependency group as members are "quite opposed to the idea that they have met for the purpose of doing work" (Bion, 1961, p. 84). In addition, the emotional tone of the dependent group is negative, guilty, apathetic, and depressed. Dependency reflects a social defense mechanism against the group's unconscious fears and fantasies with regard to its own aggression and power. Eventually, a dependent group will resent the fact that it has grown so dependent on a leader who falls short of its unrealistic and idealized projections.

Fight-Flight

In the fight-flight mode, the group on an unconscious level feels threatened or persecuted by outside forces. As Bion notes, the group assumes that it "has met to fight something or to run away from it" (Bion, 1961, p. 152). To preserve their group identity, members assume that they must protect themselves from such outside threats by either doing battle or fleeing from the situation at hand. A group that is experiencing fight-flight reactions will often look to a leader or person to mobilize the group for action. A fight-flight group is in a high state of emotional arousal. There is a sense of an adrenalin-rushed state of reaction by the group, expressed in terms of deeply split emotionally exaggerated perceptions of "us versus them," "good versus bad," "right versus wrong." Such perceptions in the fight-flight group are projected outward. Scapegoating, blaming, and verbal aggression are common expressions of fight-flight group dynamics. Given this highly emotionally charged state of the fight-flight dynamic, group reflection, introspection, or any other forms of self-diagnosis are devalued.

In learning situations, if the group is in flight, it may cease to acknowledge the existence of the official leader. The subject matter or task is ignored as the group is distracted by its concerns for self-preservation. Certainly the fight-flight basic assumption group is more active and energetic as compared to the passivity and low energy of the dependency group. However, when a group is in fight-flight, it does little work on the actual task. The fight aspect of this dynamic is obviously easier to recognize than flight. Yet the flight dynamic is distinguishable from dependency by the nature of the group's emotional expression. Even in extended periods of flight, people are stirred up and aroused, but their anxiety and aggression is expressed covertly. These periods are usually described as chaotic.

Pairing

When this basic assumption is operating, the group assumes it has met to creatively reproduce itself as a means to preserve its identity. At an unconscious group level, there is optimism and hope that the group will magically produce a new messiah or savior to solve all their problems. Members show a great deal of hopeful feeling and faith that a new leader or idea will emerge. In a pairing group, several members typically may pair up and join forces in small cliques. There is a great deal of talk among pairs and cliques, but little real action. This is because the new leader or idea must remain unborn for their hope to be sustained. And this is the defensive nature of the pairing group assumption: by not actually producing a real leader or idea, the group avoids having to confront the realities and inevitable disappointments associated with real leaders and real ideas. Instead, the pairing dynamic allows the group to remain in a world of fantasy.

Influence of Structure on Group Dynamics

While the work and basic assumption group modes exist simultaneously in any group that comes together to perform a task, certain structural influences can either help or hinder the maturation of the work group mode. Bion recognized that a structural influence was involved when he noticed that in dependent groups, "Individuals do not have a relationship with each other but only with the leader" (Bion, 1952, p. 238). Kernberg (1978) notes that while the potential for the basic assumption group mode always exists, it is more likely to be activated when the task structure breaks down.

Bion also stipulated that the ability to manage basic group assumptions and the propensity toward staying within the work group mode is a function of the group's level of sophistication. As Sullivan (1995, p. 21) points out, "The sophisticated work group, according to Bion, does not attempt to avoid the basic assumptions. Rather, it has methods or interventions that it can use either to neutralize what it considers to be the more subversive aspects of basic assumption activity or else to access those aspects of it that are useful to the accomplishment of its task."

Search Conference theory postulates that the level of group sophistication, that is, the group's ability to mobilize and use basic assumption activity for task achievement, will be influenced by organizational structure. Whether a work group can make sophisticated use of the group assumptions depends on the choice of design principle.

Under an authoritarian, hierarchical, Design Principle 1 structure, the work group mode cannot mature nor make constructive use of basic assumption group energy. Figure 6.1 illustrates the structural influence of DP1 in activating the dependency and fight-flight group assumptions. When coordination and control are strictly preserved by the levels above, the work group is effectively divested of responsibility for managing its own tasks and process. This makes the work dependent upon direction from above. In this way, the DP1 structure infantilizes the work group by activating the dependency mode. And how convenient: The strong leader that the dependent group seeks is to be found in the person who occupies the position above them—their supervisor. Indeed, dependency is valued because superiors playing the strong-leader role want unquestioned obedience and loyalty from subordinates.

Yet groups cannot linger forever in one group assumption mode, and dependency eventually merges into fight-flight. A work group under Design Principle 1 often finds itself ensnared in fight-flight dynamics. There are numerous configurations of how this may play out. For example, fight-flight group assumptions could be operating either between different work groups, or between work groups and management. In the former case, we see this play

Figure 6.1. Structure of Group Emotional Assumptions.

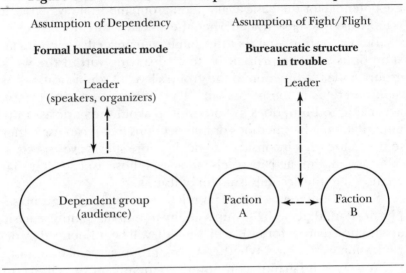

out as a war between factions and as political infighting, as subgroups lash out against what they each perceive as threats to their identity. Tensions between work groups and management are frequent in DP1 organizations as there is a tendency for one subgroup to align itself politically with the leader, while another secretly plots its strategy of attack against both. In still other cases, we see instances where work groups have gone deep into a flight mode in order to avoid such battles and conflicts. Preoccupied with defending their boundaries, these work groups retreat from their tasks and seek out little contact with other parts of the organization. Similar dynamics can be observed in large groups operating in traditional DP1 conferences.

The Search Conference, in contrast, involves large and small groups that function in a democratic, Design Principle 2 structure. Authority and responsibility for the management of tasks and process is fully invested within the boundaries of the work group. Because work groups are authorized to take responsibility for control and coordination of their own activities, they can creatively make use of basic group assumptions in the service of accomplishing their primary task. We call this sophisticated form of group level functioning the *creative working mode*.

The structural influence of Design Principle 2 upon the work group is quite different from that of Design Principle 1. With DP2, the work group is authorized to be responsible for its task; its conscious efforts go toward facilitating rational problem solving, drawing upon the members' array of individual talents and skills, and creatively harnessing the unconscious forces of the group for task achievement. In the positive sense, Bion noted that "Organization and structure . . . are the product of cooperation between members of the group and their effect, once established in the group, is to demand still further cooperation" (Bion, 1952, p. 239). Figure 6.2 illustrates that a characteristic of the creative working mode is high energy and positive emotions.

The main point here is that a Design Principle 2 system fosters the development of mature work groups that can make sophisticated

**Figure 6.2. Creative Working
Mode in a Search Conference Design.**

Design principle: Redundancy of functions
Organizational structure: Democratic

Search conference

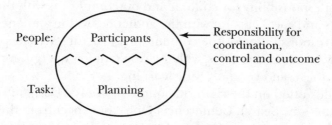

Creative Working Mode

	Affect	Energy	Learning
High			
Medium			
Low			

use of the basic group assumptions. This is in stark contrast to Design Principle 1 systems, where the negative and debilitating aspects of basic group assumptions are chronic and overpowering. In highly bureaucratic organizations when group assumptions rule, people predominantly feel helpless, frustrated, resentful, angry, paranoid, bored, depressed; or they seek forms of escape; or they fantasize that someday a new boss, a new CEO will make things right. We typically make jokes about the mental health of post office employees, but our cynicism addresses the inherent dysfunctional nature of bureaucratic structures. In sum, effective management of group dynamics is dependent upon the choice of organizational structure.

Design, Dynamics, and Learning

The diagram in Figure 6.3 summarizes the relationships among the design principles, group dynamics, and level of learning that we have been discussing. Design Principle 1 underlies the structure of conventional "talking heads" conferences. These conferences, whether they be academic symposia or professional or business meetings, are organized in a top-down fashion with hierarchies of sponsors, chairpersons, authorities, keynote speakers, lecturers—while the mass audience sits passively at the receiving end. Responsibility for content and outcomes rests with the organizers and speakers, not with the audience. As the audience has a little responsibility for the content, this structure activates dependency group assumptions, with the resultant low energy levels, negative affect, and certainly little learning.

Illustrated on the right side of the figure is a Design Principle 2 event—the Search Conference. One can expect from this structure high energy, positive feelings, a great deal of learning, and a marshaling of group assumptions toward accomplishment of the group task.

There is another structure that deliberately blurs the design principles. In practice this structure can be difficult to recognize because it attempts to mix features from both structures. Figure 6.4 shows that between the bureaucratic DP1 structure on one end, and the purely democratic DP2 structure, is the mixed mode conference design. A simple example of this would be a conference

**Figure 6.3. Comparison of Dynamics
Between Traditional and Search Conference Designs.**

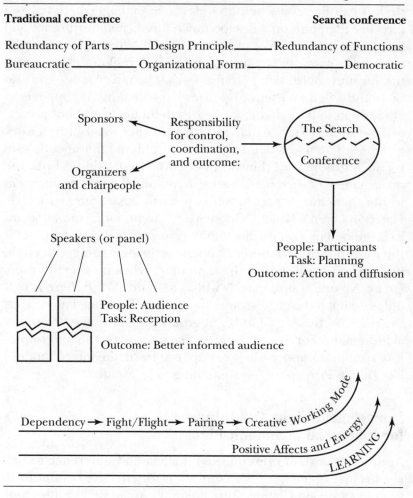

Traditional conference   Search conference

Redundancy of Parts ———— Design Principle ———— Redundancy of Functions

Bureaucratic ———————— Organizational Form ———————— Democratic

design that slots a guest speaker followed by small-group discussions. A conference that is *managed* in the mixed mode is more subtle but can be seen when a conference manager behaves as a directive therapist, provides too much unsolicited nurturance and help, or assumes the role of content expert. When this occurs, the conference manager is usurping the group's responsibility for controlling and coordinating its own work. The mixed mode can also be found when an event organizes large groups and appears to allow them to participate, but leaves them unclear about just exactly what they are participating *in*. In other words, it is a work group without a well-defined task. Bion did find therapeutic uses for such groups, but they don't get much work done! Both the management of such participative events and the groups that form within them mirror each other in a classic laissez-faire structure. Harrison Owen's (1992) "Open Space" event, for example, seems to be guided by a set of laissez-faire principles: "Whoever comes is the right person. Whatever happens is the only thing that could have. Whenever it starts is the right time. When it's over, it's over" (p. 8). No one is sure exactly who is in control, and there is very little attempt to manage group assumptions. The mixed mode runs the risk of activating fight-flight group dynamics away from task achievement. For Search Conference managers who aim to provide conditions under which groups can learn, the mixed mode— like Design Principle 1—is something to be avoided.

Management of the Conditions for Influential Communications

Another important prerequisite for a Search Conference to succeed is management of the conditions for effective communications. As noted in Chapter Two, Solomon Asch (1952) found four basic conditions need to be met for effective communications to occur in groups: *openness* (things are what they appear to be); a *shared field* (the people present can see they all live in the same world); *psychological similarity* among the participants; and *mutual trust*. By evaluating whether these conditions are present in a meeting, one can determine the potential for effective group communications. A typical business meeting rarely meets these conditions. Instead, one is more likely to see a good deal of political posturing, hidden agendas, withholding of information, stereotyping, and

Figure 6.4. Group Dynamics in a Mixed-Mode Conference.

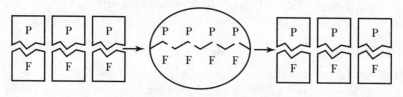

Design principle: Mixed mode conference
Organizational structure: Changes

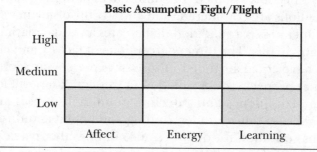

Responsibility for coordination, control, and
outcome moves during the conference

Basic Assumption: Fight/Flight

	Affect	Energy	Learning
High			
Medium			
Low			

mistrust. Asch's requirements for effective communication provide a simple diagnostic for detecting situations that will inhibit learning and impede collaborative group work. Anything that contradicts or inhibits any of these conditions will heighten tension and increase the probability of resistance.

The basic idea here is that for face-to-face learning to occur, people must enter into a relationship regarding some task in which they share an interest. It is important to keep in mind that the Search Conference is a large-group, task-oriented conversation. Most conventional strategic planning processes do not occur in a large open plenary format, where the community is the unit and free speech is the medium. The communicative atmosphere of a Search Conference relies more on the medium of spoken language, which is quite different from written language. Whereas the latter eventually has a silencing and dissociative effect, the Search

Conference restores an oral culture. Here, people convey their true thoughts, feelings, and aspirations through the power of the spoken word.

It is worth reviewing Asch's conditions for effective communications in more detail before we proceed further.

Openness

To communicate effectively, people have to know that they are in a situation that is totally open to their investigation and that things are what they appear to be. Nothing must be hidden from view. The Search Conference is designed as a learning environment where exploration of the situation from different perspectives is possible. Since it is assumed that differences of opinion will exist, all perceptions are considered valid and worthy of further examination. Openness is a condition that creates an equal playing field for all participants. The direct perceptions of factory and clerical workers have equal air time to those of experts, managers, and other types of specialists. A violation of this condition will lead to loss of self-confidence and a decline in mutual support and respect. It will also inhibit understanding and potential diffusion.

Asch's condition for openness also implies that participants have full control over all the data and information that is generated in the conference. There is no withholding of data or information from participants, and consultants do not engage in interpretation. This is in stark contrast to bureaucratic organizations—or traditional consulting interventions, for that matter—where data and information are doled out on a need-to-know basis.

A climate of openness in a Search Conference is first established with the participant briefing before the conference. Our roles, values, and expectations as Search Conference managers, as well as the underlying strategy and long-term goals of the conference itself, are put up for inspection and clarified before actual work begins. Furthermore, wherever possible, the planning for a Search Conference event must be itself participatory. At the beginning of the conference, participants receive a straightforward statement of the conference's overall purpose and design, and this statement remains in view throughout the meeting. The sponsor explains the purpose of the gathering. Participants introduce themselves and identify their expectations for the conference. Conference managers make a conscious effort to ensure that concepts are conveyed through a variety of media—visual as well as verbal—and in terms understandable to all the participants.

Perhaps the simplest yet most effective move to establish and preserve openness is the use of flip-chart paper to compile an immediate, accessible, and continuous record of work performed. Flip charts provide a common public record of information generated in the meeting. Once the group's work has been recorded on flip-chart paper, their observations, conclusions, and plans tend to be carried forward clearly and recognizably into the final report and beyond, maintaining the participants' energy level and commitment to the action they've agreed to take. In contrast, when sponsors or conference managers compile the report from private notes or information participants have recorded on individual worksheets, people often feel somewhat surprised to see what it is their group decided.

Shared Field

The very first task of the Search Conference fosters the emergence of a mutually shared objective field. In simple terms, this condition means that people will begin to collaborate when they have developed a shared context of the issue or problem they are concerned with. This arises in the Search Conference as the whole community participates in a brainstorming session to identify changes happening in the world over the last five to seven years. After all data are written on flip charts and posted on the walls for participants to see, a shift of mind occurs. Attention shifts from individual concerns and differences to a shared perception that all live in the same world. This amounts to a figure-ground reversal, as the environment moves from the background into the foreground of perception. The community may have identified a number of trends and forces that appear to be moving in contradictory directions; for example, some people perceive environmental problems are getting worse, while others perceive such problems to be lessening. However, there is still the emergence of a mutually shared field embedded in the common perceptions of such conflicting trends. For exactly these reasons, the meaning of these perceptions and their validity are established in constructing scenarios of their most probable future. Complexity is the nature of a turbulent environment, but the presence of a mutually shared field allows participants to make sense of their data and establish a hierarchy of probabilities for the future.

The mutually shared field emerges by establishing that the environment has features that can be commonly perceived. It is these perceptions that later become a shared context for planning and action. The simple brainstorming procedure for mapping the contextual environment produces a picture that contains the widest range of perceptions. Because flip charts cannot be manipulated, they remain an accessible snapshot of the contextual environment and serve to establish the validity of the notion that *we all live in the same world.* By this point, participants have accepted the democratic norms for equal participation, experienced a new paradigm of learning, and have laid the foundation for building more trust.

Basic Psychological Similarity

Most people naturally seek confirmation of their basic human similarities. Once they can see that the behaviors and motives of other people are similar to their own, they will admit that they can learn from one another. This is perhaps why the Dalai Lama urges, "It is important to realize our sameness as human beings." When, however, there is a perception of contempt or condescension on the part of one toward another, the probability of effective communication declines rapidly. Any perception of a Search Conference manager or participant acting as a self-appointed expert, talking down or displaying arrogant behavior, will inhibit learning.

The conditions for psychological similarity begin to emerge early in the Search Conference when, as participants discuss their greatest aspirations and hopes for a more desirable future for the world, they discover their similarities. Sharing these ideals makes them real, vivid, and alive. This task serves to confirm that:

- There is an underlying level of concern with humanity and the state of the world.
- Though often unspoken, human ideals transcend position, gender, race, status, or age.

- By discussing and deciding upon these matters—such as a desirable future in either global or system terms—a *modus operandi* has been established; this opens the way for cooperative work on more immediate problems later in the Search Conference.

Participants are often amazed at the extent of the overlap when they present their desirable world future scenarios. Regardless of the exact words used, the four ideals we discussed in Chapter Four usually emerge in every scenario. Building on this basic level of psychological similarity makes it possible to deal with issues and conflicts in such a way that they become channeled toward higher purposes in the process of creating a genuinely adaptive community.

Trust

When people experience an open learning environment, and come to appreciate that they share similar concerns for the state of the world, trust begins to emerge. This condition grows out of the way the other three conditions are met early in the conference. Trust accumulates over time as individuals come to experience the openness of the world they share with others and the mutual respect and consideration likely to accrue from initiating new ideas. As such trust develops, interpersonal relations strengthen and deepen, increasing the probability of mutual learning and network building. In the process, individuals themselves begin to become open systems, able to grow in response to each other.

For the management of any learning environment, the emergence of trust is a critical factor. Without a foundation of trust, joint action is nearly impossible. Trust needs to occur at both an individual and group level. The individual must develop greater trust in his or her own perceptions. The group must develop confidence and trust in its members to assume responsibility for managing tasks. The group must also develop trust in the Search Conference managers. Regarding this latter point, the relationship between participants and managers must be collaborative. Conference managers are not servants to sponsors, nor should they display any signs of superiority. They are not above participants.

Trust developed in this way allows people to open up, gradually discarding their masks of passivity, hostility, and indifference.

The resultant energy enhances group consciousness and intensifies interpersonal engagement with the task at hand. This leads to more mutually supportive action. Without this spiral of trust, learning, energy, and commitment, the process of implementation would be impossible. The presence of trust is tested toward the end of the Search Conference when participants select groups to work on action plans. Because the self-selected subgroups work on behalf of the whole, they must be trusted to do so.

In summary, the Search Conference design incorporates Asch's properties for effective communication. Table 6.1 shows how the steps of the Search Conference allow each of Asch's four conditions for effective communication to emerge with a cumulative effect over the course of the conference. The task of every Search Conference manager is to ensure that Asch's requirements are met during each progressive stage of the conference—and that they are not violated.

Rationalizing Conflict

Disagreements and conflict are inevitable, in Search Conferences as elsewhere in life. They should not be avoided. When people with diverse backgrounds come together for the purpose of deciding the future direction of their community or organization, there are bound to be substantive disagreements. The Search Conference process doesn't pretend that there can be perfect harmony in a complex world. It appreciates diversity and differences—these are what makes the world rich and exciting. Particularly when there are institutionalized adversarial positions or when people have different perceptions on issues that deeply concern them, trying to reach consensus may be unrealistic.

However, when significant differences arise in the Search Conference, the goal is not to negotiate a compromise or gain grudging agreement to support something some participants still basically disagree with. Rather, managers use a special process in a Search Conference to make differences rational, while at the same time establishing the areas of common ground—those areas upon which participants *can* agree. To rationalize conflict means to take conflict seriously, not to skirt around it or play it down—and yet not to intentionally provoke it for the sake of provoking it. By

Table 6.1. Asch's Conditions
Translated into Search Conference Design.

Conditions	Design and Management
1. OPENNESS Exploration, checking of opinions and perceptions	Prebriefing on content and process. Minimize threat to participation. Clarify roles and values. All recording is public (flipchart paper) visual, verbal, vernacular.
2. MUTUALLY SHARED OBJECTIVE FIELD We all live in the same world. Establish commonly perceived background for joint action, taking into consideration interdependencies.	Scan the external environment using the ground rule—all perceptions are valid. Environment is analyzed and used throughout as a benchmark.
3. BASIC PSYCHOLOGICAL SIMILARITY We are all human with the same human concerns. We can talk as equals and learn from each other.	Provide opportunities to see common ground—desirable futures based on ideals provide basis for cooperative work and the rationalization of conflict.
4. TRUST Communication builds self-confidence and generates energy, which leads to action and diffusion.	No status difference between participants and managers. No management interference in the content.

$$1+2+3=4$$
$$TRUST \rightarrow (COLLABORATIVE\ ACTION$$
$$+ DIFFUSIVE\ LEARNING)$$

rationalizing conflict, we mean that participants need to truly understand and clarify their real differences. They must know precisely where the boundary lies between what they agree with and what they do not agree with. If conflict is not acknowledged and rationalized when it arises, it is likely to erupt in less manageable and predictable forms later in the Search Conference.

Our experience has shown that when conflicts become clear and respected by the Search Conference community, they tend to diminish over time. The outbreak of emotional group assumptions can be prevented through the rationalization of conflict. As participants learn from the beginning of a Search Conference that all perceptions are valid, that their common ground is greater than expected, and that the differences between opinions are clear, neither dependency nor fight-flight group dynamics arise. People in the Search Conference relax once they perceive that the critical conditions for creative work are in place.

The aim of the rationalization of conflict is to precisely establish common ground, and to identify the line between agreement and disagreement (see Figure 6.5). We have found that groups tend to overestimate the area of conflict and underestimate the amount of common ground that exists. Once a group finds its common ground, the members can work collaboratively toward completing their goals. In this process, they will enlarge their area of common ground.

Figure 6.5. Rationalization of Conflict.

Total consensus   Rationalization of conflict

Two systems in conflict

Not

Toward
two systems as one

Toward
the establishment of
common ground

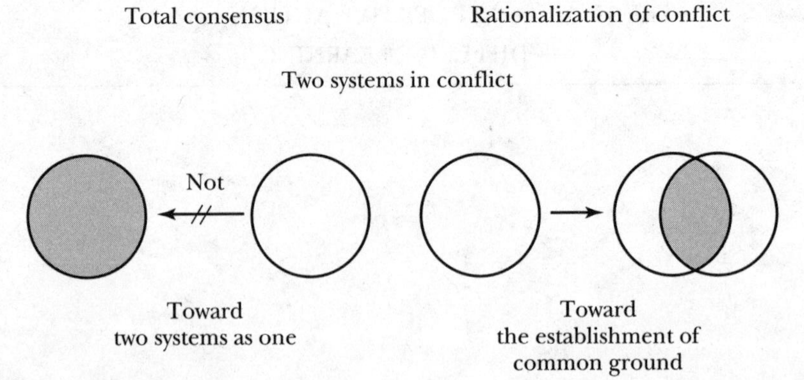

How Rationalization of Conflict Works

Here is how the rationalization of conflict works in the Search Conference. After small groups develop and generate strategic goals (the most desirable future for the system), their flip-chart reports are hung on the wall next to each other. Someone from each group gets up in front of the community and gives a summary report of the work conducted by the small group. Then the Search Conference manager raises two sets of questions. The first set consists of questions of clarification from the community. Once everyone indicates understanding of all the statements, the conference manager tests for whether the community agrees with all of the statements from the group's report. The conference manager does this by asking the entire community, "Is there any item on any of the reports that you can not agree to?" The conference manager may prod the community further by asking "Is everyone here prepared to support all the items from this report?"

When group reports are made, the commonality between them is obvious and usually much greater than anybody had anticipated. However, if there appears to be a disagreement, the statement or item is first debated fully in the plenary session. Search Conference managers allow the community to talk the matter through to clarify whether the issue being debated is one of semantics or of objective substance. If the community decides that the issue constitutes a substantial disagreement, the Search Conference manager will then attempt to rationalize the conflict. It is important to point out that the community ultimately decides (not the Search Conference manager) whether this disagreement is substantive enough to warrant rationalization. When this is the case, the Search Conference manager may request that one or two individuals from the conflicting parties temporarily leave the room to try to sort it out and see if the matter can be negotiated. In the meantime, the rest of the Search Conference community proceeds with the task of integration. If the parties return to the community empty-handed and still at odds with each other, the item is placed on a *disagree list*. It then ceases to be part of the discussion. At this point, the conflict is rationalized, acknowledged, and set aside. This simple mechanism is available for use during any phase of the process, and is quite effective when dealing with intense conflicts concerning sensitive issues.

Avoiding the Pitfalls of Consensus

To achieve consensus within a group, parties opposing an alternative are included in discussions but must eventually come around to support the decision. Edgar Schein (1969, p. 56) operationally defines *consensus* as a psychological state induced through influential discussions such that "Those members who would not take the majority alternative, nevertheless understand it clearly and are prepared to support it." This is obviously very time consuming and can be frustrating when meetings are prolonged and extended in order to reach a consensus.

The rationalization of conflict is quite different from the consensus decision-making process. With the latter method, the dissenting group's opinion or position is talked through until they feel that they have had their say and are willing to go along with the majority, perhaps having moved the majority some distance toward the minority position. With the former, items in genuine disagreement are set aside for private action, allowing the group to get on with developing action on matters they all want. Rather than spending a great deal of time and attention on a few items in conflict, the group can devote its energy to productive work.

The amount of time involved in consensus decision-making often distorts perceptions of the balance between common ground and conflict, while rationalization puts matters into proper perspective. It allows all parties to see the true ratio of agreement to disagreement, which in most cases is on the order of 85 percent to 15 percent. For example, a Search Conference community usually generates a list of strategic goals, perhaps as long as ten or fifteen items. Out of a list this size, it is rare for more than two or three items to be the object of serious disagreement. Once an item in conflict is seen in proportion to the other items in agreement, the energy surrounding the disagreement dissipates. There are usually many items for which there is agreement and common ground, and the conference community is quite eager to proceed on those, leaving the contentious items on the disagree list. The community usually moves forward smoothly; by this time, areas of common ground have already been established. These common areas, in turn, allow the community to concentrate its work on those items for which there is agreement. Once this process is complete, the plenary session integrates the group reports into one master report. Only the redundancy that exists across the various small-group reports is removed. The integrated product possesses the richness of all the small-group reports. Its language is that of the participants, in their own words.

Therefore, in a Search Conference, we are not assuming that consensus within the community will or should exist at all times. If consensus does occur, it is an added bonus, but we do not strive for it. To do so is unrealistic, certainly in cases when there are legitimate adversarial positions. Further, it is hard enough to reach consensus within a group of five people, let alone a group of twenty to thirty. Even in small groups, consensus decision-making often involves an unspoken agreement by the group to be fuzzy about what they disagree with, concealing individual differences as a means of maintaining an illusion of harmony.

Another point needs to be made here. The expression of verbal aggression in meetings is generally regarded as taboo. However, it should not be surprising that when people are engaged in planning their future, they may get excited. Indeed, they may get angry over their differences. Clearly, it is much better to have people yelling at each other than not talking at all. Wars start only after somebody stops talking. Search Conference managers must not be afraid when people express strong feelings; it means they are engaged. It would be much worse to encounter a totally dissociated and passive group. In that case, participative planning becomes almost impossible.

When all the necessary pieces of design and management are in place, there is little to fear from argument or anger—respect them for what they are, the expression of care and concern for the outcome. The whole range of human feelings can be expressed without destroying the bonds of community.

Integration Toward a Community Product

One of the major goals of a Search Conference is to build a community, so all strategies and action plans must accordingly become the property of the community. Key deliberations involving critical decisions are debated and discussed in the plenary session—that is, in front of the whole Search Conference community—not in small groups. Search conferencing is, after all, a large-group intervention. Search Conference managers often use the plenary discussion process for the rationalization of conflict and the development of crucial decisions. Plenary sessions allow the entire community to agree on the desirable and probable future of the world (and, in some cases, industry or business environment), as well as to arrive at an agreed-upon list of strategic goals that describe the most desirable future of the system. Small groups serve a vehicle to facilitate work on tasks, such as generating possible strategic goals for the system. Reports from small groups are always integrated in plenary session to form a community product.

Part Three

Strategies for Effective Search Conferences

Chapter Seven

Planning for Success

It is vital to the success of any Search Conference that planning be done well in advance and in accordance with the needs of each organization or community. This includes an assessment of needs and sponsor readiness, collaborative design, careful selection of participants, and so on. This chapter reviews the activities that occur in the planning phase.

Initial Contact

The initial contact with the prospective sponsor of a Search Conference may occur in a variety of ways. The first task of the conference manager is to determine how familiar the prospective sponsor is with the Search Conference method.

A prospective sponsor who has previously been a participant in a Search Conference is obviously highly informed, and needs no formal introduction to the Search Conference method. In contrast, a sponsor without such experience does need a formal introduction to the Search Conference method. The presentation to a sponsor who is not familiar with the Search Conference method need not be complex or theoretical. Instead, the introductory briefing should convey the essential features and benefits of the Search Conference, the minimum conditions needed to ensure a successful outcome, and the resources and activities that are required. See Resource 1 at the end of the book for a sample slide presentation designed to support an introductory briefing.

Before the briefing, the Search Conference manager should try to determine whether running a Search Conference will meet the prospective sponsor's needs. Potential sponsors need to understand both the benefits of the Search Conference for their unique situation and its long-term effects on participants. Thus, one shouldn't approach this introductory meeting as a high-powered sales presentation. This is a different approach from trying to sell the Search Conference up front as a tool.

To summarize, here are the tasks of the initial meeting:

- Assess the specific needs of the sponsor and determine whether the Search Conference method is appropriate for these needs, and also whether the sponsor is amenable to large-group participation and the completely open format that the Search Conference methodology requires.
- Make sure the sponsor understands what a Search Conference involves, using a detailed briefing if the sponsor has no direct experience with the method.
- Find out what formal authorities would be required to sanction and support the conference, and whether they are likely to do so.
- Outline the resources required to conduct the planning activities, and determine whether these resources can be made available.

Assessment of Sponsor Needs

In many cases, the benefits of conducting a Search Conference are immediately obvious to the sponsor. Where there is a clear need for planning a future state of affairs and an implicit need for high involvement for a large group of people, the Search Conference method is obviously a good match. Many of the conferences discussed in previous chapters fall into this category—consider Hewlett-Packard with its need to avoid grinding out another strategic plan that would be locked away in a drawer, Macatawa regional leaders facing complex community planning problems, Colorado water planners dealing with the legacy of a century of conflict.

In other cases, more exploratory discussions may be required to determine whether the Search Conference method is an appropriate intervention. This initial phase of exploration is crucial, for it makes absolutely no sense to use the Search Conference method when the situation requires an alternative approach. For example, a technology manager of a consumer products company heard that the Search Conference method was successfully used by one of his peers in another department. He thought that it might also be useful for solving a difficult technical problem that was occurring in product development. This problem clearly was not an issue that required long-term planning or the mobilization of large groups of people. Instead, the technical glitch in the design phase of the product was of limited scope, requiring an immediate response and a structured problem-solving process with a small group of expert design engineers.

Every proposal must be analyzed to determine whether the Search Conference is an appropriate intervention. There are several minimum requirements that must be met:

- The presenting problem or issue requires an effort to plan for the long-term future.
- The presenting problem or issue requires a systemic focus, and the need to examine the issue from multiple perspectives.
- The presenting problem or issue requires a forum for broad-based participation in puzzle solving.

Many types of presenting problems fail to meet these criteria, and thus offer little chance of serving as the focus of successful Search Conferences. Some common proposals to avoid include requests from managers looking for ways to get employees to work more as a team, requests to fix or solve a pressing and immediate problem within a department, or requests for meetings designed to get employees to buy into a management decision.

Assessment of Sponsor Readiness

Assuming that the Search Conference is an appropriate intervention for the presenting issues facing the sponsor's system, the question remains whether the sponsor truly understands how participative and open Search Conference processes really are. The sponsor may have a preconceived image of participation that conforms to previous types of large group events—other off-site planning meetings, departmental retreats, and so on. These events may not have been based on full participation, or on Design Principle 2 democratic structure. The sponsor must be informed that participation in the Search Conference means that participants will take full responsibility for the control and coordination of the entire planning process—including implementation.

The sponsor has to understand what this level of participation entails. The sponsor must be absolutely clear that in a Search Conference, there is no division of labor between thinkers and doers. This means that there are no hand-off points where people pass their creative ideas on to upper management to evaluate. Nor can sponsors or upper management manipulate the Search Conference agenda to steer participants to some predetermined destination. Openness is also a primary condition for ensuring effective communication. Sponsors must realize that everything that is discussed must be in public view among the participants; that all data generated will be recorded on flip charts; and that there will be a complete ban on expert lectures, management speeches, and so forth. Sponsors must also understand that the participants attending the conference will be the ones who take responsibility for the implementation and diffusion of action plans. After the Search Conference, to ensure a successful implementation process, action planning teams must have the autonomy and leeway to retain their self-managing structure.

Sponsors' reactions to the required conditions for running a successful Search Conference will reveal whether they clearly understand these concepts, and whether they are ready to proceed with the planning phase. One prospective sponsor, a district superintendent of Niles High School in Skokie, Illinois, was very interested in the Search Conference as a potential method for involving parents and the community more in the affairs of the school. During the initial exploratory meeting, however, it soon became evident to both the district superintendent and the Search Conference consultants that the stated need for getting parents and the community involved didn't match the high level of participation demanded by the Search Conference method. The district superintendent revealed that when the Board of Education thought of seeking more involvement from the community, their idea of involvement was to send out a formal written survey, not to invite people to participate directly in a face-to-face planning event and then begin working on various aspects of district operation. In short, the Board of Education and the superintendent weren't ready for this level of participation from the community in planning the affairs of the school district.

Obtaining Sanctioning from Formal Authorities

After an exploratory discussion with a prospective sponsor, it should be fairly easy to determine if search conferencing is the most appropriate method. Assuming that the sponsor has agreed to proceed, the next step is to obtain sanctioning from formal authorities whose support is crucial to the success of the conference. The sponsor may be one of these formal authorities, but other key managers or leaders may also need to be consulted and brought on board. Sanctioning is critical to ensuring that the action plans generated from the Search Conference will be supported by those in power and fully implemented after the event. As senior management is often asked to initiate and support major organizational changes that result from action plans, sanctioning is even more critical in the case of corporate Search Conferences.

In other situations, such as with issue-based Search Conferences, multiple parties may need to be involved in the sanctioning process. Even more complex are meetings involving traditional opponents such as unions and management, or environmentalists, land developers, and city government. Preparation for these meetings can be very time consuming. Delicate negotiations about sanctioning, membership, and conditions are frequently required.

Sanctioning is even more difficult to attain with issue-based Search Conferences than with corporate Search Conferences because of the loosely coupled relationships among organizations and interest groups. Because "leadership and power are dispersed among autonomous organizations rather than hierarchically centralized" (Cummings and Huse, 1989, p. 407), the system as defined by the organizations that need to be involved tends to be underorganized. Key organizations or interest groups that need to be part of the conference may not want to be involved in such a joint process of collaborative planning for fear of losing their autonomy. These groups may need special prodding and education on the need for their participation in the conference. The Search Conference manager plays much more of an activist role when planning with underorganized systems (Cummings, 1984). This requires extensive community organizing skills, and delicate work to establish forums in which potential sponsors can be invited to discuss the possible purposes and feasibility of convening a Search Conference for the issue under consideration. Issue-based Search Conferences are an application of transorganization development; the aim is construct a system composed of multiple organizations, alliances, and partnerships so that participants may address issues and "solve problems that are too complex and multi-faceted for single organizations to carry out" (Cummings and Huse, 1989, p. 407).

Obtaining Resources for Planning Activities

In addition to obtaining formal sanctioning, the Search Conference manager needs to ensure that the sponsor will provide the necessary resources for conducting pre–Search Conference planning activities. Among of the key resources are people from the system to help with planning of the Search Conference. In the case of corporate Search Conferences, this might amount to two or three people who can assist the Search Conference manager with such tasks as deciding on a process for participant selection, organizing briefing and education sessions, and dealing with conference meeting logistics. For example, for the Wheeling School District Search Conference, this group consisted of the superintendent, the assistant superintendent, three teachers, one member from the Board of Education, a business person, and an administrative assistant. In this case, the sponsor—the superintendent of the district—also participated in the planning sessions, whereas the official sanctioning group for the Search Conference was the Board of Education.

Defining the Purpose of the Conference

It is important that the sponsors and any others sanctioning the Search Conference attend the first planning meeting and help clarify the overriding task or purpose of the Search Conference. Defining the purpose of the conference is one of the most important planning tasks. The purpose declares why the Search Conference is being convened, and specifies the nature of the conference task. Sometimes it is helpful for people to think of the purpose as answering the question, What is our system trying to bring into being that currently does not exist? In other words, What is the planning task? An easy way to help a planning group define its purpose is hold a brief brainstorming session.

For example, a group brainstorming session with members of the Xerox conference planning committee generated a long list of phrases. After reviewing and discussing various possibilities, the group finally settled on a statement that synthesized bits and pieces of the phrases generated by the group. The planning group's purpose for convening the Search Conference was: "To develop a shared future direction for the Customer Business Unit that will enhance its market focus over the next three years." Note the planning horizon or time frame for the Search Conference task—this should also be part of the discussion in the preparation and planning stage. Many factors may have to be taken into account before a final decision on time horizon is made. For example, some factors might include the pace of change in the industry in question, the lead times for product development, the funding or budgetary cycles, and so on. The guideline here is to set a time frame that is realistic in terms of achieving long-term strategic goals.

In the case of the West Cluster Empowerment Zone Search Conference, after much deliberation, the sponsor and community activists together developed a collective purpose statement as follows: "To develop a shared vision of economic revitalization for the West Side in the year 2000, (1) with a plan for achieving the vision, (2) that identifies existing and potential resources, (3) which enhances our capacity to work together, (4) making our plan a national model."

This purpose statement clearly demonstrates that the task of this Search Conference was to develop and agree upon a long-term plan for economic development, targeting existing and potential resources. Getting the purpose of the Search Conference clear is critical because it determines the boundaries of the system and the selection of participants. These choices ultimately drive the design and activities of the entire conference.

Defining System Boundaries

Once sponsors clarify the purpose of the Search Conference, the next most important element in planning the event is the selection of participants. But before doing this, the purpose statement should be reviewed once again and used as a benchmark for defining the boundaries of the planning system. Using the case of the West Cluster Empowerment Zone as an example, the purpose of the proposed Search Conference was to develop plans and secure resources for economic development. Focusing upon this purpose defined the boundaries of the planning system in both geographic and functional terms. Geographically, the boundaries of the system were drawn around the West Cluster Empowerment Zone. The majority of participants lived and worked on the West Side of Chicago. Functionally, the boundaries of the system were economic: only individuals from organizations with a significant role to play in economic revitalization were selected.

By taking into account the purpose and by using the open systems model, a Search Conference manager works with sponsors to identify the system and specify its boundaries. This guides the process for participant selection from within the system. With issue-based Search Conferences, the selection of participants may also include appropriate *boundary riders* of the system. Boundary riders are those participants from outside the technical borders of the system who could significantly affect the planning process, or who could significantly participate in future changes in the system. In the case of the West Cluster Empowerment Zone Search Conference, boundary riders included key politicians and administrators from city, county, state, and federal agencies. These boundary riders were not West Side residents, yet their participation was necessary to back and support an economic development plan that required local, state, and federal government approvals. Corporate Search Conferences do not usually include or require the participation of boundary riders, since power and authority for approving the plan resides within the system itself.

Participant Selection

Having defined the boundaries, the next major planning task is to select and invite participants who will attend the Search Conference. There are a number of possible techniques, some more suited to community-based conferences and some to organizational or corporate conferences.

Community-Based Search Conferences

Participant selection for community-based Search Conferences often requires a process that is viewed as fair, nondiscriminating, and democratic. This could also apply to industry, network, and issue-based Search Conferences, where the notion of community is broadly defined.

Community Reference

One method of participant selection that meets the requirements for fairness and openness is called the *community reference* system. The community reference system is a referral process for identifying and selecting participants that results in a genuine microcosm of the larger community or region. The process works as follows:

1.   Those involved in planning the Search Conference must draw up a social network map of the system. A network map for a community, for example, will typically cover such variables as key interest groups, demographics, different types of institutions, such as small businesses and large corporations, social services, schools, government offices, religious groups, and so forth.

2.   Having identified the major interest groups and institutions linked to the purpose of the proposed Search Conference, planners need to develop relevant criteria against which individuals are to be selected. *Note: These selection criteria specifically should not include such factors as general articulateness, education, or even literacy— if someone has information or leverage needed for action on the system, deficiencies in traditional tokens of expertise do not matter.* Usually two or three sets of criteria are used to evaluate each potential participant. For example, for the Search Conference on the Future of Economic Development in the West Cluster Empowerment, the selection criteria consisted of several "and/or" statements. Criteria were defined as: the participant must be a West Side resident (and) be involved in current economic development programs (and/or) be a potential resource to the development of a long-term economic development plan. Search Conferences focused on the future of a geographical community may need to ensure that there is an appropriate demographic mix, diverse age range, and presence of people from different socioeconomic groups that match the census data for that community. Other special areas of expertise may

need to be sought out if the Search Conference is dealing with some type of focal issue, such as economic development. In the West Cluster Empowerment Zone case, participant selection included individuals from financial institutions with an economic interest in the West Side. Usually one selection criterion is universally applied to all potential participants in the form of a question, namely, "Is this person known to be actively concerned about the task and central purpose of the Search Conference?"

3.   Once the criteria are decided, the planning group will identify several people from different sectors of the community who appear to meet the criteria. These people are then approached, either in person or by mail or phone, and asked to provide two or three names of additional people who meet the selection criteria and who they think would be interested in participating in the Search Conference. People who are polled are not given any guarantees of an invitation at this point. This is strictly part of the polling stage of the selection process.

4.   After the first round of name generation is completed, planners follow up by contacting the new people, without mentioning where their own names came from, and asking them to provide two or three names of individuals who fit the selection criteria.

5.   After several iterations of the polling process, some of the same names should reappear. Individuals whose names are cross-referenced by their peers in the community are selected, at least tentatively. Planners need to review the names that appear on this list against the community reference system data, checking to make sure that the list conforms to the specified demographic, institutional, and geographic mix. Other individuals may need to be identified and added to the final list to achieve the desired level of diversity.

The community reference system clarifies that Search Conference participants are not stakeholders, as in public hearings or conflict resolution meetings. We view participants in the Search Conference as whole persons. Any one participant may wear many different hats—citizen, parent, manager. Despite the emphasis on diversity, people who participate in the Search Conference are not invited because they can serve as representatives, play their organizational role, or guard stakeholder interests. The Search Conference creates conditions that allow people to participate as themselves, as whole human beings, and not as representatives or stakeholders. When people are thought of as stakeholders, they are more likely to maintain their political posture, argue for their own narrow self-interests, and act within the confines of their role set—all counterproductive behaviors in terms of the purpose of a Search Conference. Once participants are selected, they attend simply as people, chosen for the sole reason that they can contribute to the task of the Search Conference.

Lottery

When selection of participants is an extremely sensitive issue, or when there is considerable mistrust and suspicion over the fairness of choosing participants, a lottery method may be used. First, a pool of potential participants from the community is generated. This is a variation on the community reference system. However, in this case, a referral procedure is not used. Instead, a pool of participants is gathered by soliciting names from community leaders. A Search Conference for a school district in southeastern Wisconsin successfully used this selection method. In preparation for a Search Conference on the future of education in this area, a participant pool was drawn up by soliciting names from school principals, PTA leaders, town officials, local storekeepers, and informal leaders in the farming community. Out of this pool of names, a lottery process was used in which a certain number of names were drawn for each of the community reference groups. For example, out of a list of twenty names of teachers who were nominated to the pool, ten finalists' names were picked at random, fulfilling the quota for the number of teachers we needed to attend the Search Conference. Likewise, out of a pool of twenty-five parents, fifteen names were randomly selected. This was done for each of the reference groups until all the slots had been filled. In the event that some people declined the invitation or were unable to attend, several additional names were also drawn from each category as alternates.

Direct Participation

Issue-based Search Conferences often call for a form of direct participation of those people critical to accomplishing the conference task. Search Conferences held to develop a domain, such as environmental management in a region, also lend themselves to this selection method. For example, the Colorado Front Range Search Conference was an issue-based conference concerned with developing a long-term plan for water usage in the region. In this case, water engineers from different municipalities and agencies in the Front Range region were responsible for water usage planning. As stated earlier, the nature of the issue determines the criteria for selection. In this case, the specialized topic of water usage planning called for a meeting of the minds of all the water engineers in the region.

Organizational and Corporate Search Conferences

Participant selection is more straightforward when planning for organizational Search Conferences. Again, the purpose of the conference should dictate the criteria for participant selection. For high-level strategic planning conferences, participants should be selected from those who hold responsibility for the direction of the corporation, namely, directors and senior managers. In this type of conference, the purpose is obviously that of strategic direction setting. It may not be appropriate for either lower-level employees or outsiders to attend such a Search Conference, as they have no significant role to play. However, this does not preclude gathering information from unions, customers, suppliers, distributors, and employees at all levels of the enterprise as part of the preparation for the Search Conference. Indeed, information gathering from all those affected will be essential.

Although the Xerox Search Conference was strategic in nature, the purpose emphasized the need to "develop a *shared* future direction for the Customer Business Unit." In this case, criteria for participant selection were much broader in scope, requiring a vertical slice of the company. In this case, half the participants were selected from the management staff, while the other half were drawn from lower and middle levels of the organization, including both exempt and nonexempt employees. Lower- and middle-level employees brought the conference essential first-hand information about actual work processes and customer requirements.

If, on the other hand, the purpose of the Search Conference is to look at the future of relationships between the corporation and its customers, then participation of outsiders will of course be required. This is exactly what occurred when Exxon Chemicals sponsored a Search Conference focused on the "Future of Customer-Supplier Relationships in the Tire Industry, 2010." Exxon Chemical managers invited their major customer, Goodyear Tire and Rubber, to participate in a two-day Search Conference for the purpose of developing a long-term strategic partnership. Again, participation is determined by the boundary of the system.

Participant Briefing

Ideally, all participants should be as fully informed as possible about all aspects of the Search Conference before they attend. Those who have been invited should be informed through face-to-face meetings several weeks before the conference. Out of such conversations, ideas for design improvements may surface. Most important, participants need to know exactly why they were chosen and what the conference aims to accomplish. They also need to know that the Search Conference is not a traditional conference, that they will be expected to attend the whole event and fully participate. Other approaches for briefing participants might involve informational meetings, or at the very least, some form of written communication. Exhibit 7.1 illustrates one approach to this preliminary briefing—the letter of invitation to the Macatawa pre-conference meeting.

Conference Logistics

The Search Conference manager and the planning group work together on the logistics for the event. It is important for the conference managers to monitor the progress of the planning group to ensure that all the minute details of the conference are attended to. These include such items as securing an appropriate meeting space, sending out invitation letters well in advance to selected participants, keeping the number of participants to a manageable level, and so on. Exhibit 7.2 provides a helpful checklist of pre-conference logistics.

Timing

Normally a Search Conference requires two days and two nights. Intensive creative work always carries with it the risk of cognitive

Exhibit 7.1. Macatawa Invitation Letter.

 **Macatawa Area
Coordinating Council**
A Cooperative Effort Among Units of Government

March 11, 1994

"Macatawa Future Search: A gathering of the diverse people of the
Macatawa area in a collaborative quest to create a common vision
developing a path to a significant future place."

The citizens and organizations of the Macatawa area are experiencing unprecedented
change and challenges. This is, therefore, an opportune time for us, as a community,
to step back and reflect on where we are, and what we aspire to be and do in the future.
We are excited to introduce a method to accomplish this which we call the Macatawa
Future Search.

Future Search is an innovative, proven approach to develop consensus about the future
among diverse interests and the means by which this future vision can be achieved.
We are writing to invite you or another representative of your organization to a
meeting on March 23 regarding the Future Search conference that the Macatawa Area
Coordinating Council (MACC) is planning to conduct. <u>Our goal is to familiarize
you with the Future Search process and then ask your organization, during the
following week, to submit the names of individuals you believe would be valuable
contributors to the conference.</u>

The enclosed document describes Future Search and MACC in more detail, but
briefly, MACC's Future Search will involve approximately 50 persons in a 2 1/2 day
gathering on May 24-26 at the Big Rapids Holiday Inn. We will work together in
small groups and collectively on two principal tasks:

1. <u>Our Desired Future</u>: What do we want our community to be in the
   future?
2. <u>Achievement Strategies</u>: How will we achieve our desired future?

The introductory meeting on March 23 that we are inviting you to attend will be held
at Holland's Holiday Inn beginning at 4:00 p.m. and adjourning promptly at 5:15 p.m.
It will begin with a brief reception followed by a program explaining the Future
Search process in more detail and answering any questions you may have. As noted
above, we will ask you to submit the names of persons who could contribute
effectively to the Future Search process. Invitations will be sent to the chief elected
official, chief administrative official, and at least one citizen from each of the seven
units of government participating in MACC. The remaining invitees and ultimate
participants will be selected by the organizing committee from the suggested persons
and are expected to represent the diverse population and interests of the Macatawa
area.

400 - 136th Ave., Suite 416, Holland, Michigan 49424 Phone: (616) 395-2688 - Fax: (616) 395-9411

Exhibit 7.1. Macatawa Invitation Letter, Cont'd.

The Macatawa Future Search is being sponsored by MACC with the assistance of the Michigan Department of Transportation, as well as contributions from private organizations. As a result, participants will be responsible only for their transportation to and from Big Rapids; all other expenses will be covered by MACC.

We invite you to join us on <u>Wednesday, March 23</u> at <u>4:00 p.m.</u> at the <u>Holland Holiday Inn</u> for the kickoff of this special initiative. We look forward to your participation and counsel.

Sincerely,

Richard Vander Broek
Chairman

Encl.

Reprinted by permission.

and emotional overload for some individuals who might be particularly vulnerable. Longer periods increase this risk. On the other hand, it is impossible to conduct a Search Conference in one work day. When the number of participants is relatively small, between fifteen and twenty, some conferences can be conducted in eighteen hours. In addition to numbers of participants, other significant variables that affect timing include the difficulty of the task and whether there has been a history of conflict. An organization attempting to develop a complex business plan, or a community that is assembling a diverse group of people with conflicting interests, will require a full two-and-a-half-day conference. Because of fatigue and overload, there reaches a point of diminishing returns if a conference is extended beyond three days.

Because the Search Conference is not an everyday type of event, it shouldn't be confined to normal business hours. Human beings are subject to circadian rhythms, and are better at performing different types of activity at different times of the day. Creative work requires the optimization of all conditions, and the best starting time has been found to be late afternoon. It is essential to create a relaxed social atmosphere in which people can become acquainted. Introductions, briefings, and discussions of expectations for the conference can go before drinks and dinner, preferably served informally, buffet style. Formal work should start after dinner and continue to 9:30 or 10 P.M. The conference begins again early the next day and continues into the evening of the second day. It comes to a close around lunch or midafternoon on the third day.

Flexible arrangements also help. Continuous access to tea, coffee, juice, and snacks is preferable to fixed break times. Search Conference managers cannot predict exactly when a group will need breaks. Buffer periods should be built around meals so that more time will be available for work if it is required.

Venue

People cannot be expected to work intensively and creatively in their normal office environment. They require time free of the distractions of phones, messages, faxes, families, and so forth. They need to retreat to a place removed from their daily round, such as a hotel or a conference center built to establish a social island for groups in attendance.

The ideal facility offers access to the outside and fresh air, and has natural or near-natural light, plenty of wall space, and reasonably comfortable furniture. Tables are unnecessary—all the data and information will be written on flip charts—but not usually a problem. People like them. However, if the conference involves groups with a bitter history of conflict, set up the room without tables so they won't be available to use as barriers. Make sure the room is big enough for the entire group to meet together, and also for the participants to meet in small groups with a reasonable amount of air space around them. Despite the noise level, small groups should stay in the main room—break-out rooms are undesirable for small group work, as their use splinters the community spirit and makes it difficult for a Search Conference manager to coordinate and keep track of the progress of various groups. A large square room is ideal, as it provides plenty of working space and allows participants to see and hear reports from any point in the room.

Helpful as the physical environment can be, bear in mind that venue is far less important than design and management. In fact, despite the importance of the conference venue, many successful Search Conferences have been held in far from optimum conditions. It is not the meeting space that makes or breaks a Search Conference, but the quality of preparation and planning, the soundness of the design, and the competency of conference managers. An expensive hotel meeting space with a panoramic view, gourmet meals, and all the other frills cannot rescue an ill-conceived conference that is poorly designed and managed.

Numbers

The optimum number of participants for a Search Conference is between fifteen and thirty-five, although the lower limit is better around twenty and the upper limit has on occasion been extended as far as fifty. Below fifteen, the meeting takes on the character and dynamics of a small group. With a small group, there is an insufficient critical mass of data and perspectives to produce the energy, excitement, and sparks for creative thinking that characterize a Search Conference. When the number of participants exceeds thirty-five, one begins to run into a problem of time management, with too many small groups having to report out their work at various intervals.

As the number of participants and small groups in a conference increases, so does the amount of time required for reports. The small groups come under pressure to keep their reports short, and discussion becomes severely compressed. Without enough time to engage the whole community in the process of integration, the result is apt to be a laundry list of items and an array of data from each of the small groups rather than a true community product.

We have found that the energy in a large group tends to diminish after about the fifth report. Thus the realistic expectation for reports that can be considered thoughtfully during any one plenary session is four or five. If small groups have been working in parallel on the same task, it is useful to take one full report, and then ask the other groups to add any different points they might have on their report. Building such a cumulative picture serves the purpose of integration as well as saving time. However, it cannot be used for groups working on different tasks.

For those tasks that require small-group work, the groups should not be larger than ten people. Groups of five to seven are optimum. If the small groups are too large, their work takes longer and the quality of discussion often suffers. When the number of essential participants for a Search Conferences exceeds thirty-five, depending on the scope of the system, it may be preferable to design a series of Search Conferences that can be integrated in various ways. Some companies, such as the Microsoft Corporation, have held contiguous Search Conferences, where the cumulative data from each conference was fed into the next. There are many variations on this theme, and these are all questions of design.

Judgments about the selection of participants, numbers, timing, and venue are a critical component of the planning and preparation stage. Good judgments require a collaborative relationship among the Search Conference managers, the sponsors, and those people from the system who are assisting with the planning tasks.

Exhibit 7.2. Search Conference Logistics Checklist.

For Participants:
- Invitation letter
- Name badges
- Rough agenda

Location and Conference Set-Up:
- Preferably off-site conference facility
- Adequate room size with plenty of wall space
- Ideally at least one wall with large windows
- Round tables if possible
- Flexible break and refreshment arrangements
- Registration table for check-in

Materials:
- Flip-chart pads and easels for every table
- Two flip-chart pads and easels for conference managers
- Chart pens of different colors for every table
- Several rolls of masking tape

Planning in Practice: Case Examples

Each of the following cases illustrate the planning processes involved in preparing for a Search Conference. Each case also shows that a decision to convene a Search Conference is always in response to a felt need of some kind. We have found that the most successful Search Conferences tend to be those that pay attention to such issues as getting clear on the conference purpose, inviting the right participants, and making sure that participants are well informed about the reasons why they were selected.

Nebraska Mental Health

Sponsor:	Nebraska Department of Public Institutions
Purpose:	Develop a unified adult mental health system
Selection Method:	Community reference system
Participants:	Administrators, psychiatrists, mental health counselors, agencies from urban and rural areas, and consumers
Length:	Three and a half days
Place:	Arbor Day Farm Conference Center, Nebraska City, Nebraska

The Nebraska Department of Public Institutions (DPI) was organized in 1974 to provide state leadership, planning, and coordination for six mental health regions. Each of the six regions needed to optimize local delivery of services. The core organizations of the mental health system were three regional centers, formerly called state psychiatric hospitals, which provided short-term and extended inpatient service. Program offices coordinated services with local community mental health resources to provide a continuum of care, acting as alternative vehicles to hospitalization. Patients, now called consumers, felt that this system of care did not satisfy their needs. Prior legislation mandated the creation of mental health citizen advisory committees to provide citizen input at local levels. Thus, DPI has had a tradition of actively soliciting input from citizens, including mental health consumers and their family members.

Administrators at DPI were cognizant of the changing nature of health care and the potential for health care reform well before these issues became a focus of national debate. They saw the writing on the wall; future health care reform would call for more direct, localized service delivery. DPI administrators engaged in strategic planning efforts periodically over the years but they had never involved people from the whole system to the extent feasible in the Search Conference. In previous years, they had brought together mental health administrators from around the state for interagency strategic planning. This process was not considered to be very effective. Administrators suggested that DPI find a method to expand the strategic planning process to include a wider range of people, including consumers, local private and public agencies, and direct care staff.

In 1992, Governor Benjamin Nelson requested that DPI and other state agencies begin strategic planning activities to prepare for the 1993–1995 budget cycle. As a long-range planning method, the Search Conference appealed to DPI administrators, especially because of its open process, designed to produce a strategic plan that all parties could accept and implement. They also considered the utility of the Search Conference in terms of how the method would allow many different interest groups to participate in the development of the strategic plans.

DPI administrators wanted a process that would be more inclusive, but not unwieldy. Even consumers, that is, recipients of mental health services, would be invited to participate in the conference. The administrators had always been looking for a way to receive substantial input from people with diverse perspectives.

A planning group was formed consisting of administrators, health care providers, and consumers. A few weeks were spent on clarifying the overall purpose of the Search Conference, and identifying criteria for participant selection, as well as creating an invitation process. The purpose of the Search Conference was defined as "To develop a shared commitment to specific action steps for building a unified mental health system that is driven by consumer needs."

Looking on the mental health system as a complex puzzle, the planning group looked for participants with knowledge of at least one piece of this puzzle. Key interests included administrators and staff of public and private sector health care providers and institutional and community-based agencies from urban and rural areas in the state. As the ultimate customers of the system, consumers were included as well. Commitment to attend the entire Search Conference was also considered an important criterion for selection.

The community reference system was used to invite people to the Search Conference. Key people from each of the relevant sectors were asked to nominate several people they regarded as meeting the search criteria as potential participants in the Search Conference. Based on the list of nominations, the planning group identified and selected the names of people who were frequently mentioned by their peers. These people were then formally invited to the conference. In most cases, a community reference system selection process is used in underorganized community settings, which requires going through several iterations of soliciting referrals before settling on a final list. In this case, however, the nature of the mental health system was well bounded; this allowed planners to identify duplicate names of nominees that appeared on the first batch of referrals. The planning group also considered it important to put together an information packet for each participant to read before the conference. This packet consisted of general information related to the mental health system of Nebraska, along with a short explanation of the Search Conference method and process.

The Search Conference was held at a remote conference site. With time built in for recreation and presentation to government officials, the conference occurred over three and a half days, beginning after dinner on a Tuesday evening and finishing late Friday afternoon with the last presentation to government officials.

Future of the Macatawa Area

> *Sponsor:* Macatawa Area Coordinating Council
> *Purpose:* Develop a community-based vision for the future of the region
> *Type:* Community development
> *Selection Method:* Community reference system
> *Participants:* Mayors, town officials, school superintendents, bankers, local business owners, health care providers, religious leaders, social service agency directors, realtors, and local citizens.
> *Length:* Two and a half days
> *Place:* Big Rapids, Michigan

In 1993, community leaders in part of western Michigan formed a new organization called the Macatawa Area Coordinating Council (MACC). The purpose of the council was to provide a new cooperative framework for regional planning. As the 1990s unfolded, leaders in the communities were increasingly aware of the uncertain, turbulent nature of their environment. Population was booming, big companies such as Hermann-Miller and others were growing and new ones moving in, juvenile crime was on the rise, traffic was becoming congested, and quality of life seemed to be deteriorating in this once-pastoral Dutch community. The newly appointed Macatawa council knew something had to be done and that careful planning would be required if the region were to regain control of its destiny. The council wrestled with the options of using a traditional expert urban planning process or the Search Conference method.

Many of the council members had worked with expert urban planners in the past and knew that traditional planning approaches tended to exclude the community. They wanted a process that would produce a plan the community would be committed to implementing. The capacity of the Search Conference method to mobilize broad citizen participation had instant appeal to council members, and a planning group was formed.

The planning group consisted of ten people, including the mayors of Holland and Zeeland, Michigan, representatives from the Holland and Zeeland chambers of commerce, two members of the MACC, a county commissioner, a university official, a church leader, and a business person from the region. The main planning tasks were to develop the purpose of the Search Conference, inform the community, and design a fair and reasonable way to attract and select the right participants.

The planning group used a modified version of the community reference system for selecting participants. This was done by first inviting leaders from the entire area to a special luncheon at a local hotel where they introduced the Search Conference idea. During the luncheon, the planning group led people through a process of identifying those people whose participation would be critical for the success of the conference. The criteria they used for this purpose were clear and simple: they were looking for intimate knowledge of the community, a variety of individual perspectives, and potential for carrying out the plan developed at the conference. Based on the list of names generated at the luncheon, a group of participants was selected and invited. (See Exhibit 7.3.)

Exhibit 7.3. Macatawa Press Coverage.

Planning group picks participants for goal-setting conference

HOLLAND

The Grand Rapids Press

A seven-community coordinating agency has picked a group of people to participate in a three-day conference later this month to identify long-term goals for the area.

The 62 people that make up the list range from a high school student to an environmentalist to a bank CEO.

But MACC Director Sue Higgins says titles will not be part of the focus of Future Search conference; the organization, in fact, released the names of the participants without their occupations or titles.

MACC had been expected to release the names two weeks ago after receiving more than 200 names applications.

Higgins said the planning committee had a list two weeks ago but at the last minute decided to revamp a portion to add more diversity.

The final total is more than MACC had planned on inviting but decided to include the 10-member planning committee.

The Macatawa Future Search conference will be held in Big Rapids May 24-26.

The conference will focus on setting goals and coming up with plans to achieve them on issues such as coordinating land use, preserving green space, reducing crime and looking at housing needs, Higgins said.

Source: Grand Rapids Press, Tuesday, May 10, 1994, p. L2. Reprinted by permission.

The Macatawa Regional Search Conference was held in May 1994 over the course of three consecutive days in Big Rapids, Michigan. The planning group selected a hotel for the site that was an ideal social-island setting, fifty miles away from the area. This required all participants to stay at the conference facility for two full nights, minimizing the distraction of normal daily affairs.

Workforce Empowerment at Hewlett-Packard

Sponsor: Hewlett-Packard Manufacturing Plant
Purpose: Develop a strategy for empowerment of the workforce
Type: Corporate/Organizational search
Selection Method: Direct participation and community reference system
Participants: Manufacturing managers, supervisors, production line workers, and human resources staff.
Length: Three days.
Place: Greeley, Colorado.

Search conferencing was a natural fit for Hewlett-Packard, a global manufacturer with a long history of progressive management practices. In this case, a plant manager saw the utility of the Search Conference as a method for developing a long-range plan for empowering the workforce. He envisioned that this approach would lead workers to take more ownership of the business.

A small planning group consisting of a human resources specialist and several manufacturing managers and first-line supervisors met periodically over the course of a month to plan the conference. They decided to invite all the managers in the plant, since their support for empowerment of the workforce was critical. Line workers were selected through a community reference approach. Work groups on the production floor nominated people from their respective areas. The planning group took special care to make sure that the selection process didn't become politicized. Prospective participants attended special informational meetings prior to the Search Conference. The Search Conference was held for three consecutive days at a remote conference center high in the Rocky Mountains.

Summary

Planning is the key to success for a Search Conference. Special efforts must be made to ensure that the Search Conference has the sanctioning of sponsors, whether they are community leaders, politicians, or senior management. The purpose and overall task of the Search Conference must be clearly defined and relevant to the participants. The planning of the conference must be well thought out, since there are numerous logistical items and minute details that require a good deal of attention and follow-up work. It is also crucial to select and invite the right participants. Once these planning tasks are executed successfully, the next step is to design the Search Conference itself.

Chapter Eight

Designing the Search Conference for Effectiveness

As Julia Child says, "Good cooks don't follow recipes, they use principles." Good Search Conference managers don't follow recipes, either. There is no single, all-encompassing Search Conference design that can be applied to all situations. This does not mean that there isn't a basic plan, of course. There is. However, the design of any Search Conference should follow its purpose, guided by theoretical principles.

Search Conference managers use the principles underlying the method—open systems thinking, theories of democratic structure, and conditions for effective communications—when they go about the task of design. The resulting design will differ from case to case, depending on the needs of each system. Thus, Search Conference design requires not only a knowledge of principles, but an ability to creatively match these principles to the specific purposes of the immediate task. A conference design requires a well-thought-out game plan, with slack time built into it. In all likelihood, there will be situations where the conference manager needs the skill to redesign on the run, that is, to adjust the design as the conference unfolds. The design of the Search Conference must take into account all the relevant factors, including the purpose, participants, time available, and history of the sponsoring organization—not just the presenting issues.

In this chapter, we provide an overview of the classic Search Conference design, describing each of the various design elements. These design elements are the basic building blocks of any Search Conference, whose arrangement may vary depending upon the specific nature of the situation. Next, we consider the various ways in which Search Conferences can be designed to reflect the needs and unique circumstances of different systems. Several brief cases illustrate the common and unique features of various Search Conference designs. The purpose of this chapter is to explain the basic external structure that outlines the design of a Search Conference, and also to give the practitioner some criteria and standards to apply to design options.

Classic Design and External Structure

A classic design for a Search Conference takes into account the interrelations of necessary components that make up the major tasks for the community to work on. Every Search Conference should contain components that allow participants to:

- Learn about changes in the external environment
- Search for the desirable future for the world and discover common ideals, at the same time becoming mindful of the probable future
- Gain a shared appreciation of the history of their own system
- Critically analyze the functioning of their system
- Search for the most desirable future for their system, which includes the development of strategic goals that are achievable, taking into account likely constraints
- Develop precise and concrete action plans that can be implemented in ways that are consistent with the ideals and purposes outlined earlier in the conference

Clearly, every Search Conference must be designed in such a way as to allow participants adequate time for data generation, diagnostic activities, and action planning. Rest periods and free time are also very important and must be considered when designing the conference.

The external structuring of these components can vary considerably, but—as mentioned earlier—a classic Search Conference design can be visualized as a funnel. Figure 8.1 elaborates on the funnel design introduced in Chapter One. The conference is structured into three broad phases: environmental appreciation, system analysis, and strategic action planning. The broad top of the funnel signifies that the conference is designed to begin with the widest possible perspective. Participants identify trends, events, and significant changes occurring in the external environment that are important to the future of their system. As the funnel narrows, the Search Conference community shifts to examining the evolution of its own system, from the past to the present. From there, as the funnel narrows further, the community turns to developing shared visions for the future of the system, converging upon an agreed set of strategic goals and action plans. The diagram also shows the diffusion of the plans into the system at large at the mouth of the funnel, as participants leave the conference carrying its achievements with them.

Traditional strategic planning sessions usually start with a focus on issues, problems, and constraints, but the Search Conference turns this sequence on its head. The Search Conference is designed to have participants focus on just the opposite: to concen-

Figure 8.1. Classic Search Conference Funnel Design.

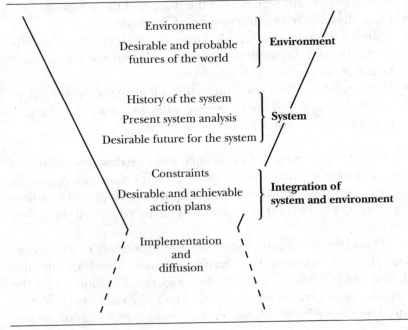

trate on identifying the broader context and its changing trends. Only after opening up to the influence of the world outside does the conference proceed to look at issues that are close to home. Thus, the Search Conference design requires people to suspend judgment about what specific outcomes should occur until a shared, overall picture has emerged. In simple terms, the funnel design conveys that in the Search Conference, participants first take a broad look outside themselves, and then gradually narrow in to the agreed set of purposes and actions.

The design of a Search Conference essentially is a translation of open systems theory, as we discussed in Chapter Four. We will now examine some of the choices typically involved in the design of Search Conferences.

Phase One: Environmental Appreciation

Phase 1: Environmental Appreciation

Task: Identify changes in the world that have occurred in the last 5–7 years that are significant or novel

Outcome: Creation of a shared context; establishing Asch's first and second condition for effective communications

Format: Large-group community brainstorming session

Average Time: 1 hour

Most Search Conferences should begin with a perspective session or environmental scan. We have found that people's circadian rhythms make this first session most effective if it begins either in the early evening or the afternoon rather than first thing in the morning. The basic objective during this phase is for the Search Conference community to gain a shared appreciation of their external environment by identifying changes in the world important to their system's future. Establishing that a system exists and functions in the context of a larger environment is the basic underpinning of open systems planning. During this task, participants come to perceive the interdependencies among and between different trends that are the cause of turbulence and uncertainty. As this larger field of trends and forces comes into focus, those in the room who serve as the eyes and ears for their system quickly realize that their new plan will be effective only if it is proactive rather than reactive to these environmental forces.

This first task usually takes no more than thirty to forty-five minutes. And since it is conducted as a large-group brainstorming session, substantial amounts of data are produced very quickly. People voice their perceptions of the significant or novel changes that they have seen happening in the world over the past five to ten years. As the list grows longer, the changing world appears before everyone's eyes. Conducting this session as a large-group event is essential, for it conveys the message that the Search Conference is about building a community that can learn and plan together.

This is an important and exciting session, bringing many of the Search Conference principles to life. Participants begin to stop focusing inward and to develop a shared appreciation for the changes happening in the environment. They begin to live the open systems concept as they recognize the fact that their system exists within a much larger context. They also recognize that this is no traditional meeting or conference. The participants all begin to feel that their own personal perceptions are valid, and they really can shape the outcome of this conference. Participants also come to appreciate how changes in the wider environment affect their own system. The realization that this event is not a traditional conference usually hits home toward the end of the first session. Participants truly see that they have to take responsibility for their own data, and, by placing all their data on flip charts, they establish Asch's conditions for openness and begin to build trust in their planning community.

Analysis and Synthesis of Data

Following the environmental scanning session, if time permits, we usually design in a task that has the community analyze the meaning and significance of the trends from the data. This subtask typically is assigned to small groups. First, small groups are told that they should identify and analyze the most significant trends in the data. This includes examining recent events or emergent trends that may be signs of things to come. We refer to these trends as *social embryos of change* because they represent new developments on the horizon that are just beginning to emerge. These trends are important because they may be indicators of impending changes in the socioeconomic environment, as well as major shifts in societal values. Small groups choose their own recorder and presenter. We do not assign such roles, for such instructions would contradict the stated intention to foster the growth and development of a self-managing community. If time permits, the most significant trends and social embryos of change that have been identified and analyzed are reported out in a plenary session to the Search Conference community.

Desirable and Probable Futures of the World

> *Phase 1:* Environmental Appreciation
> *Task:* Identify desirable and probable future of the world ten years out.
> *Format:* Small task groups analyze the data and report out four or five descriptive scenarios; findings from each group are integrated into a community list.
> *Outcome:* Expression and recognition of shared ideals; emergence of Asch's third condition.
> *Average Time:* 2–3 hours

Phase One of a Search Conference should always include a session that engages the conference community in searching for the desirable and probable futures for the world. Trends that reflect the conference community's shared human ideals for a more desirable future for the world are articulated and presented in scenario form, along with those trends that seem likely to extend into the future and define its probable shape.

Because this session is usually conducted in small groups, followed by report outs and integration with the whole community in a plenary session, several hours should be built into the design for it. The amount of time to conduct this session will depend on the number of participants, the number of small groups, and the depth of analysis that ensues. For example, with forty-five participants in the Search Conference for Economic Development for the West Cluster Empowerment Zone, this session required two hours. This consisted of six small groups of seven or eight people. Three of the groups were designated to work on generating desirable future scenarios, while the other three worked on generating probable future scenarios. Our design allowed forty-five minutes for the small groups to complete their work. With six small groups having to report out to the larger community, we allowed seven or eight minutes for each report. With questions, comments, and discussion that followed each report, the reporting session actually took about one hour and fifteen minutes.

In cases where the first session begins in the early evening after dinner, it is often desirable to have the small groups work on this task until quitting time, and report out the next morning. The idea here is to generate a *Zeigarnik effect* (Marrow, 1969; Zeigarnik, 1927). According to this theory, the excitement generated during the evening session will be sustained, pending completion of the unfinished task in the morning. The Zeigarnik effect occurs when intensive work on a task is interrupted, leading to a heightened motivation to complete unfinished business. Even giving notice that there will be a recap of the earlier work done first thing in the morning is sufficient for producing the Zeigarnik effect.

Beginning on the second day, we always include in the design some time for a recapitulation of the previous day's activities, as well as an overview of the current game plan. In practice, this is purely an information update, so the review usually does not take more than fifteen minutes. However, we always attempt to design in additional buffer time. Because we have built buffer time into the plan on paper, if things don't get moving or started exactly on time, we are not thrown off schedule. Alternatively, if the session starts promptly, we know that if some other task runs overtime we will have additional time to cover ourselves. These time cushions and buffers are like insurance; while tasks may go according to plan and not run off schedule, it is still good to know that you have flexibility.

Scan of the Task/Industry Environment

In corporate, industry, and issue searches, a more focused task environment scan may need to be included. The task environment lies between the broader social environment and the system itself (as described in Chapter Three). This scan is also conducted as a large-group brainstorming session aimed at identifying those changes just outside the boundary of the system that are having the most immediate and proximate impact on the future of the system. Changes in the task environment of a corporate Search Conference might include marketing and industry trends, changing costs of raw materials, information about labor pools, pending government regulations, probable product strategies of competitors, new technical innovations, changing industry standards, social problems in the workplace, and so forth.

Phase 1: Environmental Appreciation

Task: Scan and identify current and emerging trends and demands in the business, industry, or regional environment the system must plan for and respond to

Format: Large-group community brainstorming session

Outcome: A systemwide view and forecast of environmental demands in the immediate context; a strong case for change

Average Time: 1 hour

In corporate Search Conferences, the initial scan of the business environment is often followed by an additional subtask of analyzing the probable future of the system. This is especially useful if the organization is trying to build a strong case for change or to overcome resistance to the need for systemwide change. Analyzing the probable future of the system in light of emerging trends and environmental demands presents a realistic scenario of what is likely to happen to the organization if it continues to operate with a "business as usual" mind-set. It awakens people to the fact that proactive and planned change is in their best interest and that to survive the wake of turbulence requires creative collaboration and innovative responses.

Phase Two: System Analysis (Past, Present, and Future)

After having developed a shared appreciation of the global environmental context, a realization of shared ideals for a more desirable future for the world, and the identification of significant trends relevant to the formulation of long-term strategic goals, the community is ready to enter the next analytical phase. The stage is now set as the focus shifts to examining the past, present, and future of the system, in a shared context of a changing environment.

History Session

Phase 2: System Analysis
Task: Review the history of the system—major events, milestones, achievements, tragedies that have shaped the character of the system
Format: Large-group session
Outcome: Affirmation of Asch's second and third conditions for effective communications; emergence of the fourth condition (trust)
Average Time: 1–3 hours

Surveying significant historical events and changes is a critical phase for any preexisting community, network, organization, or industry. Gaining a shared appreciation of the system's origins and past is an important part of the planning context. Leaving this phase out altogether leaves the group at risk of developing plans without continuity linking the past to the future. History sessions should be customized and flexible. These sessions can last anywhere from forty-five minutes to several hours.

While the format of the history session may vary, its underlying purpose is to develop a shared appreciation of how the system has evolved and developed over time. The history session is almost always conducted as a large-group community session. There are many creative variations on how the history session can be designed. One design option is to conduct the history session simply as an open community discussion, allowing people to talk about the historical events, turning points, crises, achievements, milestones, or legends that have had a significant influence on the development of their system. With this design option, it is sometimes advantageous to have the whole community seated in a large circle (without tables, of course). We often start the session by inviting the oldest and most experienced members of the community to speak first. Their organizational experience and memory of events are recollected and told so that others in the community can learn about its past.

Another option is to assemble six or seven flip charts side by side in front of the room, drawing a horizontal time line across the middle of all the charts. The time line can begin when the organization started, or, in the case of a community, as far back in time as participants can go to provide historical background. The arrow at the end of the time line should stop at the current year. The elders of the community are asked to start the history session by coming up to the front of the room, and marking the year on the time line. Usually there are a few good-natured remarks or jokes made about the people who are considered the elders in the room. In most cases, the elders can be counted on to tell a few colorful tales of the good old days in the community as they remember them. Once this process is initiated, other participants will voluntarily step up to tell their stories, either revealing personal experiences, or adding their interpretations of why the milestones in the history of the system are significant to the planning of their future. The process need not follow a rigid linear progression, as people will tend to remember significant events that have occurred at various points in time.

The history session often is remembered by those who have participated in a Search Conference as the session that pulled people together as a community. In a way, the history session restores the oral tradition that once thrived in preliterate cultures, where people shared their common history, celebrated their customs and rituals, and paid homage to their ancestors all with the spoken word. The history session reinforces the ideal that expresses the need for belongingness—the communal sense that this is *our* place, this is *our* history.

A history session can be compared to a form of learning that mobilizes the collective memory. As the time approaches the present in the history session, more members become involved in contributing to the community story. The weaving together of different experiences makes the history session a fully participative community event, amplifying the common ground established in the previous phase.

In the history session, the community begins to explore the unique character of its system, its distinctive competence (Selznick, 1957, pp. 42–56), and its other familiar features. One of the Search Conference managers usually records the significant events and changes that have shaped the system's culture. The history session is important as it helps to identify the continuities that need to be extended from the past into future, so that the strategic plan reflects and respects the culture of the system.

Present System Analysis

Phase 2:	System Analysis
Task:	Present system analysis—strengths and weaknesses, what to keep, drop, and create
Format:	Large-group brainstorming session
Outcome:	Open and honest examination of the system
Average Time:	1–2 hours

Here the community begins to build on the learning from the history session. At this point in a conference, there should be sufficient trust among participants for them to be willing to openly acknowledge the weaknesses and strengths of their current system. This task brings things closer to home. However, rather than narrowing this session down to a familiar SWOT analysis—looking specifically at strengths, weaknesses, opportunities, and threats—it is more useful to take a broad look at current system functioning.

The present systems analysis is conducted as another large group brainstorming session that moves along rather quickly. In front of the room, the Search Conference managers stand by three flip-charts that contain the headings KEEP, DISCARD or DROP, and CREATE. Depending on the complexity of the system, this session is designed to last anywhere from thirty minutes to a few hours. The session provides immediate data on what items or facets of the system needs to keep and carry forward into its future, usually those features that have been working well; what needs to be changed or done away with, that is, the weaknesses in the system; and finally, what features don't currently exist and need to be created. During the brainstorming session, people do not have to agree on where a particular item belongs; an item could conceivably appear on all three flip charts. Using the same ground rules and format as the original brainstorming for changes in the wider environment, the Search Conference managers record all items that participants identify. This again reinforces confidence in people that their direct perceptions are valid. People may disagree on certain items, but those disagreements too are simply recorded on flip-chart paper. After the brainstorming session, the conference managers return to the items in conflict. For example, someone may have said, "Keep the TQM program," while someone else countered with "Drop the TQM program." The conference managers rationalize the conflict by inviting both parties to discuss their positions. If their difference turns out to be irreconcilable, the item is moved over to the disagree list.

Desirable Future of the System (Strategic Goal Setting)

Phase 2:	System Analysis
Task:	Describe the most desirable future (strategic goals) for the system
Format:	Small task groups develop scenarios that describe the most desirable future and strategic goals for the system; agreements on strategic goals and future directions are integrated into a community product
Outcome:	Common ground around a shared direction, backed by momentum of high energy and group creativity
Average Time:	3–4 hours

This phase of the Search Conference shifts attention explicitly toward the future of the system. The objective of this task is to develop a set of strategic goals that will bring about the most desirable future for the system. The output deriving from this task should be able to provide future strategic directions for the system. The question to be asked and answered during this task session is What is a desirable future for our system in 2005? (Or some other appropriate time frame.) During this task, people should set all constraints aside, exercise their creativity and imagination, and dream large. Remember, by definition a desirable future is based on ideals; it cannot be fully realized or attained. The task of describing a desirable future for the system should yield a set of strategic goals, long-range targets, and descriptions of desired end points. The West Cluster Empowerment Zone Search Conference spent approximately three hours on this task, focusing on what the West Side of Chicago would look like with good economic development in the year 2005.

During this session, small groups work in parallel on the same task. Participants are by now well prepared to work on the task of formulating the most desirable future directions for their system. Typically the manager simply asks the participants to prepare on flip charts a list of four to seven key points that best describe their most desirable future system, as it would look at a certain point in the future. For example, in the Xerox Search Conference, we opened the small-group session by saying, "Come up with a list of four to five points that describe the most desirable future of the Customer Business Unit in 1997. Consider these to be your strategic goals." The small groups then report and integrate their results. From there, the entire Search Conference community decides on specific desirable strategic goals.

Occasionally, there may be a situation where there are more strategic goals than the community can comfortably manage. The community will then need additional time to integrate and decide on their highest priority strategic goals. One option is to have the community integrate their list of goals around those that have strong interrelationships. Alternatively, various strategic goals can be assigned priorities. This can be one of the most important tasks a community faces, and yet it is one of the areas where it is easiest to slip away from Design Principle 2. The course of action that tends to come to mind first is some form of voting, but the expectation that the minority should accept what the majority comes up with actually derives from Design Principle 1. An aggregate of individual votes will yield an entirely different product from a set of democratic deliberations that represent a community view. In addition, organized voting usually bypasses the step of developing criteria for establishing priorities.

Such an important task requires serious reflection and work. First, the community should go back into their previous groups and decide the three or four most relevant criteria to be used in deciding the priorities. Then, using these criteria, they should assess each item (strategic goal) and arrive at the required number of priorities. Reports are taken in the normal manner followed by community discussion and negotiation of the final set. For example, in the Nebraska Mental Health System Search Conference, by merging strategic goals that were similar and leaving those that were not as stand-alone items, participants integrated thirty-five separate strategic goals. After a lengthy discussion to understand each of the strategic goals, the community organized them into ten clusters. Small groups developed three criteria to evaluate the priority of each of the strategic goal clusters. Using these criteria, the five highest-priority clusters were identified by each group. The results of this were then tallied in the large group. The top ten strategic goal clusters were then presented to the entire community for confirmation and clarification. The whole community decided in the plenary session which strategic goal clusters should be on the final list. The final list of strategic goals constitutes another community product, which guides the direction and activity of the action planning phase.

Phase Three: Action Planning (Integration of System and Environment)

The previous task of creating a desirable future for the system describes what the system will look like five or ten years from the present. In the final phase, participants draw on data and work from all previous sections to devise means of achieving the desirable future for the system. The time available for this third phase should approximate one-third of the total working time of the Search

Conference. It is in this phase that participants decide upon practical strategies that will move their system from the present to the desired future state. The components of this phase are:

- Dealing with constraints (by the strategy of the indirect approach)
- Actions we need to take to achieve strategic goals
- Next steps and follow-up action

Dealing with Constraints

> *Phase 3:* Strategies and Action Plans
> *Task:* Identify constraints to achieving desirable future and strategies for getting around them
> *Format:* Can be done in large-group brainstorming or small task groups
> *Outcome:* Indirect strategies for overcoming constraints, leveraging resources, and diffusion
> *Average Time:* 1 hour

Unlike traditional strategic planning sessions, a Search Conference deals with constraints as close to the end of the event as possible. Concentrating on constraints in earlier stages tends to inhibit the growth of confidence and creativity in large groups. Dealing with constraints is an important step, however, as it is the process by which the system begins to establish an adaptive relationship with its environment.

Before the community sets out to work on constraints, the Search Conference manager should provide a very short informational briefing on the strategy of the indirect approach (see Chapter Three) as a helpful tool for considering the ways and means for getting around constraints. To recap briefly, indirect strategies are devised to control maximum territory with minimum resistance to the strategist. As the name implies, indirect strategies either en-circle, get around, or undercut the key constraints that exist, as op-posed to directly confronting them. They involve the application of effort first in those areas where there is likely to be the least re-sistance to change. Moreover, the most effective strategy will be that which increases the ratio of success to effort.

By this point in the conference, the Search Conference man-ager has established a trusting and equal relationship with partici-pants. Nevertheless, to inject external information into the conference represents a major role shift on the part of the Search Conference manager, from that of designer and manager to that of expert presenter. A public acknowledgment of this role shift should be made before the briefing.

Besides discussing indirect strategies, the briefing also clarifies the task instructions and places emphasis on generating positive ac-tions. We never ask groups to simply list the constraints. Rather, we always say something along the lines of, "Bring back a list of the most serious obstacles, together with a way of dealing with each of them."

There are two options for conducting this phase. First, con-straints and strategies for dealing with them may be identified by conducting a brief brainstorming session with the whole commu-nity. These ideas and plans are then available for all the small ac-tion planning groups to use during their subsequent tasks. The other option is to have small groups identify constraints associated with particular strategic goals, as part of their action planning process. In establishing constraints, participants need to review trends in the global and task environments. To identify major con-straints, participants survey previous work, particularly their analy-sis of the most probable future of the world (environmental constraints), and the present system analysis items that appear on the discard list (system constraints). As participants are encour-aged to find indirect strategies for maneuvering around con-straints, they also find it useful to reexamine their system strengths for potential leads that can exploit new and as yet unforeseen op-portunities. Strategies are the means for accomplishing the ends specified in the previous phase, as well as the basis for generating more detailed action plans. Good strategies ultimately should gen-erate rather than consume resources.

Developing Action Plans

> *Phase 3:* Strategies and Action Plans
> *Task:* Develop detailed action plans with project milestones, commitments, and progress review checkpoints
> *Format:* Small task forces self-select around strategic goals to develop action plans that are later reported back to the community
> *Outcome:* An achievable plan backed by commitment, enthusiasm, and energy for diffusion
> *Average Time:* 4–8 hours

After work on constraints, conference participants move very quickly forward on the task of nailing down strategic action plans to be accomplished in both the short and long term. It is essential that the design allow enough time for this task. Strategic action planning is a task that integrates all the previous work, linking the system with the environment. Therefore the design of the Search Conference must ensure adequate time to be devoted to the development of detailed action plans. Time allotted for this phase can range anywhere from four to eight hours. Participants usually self-select themselves around those strategic goal areas that involve their expertise, and the ones they are committed to implementing. This results in the formation of a number of task forces dedicated to working on the development and implementation of detailed action plans on behalf of the whole community. For the West Cluster Empowerment Zone Search Conference, we gave the small groups working on this task a number of guidelines to help them as they developed their strategic action plans for economic development. In this case, work on constraints was combined with the task of action planning. Each small group was instructed to produce action plans that would be long-term and strategic in nature, capitalize on existing and potential resources, and overcome constraints and deal with issues that were likely to present obstacles to goal achievement.

Participants must develop action plans that outline the specifics of what needs to happen to accomplish their strategic goals. Thus, action plans need to be concrete and precise, with programmatic steps. We often use a *3–3–3* framework, which has action planning groups specify the tasks they will accomplish in the next three weeks, three months, and three years. This task session is also where participants must develop detailed action plans on how to spread the learning from the Search Conference to the rest of the people in their system. Make sure to include time for an interim plenary session to ensure coordination of the task force plans with the interests of the total community.

Follow-Up Session

Final task force reports lead to a large-group session where the community plans its continued life. This is the follow-up session, and it is here that the community decides what to do with all the data generated during the conference. Usually the community desires to publish some sort of report or proceedings on the conference. In some cases, a voluntary group forms to handle the job of transcribing data from the flip charts and editing the results into a report. Based on their action plans, the community also at this point decides if and when they will need to meet again, and in what type of structural configuration. This follow-up is the work of the community, not the conference managers.

Both the sponsor and the participants should know beforehand that they are basically on their own to carry their results forward into implementation. The Search Conference manager does not normally become involved in report writing, follow-up activities, monitoring, or facilitation during the implementation phase. During the closing phases of the conference, managers should reinforce this understanding. By the time the conference ends, the community should have developed into a confident, self-managing group that is ready to begin implementing its plans. However, it is very important that the Search Conference community sustain this self-managing structure through the implementation and diffusion phases.

Design as a Flexible Process

It is important to note that the design for a Search Conference includes only a minimal set of signposts. This is very different from a programmed agenda as found in trainer-led workshops. It defeats the purpose if the managers try to run people through tasks so as to adhere to a time-rigid agenda. Rather, the design must be seen as secondary to enabling a self-managing community to come into being, a community that can learn and plan together. To appreciate this is to understand the difference between community building and programming.

It is almost impossible beforehand to estimate the exact amount of time for each phase. When groups work on formulating strategic goals, they often need to revisit the data generated in the first session. In some cases, participants may find that they need to do further analysis on environmental trends in their task environment. While the design of the Search Conference may look fairly linear and concrete on paper, it is not necessarily so—the plan does not reflect the adjustments and design changes that almost inevitably occur. Search Conference managers must build time buffers into their overall design. The community may need to spend additional time on one of the phases, and a judgment must be made by the conference manager of the trade-offs involved. This is why designing and managing on the run is perhaps the greatest test of a Search Conference manager's skill. And we can assure you that the design of any Search Conference *will* change once things are under way, sometimes dramatically, and other times with only minor fine-tuning or adjustment. In either case, such design changes can make or break the conference.

As conference managers, what we present to the sponsor is usually a sketch of the game plan that specifies only the rough stop and start times for each phase. We never post a detailed design with exact times for each task. Such a practice would be counterproductive for both conference managers and participants. Conference managers should not rigidly adhere to a detailed paper design. Similarly, posting a detailed design in front of participants would make some of them worry unnecessarily if tasks were not completed by the time specified on the design.

Good conference managers are like skilled and talented jazz musicians—they know the basics so deeply that they can let go of them and improvise. Jazz musicians spend a great deal of time mastering the basics of jazz chord progressions. Yet when they actually perform live, it is their improvisational skills that count. Similarly, competent conference managers must know in detail the timing of tasks that follow the basic Search Conference funnel design—then adjust the timing as needed in practice to match the rhythms of learning unique to that particular set of conference participants.

In the next section, we walk through a corporate Search Conference that was conducted at Xerox. This case illustrates how a Search Conference was designed and some of the choices and options that were considered, and also gives a synopsis of the actual data and group reports that the participants generated.

Xerox Organizational Renewal Search Conference: A Case Study

Dan Dotin, vice president of Xerox Company's largest Customer Business Unit (CBU), expressed a strong need to develop a strategic business plan from the bottom up. A recent reorganization and downsizing effort had consolidated three sales and service districts into his centralized operation. The Search Conference was considered to be a timely and appropriate method for organizational renewal and for developing a common vision for the newly formed business unit. Dan Dotin recollects his challenges:

Xerox had its first major restructuring of field operations. It was top-down downsizing. People were reeling and we had to find a way to get them reconnected in a new organization. I didn't want to work through the layers of management. I wanted leaders to emerge and faster decisions to be made. That meant bringing managers and employees together around a common set of strategic goals. I chose a Search Conference as the planning method to make that happen. Our task was to form strategies that would earn our customer's loyalty. It had to be a strategy worthy of being deployed. We discovered that a Search Conference speeds up the planning cycle so we can act quickly to start implementing the plan. It works because it plants the seeds of deployment into how you develop the strategy.

The planning group for this case (as described in Chapter Seven) elected to hold the Search Conference at a remote conference center for two and a half days. Exhibit 8.1 illustrates the letter of invitation. Exhibit 8.2 gives the detailed design for the Xerox Search Conference. We stress that the specificity of time allotments as shown here is strictly for educational purposes. The times allotted for various tasks are approximate. Experienced conference managers usually know when phases begin and end and make ongoing adjustments to actual time allotments as activities unfold.

**Exhibit 8.1. Letter of Invitation:
Xerox Customer Business Unit Search Conference.**

~IN THE NEWS~
Special Edition

Volume 1 Issue 1	July 14, 1995

XEROX OF ILLINOIS CBU PLANNING EVENT SCHEDULED!

Search Conference Scheduled!

Xerox Of Illinois is in the final stages of preparing for a bottoms-up planning event scheduled for July 25 - 27, at the Northwest Wyndham Hotel near Schaumburg. The event is called a Search Conference and according to Dan Dotin, CBU VP/GM, and Chet Terry, EDM, it will be an important tool in helping the combined Xerox of Illinois CBU set goals and establish strategic direction for the future. Employees from all functions and job levels within the CBU will be asked to participate. It will be "planning for the people, by the people". Outputs will be integrated into the CBU Business Excellence process for 4th quarter and 1996 implementation. This event will tap the intellectual capital of the whole organization in moving the CBU toward Xerox 2000 endpoint.

"Xerox of Illinois is Best in World"

Who will Facilitate?

The Search Conference will be facilitated by two experts: Ronald   Purser,   Ph.D. Associate   Professor   of Organizational Development, at Loyola University, and Frank   Heckman,   MA, President of consulting firm Frank   Heckman   and Associates. They both have lots of experience and have achieved excellent results using this methodology. Their clients include Amoco Oil, General Electric, Procter & Gamble, United Airlines,

Whirlpool, Arthur Andersen , and Storage Technology. We will also benefit from the experience of one of our own - ASM Kathy Grady, a Masters   in   Organization Development candidate   at Loyola University. She has participated in 3 external sessions and brought the idea of a Search Conference to our attention. (*Thanks, Kathy*!).

More . . . . .

Selection of participants has just been completed, and if you are not one of the 50 or so participants, please ask your manager for the names of those who are so that you can keep abreast of events. This is important because although everyone will not be directly involved in the actual Search   Conference,   the outputs are likely to require the involvement of many others for action planning and implementation. We will be counting   on   everyone's support and contributions!

Reprinted by permission.

Exhibit 8.2. Rough Time Plan:
Xerox Customer Business Unit Search Conference.

Day 1

6:30 P.M.	Introductions, Conference Briefing
7:00	Expectations of the Conference
7:45	Plenary: Environmental Scan—Changes in the World (Large-Group Brainstorming Session)
8:15	Small Groups: Desirable and Probable Futures of the World
9:00	Plenary: Task Group Reports
9:45	Adjourn

Day 2

8:00 A.M.	Recap and Review of Game Plan
8:15	Plenary: Changes in Xerox Business Environment Directly Affecting the CBU (Task Environment: Large Group Brainstorming Session)
9:00	Small Groups: Identifying Most Important Trends and Changes • Identify 4–5 key trends that are important to the CBU's future • Probable Future: If we do nothing and trends continue on their present course, what is the probable future of the CBU? • What the CBU is NOT currently doing, but should be doing, to respond to these trends
9:30	Plenary: Post Key Trends on Wall—Report Out Planning Implications
10:00	Break
10:15	History Session (Last 15–20 minutes, "What is the best of our past that we want to carry forward as we plan for the future?"
12:00	LUNCH
1:00 P.M.	Present System Analysis (What to Keep, Drop, Create)
1:30	Small Groups: Identify "Quick Hits"—items and potential opportunities for change and improvement that can be implemented immediately
2:00	Desirable Future for the Xerox CBU in 1998 Generate 4–5 key strategic goal statements/scenarios that describe what the CBU will be like in 1998—describe the future state
4:00	Reports (limit 10 minutes per report)
5:00	Setting Criteria for Prioritizing Strategic Goals
6:00	Break (Free Time) (DINNER PERIOD)
7:30	Plenary: Prioritization and Integration of Strategic Goals Plenary: Testing for Agreement Around Desirable Strategic Goals for the Xerox CBU
8:30	Adjourn

Day 3

8:00 A.M.	Overview
8:15	Self-Selection into Action Planning Groups Briefing: Strategy of Indirect Approach
8:30	Action Planning Strategies and actions for achieving strategic goals to be implemented within the next 3 weeks, next 3 months, and next 3 years. Specify how strategies will overcome likely constraints.
11:00	Interim Report Out on Strategies for Dealing with Constraints
12:00	LUNCH
1:00 P.M.	Action Planning Fair
3:30	Follow-Up
4:00	Adjourn

After introductions, briefings, and expectations, Xerox participants moved into a standard first phase, an exploration of the global (contextual) environment in a large-group brainstorming session. Specifically, Xerox participants were asked to identify changes, trends, events, and forces in the contextual environment that they perceived as being significant or novel over the last three to five years. We immediately began to record their perceptions of trends on flip charts:

Virtual office. . .

Dual-income families. . .

Decreasing trust in authorities. . .

Increased insensitivity to differences. . .

Political correctness. . .

Business moving to suburbs. . .

Business moving to less expensive locations. . .

High taxes. . .

Too much waste and garbage. . .

Terrorist activity on our own soil. . .

New diseases. . .

New cures for diseases. . .

Prison overcrowding. . .

Gulf War. . .

People are living longer. . .

Americans with Disabilities Act. . .

Next, in small groups, our design allowed forty-five minutes to formulate desirable and probable futures for the global environment in 2005. Half the groups in the conference room were told to focus on developing desirable future scenarios and the other half were asked to concentrate on probable future scenarios for the world in ten years. The design called for each of the small groups to present their report in a plenary session at around 8:15 P.M. Part of the job of the Search Conference manager is make sure that the conference design allows for an ample amount of time for small-group reports in a plenary session. With Xerox, we knew that approximately forty-five to fifty participants would be attending the Search Conference. Given this number of participants, we decided that we would need no more than six small groups; each group consisting of seven or eight people around a table. We allotted five to seven minutes for each task group report, or about forty-five minutes for all the reporting. These are the kinds of logistical design details that every Search Conference manager must attend to. However, one must keep in mind that one can only estimate the amount of time allotted for tasks and group reports.

Xerox participants expressed their shared ideals for a desirable future for the world as captured in these statements:

- Resurgence of the family unit; education, religion, family values, and discipline.
- Densely populated areas will be able to spread out and reduce congestion; the workforce will be able to work from any geographic point.
- Affordable health care and housing for all of the population.
- Technology explosion will yield safer fuels, efficient electric vehicles, and virtual office will become a way of life.

Their probable future of the global environment painted a different picture:

- There will be an increase in poverty, making it tougher for people to meet their retirement income needs, and economic power will shift from G7 countries to Third World and Pacific Rim.
- There will be an increase in religious conflicts, but at the same time a revival of grassroots movements.
- There will be technological innovations that increase the speed of communications, less privacy of data, and people will be overwhelmed by too much information.
- The number of people receiving a college education will decrease, while the high school and even grade school drop-out rate will increase.
- There will be increased pressure and stress put on families, and the family as we used to know it (strong bonds and ties between children, parents, and grandparents) will be eroded.

The design then included a session to scan the task environment surrounding the Xerox Customer Business Unit (CBU). Why was this deemed necessary? A scan of the task (or business) environment is usually included when we conduct corporate Search Conferences. This event planned to bring to-gether employees from each of the functions—sales, service, and administra-tion—for the purpose of developing common strategies for becoming more market driven. It was very important for these conference participants to de-velop a common data base of the market trends and changing features of their industry and business environment. Having a clear picture of the changing trends in the immediate task environment (those with direct impact on the customer business unit) is a key component of the strategic planning process. Reviewing the task environment ran in the same manner as the large-group brainstorming session for the previous environmental scan. Figure 8.2 pro-vides a summary of the trends in the task environment that were directly affecting the Xerox of Illinois CBU.

Immediately after this task, we also designed in a subtask that required small groups to identify the most important trends in their task environment. They analyzed these trends in terms of a probable future for the CBU, that is, the implications for the CBU if it did not strategically respond to these trends. What was the CBU not currently doing that it should be doing to respond to these trends? Following this small-group work, plenary reports were taken at approximately 9:30 A.M. Here is a synopsis of reports on the probable future for the CBU in 1998, if trends were to continue unabated:

- There will be a loss of market share, more customer pressure, and a decrease in customer satisfaction.
- Role of CBU will be diminished both in personnel and responsibility.
- CBU revenue will decrease, and we will continue to lose people. There will be a rapid increase in alternate distribution channels.
- There will be a depersonalized work environment; technology will provide the opportunity to market intellectual capital, but our size prohibits the rapid reaction critical to survival.

PHASE TWO: SYSTEM ANALYSIS

By midmorning of the second day, the Search Conference design shifted to a focus on the internal affairs of the CBU, beginning with a look at the history of the Xerox sales, service, and administration organizations. This design allowed well over an hour for an open, large-group history session. Toward the last fif-teen or twenty minutes of this history session, we decided to have participants highlight the best aspects of their history that they should continue forward as they plan for the future. This not only acted as bridge between the history

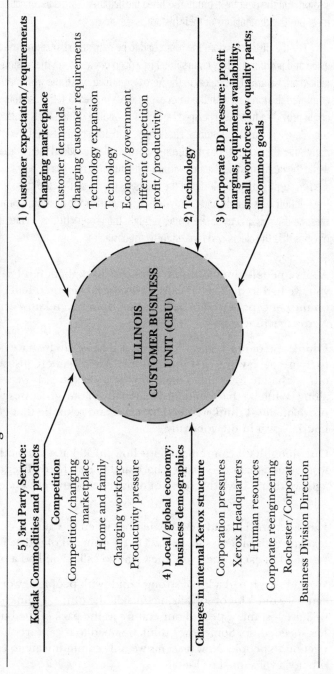

Figure 8.2. Xerox Task Environment.

session and the next task, but it also lifted participants' spirits to reflect on the most positive dimensions of their history as a system.

For the history session, the room had to be rearranged, pushing the tables aside and positioning fifty chairs in a large open circle. To get the session kicked off, we asked the elders of the Xerox organization (those who have been employed the longest, with the most experience) to speak up first, so they could provide a historical perspective on the founding values, early work culture, developmental milestones, challenges, and achievements in the company. After the elders began, medium-service employees added their voices, while the newest people listened with rapt attention. A number of people seemed surprised by the stories of the elders, as they described the close working relationships people had twenty-five years ago. For the next ninety minutes, we listened quietly as the stories brought the group's history to life. It was obvious that the elders had faced significant obstacles:

A lot of people think our jobs were easy back then, but I can tell you, we had to make cold calls. Customers back then had to be sold on the concept of photocopying, they didn't even know what a Xerox machine was.

I think one of our biggest strengths is that we always have been able to figure out a way to get things done. When we were just starting out, we had to invent and make up the procedures as we went along. While we have standardized many of our processes to improve quality, I think we need to revisit and rekindle that entrepreneurial spirit in the company.

One thing that I can remember is how we all knew each other and worked as a team. We worked hard and played hard. Twenty years ago, we didn't have this sense of divisiveness between service and sales.

I am a technician and I can remember when the sales agent used to take me with him on sales calls. That is unheard of today. Because we all knew each other, you knew who to call if you had a problem.

We had developed a lot of strong bonds with people at work because we did a lot of socializing outside the office. I think somehow we have lost this aspect of our culture as the pace of the business has speeded up. Somehow I think we need to recapture that connection to people. Now it seems we only communicate to each other via voice mail or E-mail.

Knowledge of the past usually seems to bring participants closer together; in this case, the stories they told helped them to gain a deeper appreciation for the work of their peers, the challenges they faced, and the amount of pride people have in working for Xerox over the years. The telling of past events, reminiscing about the details of significant turning points and their relation to how the company has evolved over time, brought out the total meaning and rich context behind the work these people do. As the time line of storytelling approached the present, we asked them to consider the best aspects of their history, the things they wanted to preserve and continue forward as they planned for their future. This actually was a prelude to the next task. We also reminded people that the purpose of a history session is to develop a shared knowledge of where the system has come from, and all the major formative events or changes that it has gone through, so people can work from the same body of knowledge. The history session focuses on learning about the organizational system's evolution—it is not about an individual's personal history, although individuals are emotionally and intimately involved in the history of their organization.

After lunch, we scheduled the present system analysis for a one-hour period. During this large-group brainstorming session, participants identified aspects of the CBU system that they wanted to keep, drop, and create. Another innovation we added to this design was to have participants examine the present system analysis data and then identify a short list of *quick hits*—items and potential opportunities for change and improvement that could be implemented immediately without a lot of time and additional resources.

- What do we want to keep? For Xerox, there were key aspects of the system that the participants wanted to carry forward:

  Pride in the company and one's work. . .

  The caliber of people. . .

  Our innovative spirit. . .

  Our respect for the individual. . .

- What do we want to jettison and discontinue in the present system?

  Line item budgets; discontinue all budget centers and geographic boundaries. . .

  Discontinue month-end reports. . .

  Drop the "district names". . .

  Get rid of the red tape on Total Satisfaction Guarantee. . .

  Eliminate functional roles. . .

- What do we need to create or invent? (This flip chart usually fills up quickly and contains the most items. There's room here for only a small sampling of items from this conference.)
Better sales structure to gain new customers. . .
New Sales Guarantee letter. . .
Improved communication process between sales and service. . .
Better work process for meeting deliver dates. . .
More bench strength in Service expanded to entire CBU. . .
Better customer service response system. . .
Open access to information—budget, plans, operations, data bases. . .
Community involvement, get Xerox more out into the community. . .
Local service on low end products. . .
Embrace partnerships with alternative channels. . .

By 2:00 P.M., the conference design shifted to the future of the Xerox CBU system. Small groups had a good two hours to work on developing four to five strategic goals describing the most desirable future of the Xerox CBU system three years out. Enough time also had to be allowed in the Search Conference design for report outs and prioritization of the strategic goals. The design plan allocated an additional hour for report outs and then another hour for the task of developing criteria for prioritizing strategic goals. The Search Conference manager asked the whole community to generate the criteria by which they will prioritize strategic goals. After dinner, the conference reconvened to do the actual prioritization and integration of strategic goals. The high-priority strategic goals were then integrated by the whole community into a common list by merging similar items, separating unique stand-alone items, and identifying conflicting items from different groups. The common list had to be the product of the whole community. These tasks are time consuming; this design allowed for the possibility of having to work overtime into the evening.

In the Xerox Search Conference, the fifty participants voluntarily reformed themselves into six small groups to spend intensive time on developing four to five strategic goals that—if achieved—would result in the most desirable future for the Xerox of Illinois CBU in 1998.

After integrating and prioritizing some ten different long-range goals, the top five strategic goals for the desirable future of the Xerox of Illinois CBU for 1998 were agreed upon by the whole conference community:

1. Fully empowered employees who are accountable and have incentives to meet their customers' requirements with the only boundary being ethical behavior.

2. An organizational design based on cross-functional work groups to increase profits by 15 percent, and revenue growth by 20 percent.

3. Bottom-up planning is used with all employees and managers as a means for continuous learning and improvement.

4. The CBU is market driven and recognized as the vendor of choice in the local market.

5. Mastery of technology tools that fully support our business needs throughout the organization.

PHASE THREE: ACTION PLANNING

The last phase of the Search Conference began the next day as participants reconfigured themselves into new small groups, organized around the different strategic goals. Over the course of this last set of tasks, participants developed specific strategies and action plans for implementation.

This conference design followed our usual practice of addressing constraints toward the end of the Search Conference, to avoid inhibiting creative thinking by narrowing the focus to solving current problems. When we began work on constraints, the conference managers gave the plenary session a fifteen- to twenty-minute briefing on the strategy of the indirect approach, followed by guidelines for creating action plans. Then small groups plunged into the task of developing their major strategies and action plans. This design began the action planning process in the early morning, and groups worked all the way through until lunch. Small groups had a good three hours to develop specific strategies and action plans that outline how constraints and obstacles would be overcome or addressed. This is in essence the integration of the system's capacity for perceiving strategic opportunities in the midst of environmental constraints. The action planning groups gave interim reports in the hour before lunch. The group working on the strategic goal of designing cross-functional work teams with common goals and shared compensation systems within the CBU identified these obstacles and strategies for overcoming them:

- Obstacles:
  Vague concept, lack of knowledge
  Huge task
  Significant cultural change
  Some managers fearful of the idea
- Strategies:
  Benchmark other companies using cross-functional teams
  Pilot test cross-functional teams based on local needs
  Define all options and determine which is best
  Use a phased approach
  Design logic for cross-functional teams should be based on fulfilling customer needs
  Designate a high-profile manager to lead and champion the change
  Build a case for the change based on internal and external analysis of issues

By 1:00 P.M. on the third day, action planning groups had finished their work. With this particular design, we set up an "action planning fair" (see Figure 8.3) after lunch on the third and final day of the conference. An action planning fair works as follows:

1.   In preparation for the fair, each action planning group prepares a brief report on a flip chart.

2.   The action planning groups break up and reform as mixed groups, each including at least one person from each action planning group. (For example, if there are six action planning groups with six members each, then the Search Conference manager can create six mixed groups simply by having everyone in the room count off by six.) Each of the newly formed mixed groups takes their seats at one of the action planning tables.

3.   Following the formation of mixed groups, the representative of the action planning team whose flip chart is at the table provides a brief report, and solicits suggestions and feedback from the rest of the mixed group. (All the groups go through this step at the same time.)

4.   After the first report is finished, each mixed group rotates to the next table to hear a different report. This time a new member from each action planning group will provide a report and solicit feedback. This process continues and cycles through until each mixed group has moved around the room and heard all of the action planning reports.

Figure 8.3. Action Planning Fair.

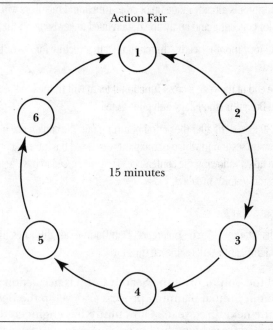

There are several advantages of conducting the action planning reports in this format. First, it breaks up the rhythm of the conference, allowing for more informal exchanges. Second, it forces more people from each action planning group to own the reports, because every group member must present the results of the action planning report to some of their peers. Third, it provides an opportunity for the cross-fertilization of ideas across action planning groups.

The action planning group responsible for diffusion of the cross-functional team strategy proposed:

1. Within three weeks, members of the team will engage the rest of CBU, communicating the intended strategies for redesign into a cross-functional team structure.

2. Within three weeks, members of the team will benchmark other companies.

3. Within three months, other key players and voluntary members will be recruited to assist with the planning and redesign effort. Action team members will create a newsletter to keep all CBU employees informed of the redesign process.

4. Within three months, existing Quality Improvement Teams (QIT) whose composition is already made up of cross-functional members will be utilized for collecting and analyzing data related to key issues in the CBU.

5. Within four months, a cross-functional team structure for the CBU will be defined.

6. By the end of the year, a cross-functional team will trained in the Participative Design methodology and pilot-tested.

At 3:30 P.M., right after the action planning fair, the conference held a plenary follow-up session in which participants discussed the future steps that need to be taken following the conference. They all agreed to have a progress review session in forty-five days.

A BRIEF ASSESSMENT

Six months after the Search Conference, Dan Dotin made this assessment of the most significant results achieved thus far:

We used the output from the Search Conference action planning teams in our annual planning process to develop the business strategy for the next three years. Our culture has engineered a big shift. We've moved from being highly dependent on top-down planning to acting like entrepreneurs. This is an incredible breakthrough for our front-line employees. Each action planning team and the associates they recruited devoted countless hours to integrate their output into the business plan. I put one of our top sales managers on special assignment to work full-time to integrate the work of all the action teams into our business practices. From a best practices point of view, the Xerox World-Wide Service chose our CBU as one of two sites as a pilot for further work to improve customer loyalty because of the results we achieved with the Search Conference. We are now implementing the cross-functional design strategies that came out of the Search Conference so Xerox can organize around tasks rather than functions. I am excited about the next year as people carry the plan forward.

Design Pointers and Design Pitfalls

While some elements of the Search Conference, such as the number of days, are flexible, others are not. A Search Conference is a whole entity that must be carefully designed in advance to fit the unique circumstances of the organization or community. Here is a list of pointers and pitfalls that one should be aware of when designing a Search Conference.

Design Pointers

Keep track of the following aspects of the design:

- *Maneuvering room.* Make sure to design buffers and adequate slack time into the Search Conference plan. These provide the necessary flexibility and room for maneuver when needed.

- *Fine tuning.* Always take into consideration the interdependent variables when making design decisions: difficulty of the Search Conference task, history of conflict between participants expected to attend, number of participants, amount of time needed for adequate reporting, and so on. Different circumstances will call for finely tuned judgments with regard to numbers, timing, and venue.

- *Sound innovation.* Search Conference design is an art, not an exact science. Think of design in terms of jazz improvisation. You will need to be flexible and innovative, and sometimes you'll find it necessary to break the rules. However, like jazz, this freedom and flexibility still needs to sound good. The principles and theories are the boundaries within which one can be flexible with the design. Other theories may well lead to a different type of conference entirely.

- *Flexibility.* Once the conference is under way, trust your intuition and perceptions. The design is only a game plan, not a rigid formula enslaving you and the participants. If you sense and feel that people need more time to complete a certain task, then don't interrupt them (so long as you are able to recover or buy time from your buffers or by making adjustments in the plan).

- *Genuine democracy.* Clearly understand the implications of what it means to design a conference structured in accordance with Design Principle 2. The role and function of democratic design is to create the best possible learning environment for conference participants to take responsibility for the control and coordination of their own work.

Design Pitfalls

Avoid letting any of the following creep into the design:

- *Surveys.* Preparing or polling participants in advance by using a survey is unnecessary and may send the wrong the message to those unfamiliar with the Search Conference. In a symbolic sense, surveys elevate the isolated thinking of individuals over the social nature of creative working groups. Distorted expectations or misconceptions among participants could potentially inhibit Search Conference processes.

- *Speakers.* Don't invite keynote speakers or guest lecturers. Any events—either at the conference or before it begins—that focus participants' attention too narrowly upon system issues or concerns can reduce the chance of finding common ground in the beginning stages of the Search Conference.

- *Fantasy and games.* The use of simulations, icebreakers, or other types of experiential exercises is directly in conflict with the purpose of a Search Conference: to be a real-world, task-oriented, participative planning meeting. Because the Search Conference design already meets Asch's conditions for effective communications, these training props are distractions and are completely unnecessary.

- *Preassigned roles.* The appointment of chairpersons, small-group facilitators, or other quasi supervisors will lead to a mixed-mode design. The Search Conference is a democratically structured learning environment that doesn't need guardians to watch over people. Search Conference managers are concerned about enabling a self-managing community to come into being. By definition, self-managing groups can take responsibility for the management of their tasks and their processes.

- *Communications skill training.* We have found that a Search Conference develops a creative planning community in which people consistently display communications skills entirely adequate to their task, without prior training. Although useful in DP1 structures, communications exercises are only distracting in the Search Conference context.

- *High-tech toys.* Resist the temptation to use sophisticated audio-visual aids. The Search Conference is designed to promote face-to-face spoken communications; it is not possible to use the method successfully through the medium of video-conferencing.

- *Hidden agendas*. Watch out for sponsors who want you to use or design the Search Conference to finalize a solution or decision they have already decided in advance. Any attempt to use the Search Conference for this end will result in long-term frustration and disillusionment.

Chapter Nine

Managing the Search Conference

Search Conference management is not for the faint of heart. Because Search Conferences are highly participative in nature, they have the potential to generate a great deal of emotional intensity. Those who wish to become Search Conference managers must learn the relevant skills—managing time, tasks, and boundaries. Beginners who attempt to manage Search Conferences on their own, without having first apprenticed with someone more experienced, are likely to find themselves in an overwhelming situation.

Role of the Search Conference Manager

The openness, democratic structure, and overall open-ended design of a Search Conference require a great deal of unlearning among those who have received professional training in organization development consultation methods. This is because the role of a Search Conference manager is fundamentally different from that of helper or change agent.

These two terms are often used to describe the role of organization development consultants, and they catch the essence of the job as it is usually viewed. For example, process consultation is primarily concerned with developing a "helping" relationship with the "client" (Schein, 1969). This notion of developing a helping relationship with the client has a long heritage rooted in the Judeo-Christian tradition and the liberal social services view of human development. Consider these opening lines from a classic text on organization development consultation:

Throughout history there have been individuals who acquired or were given status and credibility in groups as helpers in solving problems. Tribal wise men, medicine men, and priests often developed special skills as helpers in personal or group problem solving. . . . Later, charismatic leaders, such as Buddha, Christ, Mohammed, and Confucius developed circles of followers who, through role modeling, conceptual training, and some supervised practice, developed helping orientations and skills, and presented themselves to people as helpers and change agents. Formal training programs and internships developed as preparation and certification, first for religious ministries and for medical practice, then for psychologists, social workers, and public health workers. Helping tended to be differentiated into consulting and training [Lippitt and Lippitt, 1978, pp. 1–2].

According to Frances Moore Lappé and Paul DuBois (1994), the Judeo-Christian image of the caregiver providing care to the needy converged with the emerging social sciences. "Psychology, for example, helped establish the role of the professional therapist who diagnoses an individual's illness and guides the cure" (Lappé and DuBois, 1994, p. 138). While organization development and process consultation methods represented a shift away from the doctor-patient model of consultation, focusing instead upon the importance of developing a collaborative relationship with the client system and conducting a joint diagnosis of the problem, these methods retained the clinical language—and thus the mental outlook—of psychiatry and psychology. The social services paradigm embedded in such terms as helper, change agent, client, and diagnosis is familiar to all who work in organization development. In their own context, the terms provide a conceptual base for many useful interventions. Nonetheless, they also influence the relationship involved in those interventions in subtle ways. Terminology does a great deal to shape perception and social processes. When we speak (and think) of people who participate in Search Conferences as concerned citizens who want to create a more desirable future, rather than as clients with problems, many aspects of our own behavior—and theirs—shift as a result. By viewing our role as that of collaborator and community organizer rather than that of helper or change agent, we tend to evoke the most adult and independent sides of conference participants' natures.

Another major difference with a bearing on role definition is the degree of reliance on the consultant's direct activities and contributions. For example, with process consultation, the consultant is actively involved in gathering data for the client, usually by conducting interviews, administering surveys, and observing group meetings. The process consultant also makes a diagnosis (albeit jointly with the client) and offers interpretations of the data. The same is true of most action research interventions—the consultant manages the data collection and diagnosis (Burke, 1987; Neilsen, 1984).

Schein (1969, p. 9) reflects the clinical orientation of his view of consultation when he states, "The process consultant seeks to give the client 'insights' into what is going on around him, within him, and between him and other people." This notion of group facilitation focuses mainly upon the *interpersonal processes* occurring among members in a work group. It is an outgrowth of the training methods (T-sensitivity groups) developed at the National Training Laboratories (Bradford, Gibbs, and Benne, 1964). Here, "The trainer sees himself not as a teacher or expert, but as someone who helps group members to discover what kinds of events are occurring in the group and what effects such events are having on themselves and other members" (Schein, 1969, p. 12). Unfortunately, some process facilitators have overplayed the idea that they are not experts to the point that they have become overly timid and self-effacing with their clients (Freedman, 1995). Others have abused their role as process helper, perhaps enjoying the status and power of leadership, while consciously or unconsciously manipulating the situation so that a hierarchical distinction between them and the group is maintained. As Schein (1969) suggests, skilled process facilitators must have a high degree of self-knowledge and exceptional skills and abilities to avoid falling into the doctor-patient model of consultation.

The Search Conference manager's role is certainly that of an expert, but one whose expertise is limited to the design and management of the Search Conference itself. We clarify this with prospective Search Conference sponsors by establishing a very clear division of labor. As Search Conference managers, we are the experts at running the meeting. Participants are the experts in determining the issues and problems of their organization or community. Search Conference managers do not offer their interpretations or get involved in the analysis of data.

Whereas the focus of traditional forms of process facilitation is on the interpersonal processes occurring within a group, the focus of the Search Conference manager is on designing and managing the context in which a collaborative community can emerge. Managing context means that Search Conference managers create and maintain a nonthreatening situation where participants can pool their perceptions, build a common data base, and express their shared ideals for a more desirable future. The emphasis on context rather than interpersonal processes allows participants to develop confidence in their direct perceptions of the dynamics occurring between their system and its environment.

Maintaining the Community Organizer Role

Search Conference managers should view the whole community as one unit, and not as a collection of factions, groups, or individuals. This means that Search Conference managers should guard against aligning or overidentifying themselves with one party or group. Search Conference managers, whether working solo or in tandem, should especially avoid taking sides with the sponsor or other persons or groups within the community.

The worst-case scenario is when one of a pair of Search Conference managers becomes an advocate for one faction, while the other takes sides with an opposing faction. This is an embarrassing and awkward situation for both Search Conference managers, as they will lose any semblance of objectivity. They are supposed to be there to help the community sort out any conflicts that might arise, but they now find themselves divided, having fallen prey to the temptation of becoming advocates for the various causes within the community, deepening the splits within it.

It helps maintain both the appearance and the reality of objectivity and neutrality to have at least one of the Search Conference managers come from outside the system sponsoring the conference. If both Search Conference managers come from inside the system, there is a risk that participants may become suspicious and paranoid. The conference managers might be suspected of having arranged a secret pact with the power brokers to bias the agenda and outcomes in a predetermined direction. At the very least, they might be misperceived from the outset as being affiliated with a particular faction or group within the organization.

Further, if a Search Conference manager has a strong personal interest in the content or any stake in the outcome of a conference, there is very strong likelihood that he or she will become distracted from the primary task, that is, conference management. Search Conference managers cannot remain objective and impartial when they are emotionally invested in the actual outcome of a conference. It is one thing to wish for a successful conference event, and quite another to begin to exert influence in an attempt to steer participants toward certain outcomes, or to push a private agenda. Certainly it is difficult enough just to pay attention to design and management issues of a Search Conference, let alone attempt to intervene in the content. Besides, managers who lose themselves in the content run the risk of provoking Bion's fight-flight group assumptions.

Sound Knowledge Base and Theoretical Framework

A competent Search Conference manager must have an in-depth understanding of the theoretical framework (Chapters Three through Six) upon which the method is based. On the surface, it looks possible to conduct a Search Conference in a fairly mechanical manner, running participants through the tasks and treating the event as if it were just another conventional training session. However, imposing activity upon the participants without reference to what is needed at the moment can have severe side effects. Also, in the absence of a clear understanding of the reasoning behind the process, it becomes tempting to take control of the group for the manager's own comfort, or to forcibly suppress dysfunctional group dynamics when they erupt. In either case, these moves defeat the conference's basic purpose of helping the participants form a community and learn to take responsibility for their own work.

However, this emphasis on theory before practice does not mean that the Search Conference method is rigid and inflexible. Far from it; the method itself offers tremendous flexibility within the limits set forth by the theoretical framework. The warning only underscores our emphasis on the need for the work to be informed by a base of theoretical knowledge.

Comparison of Differences in Conference Management

To illustrate the effect of theory on the conduct and outcome of large-group interventions, this section compares search conferencing with the Weisbord and Janoff (1995) Future Search process.

Basic Assumptions about Human Capacity

As discussed earlier, any group intervention theory begins with basic assumptions about people. Search conferencing assumes people to be purposeful (Ackoff and Emery, 1972), and to actively want to learn and take responsibility for their future. It also assumes that people can, under suitable conditions, become ideal-seeking, making choices among purposes in the interest of the total system. It thus has a built-in expectation that participants will welcome the conference process.

The Future Search literature takes a more psychotherapeutic view of humanity, regarding anxiety and the reduction of anxiety as major factors in planning and decision-making. "Every discovery brings heightened anxiety" (Weisbord, 1992, p. 103); eliciting values, dreams, and the like is an "enormous anxiety reducer" (p. 10); structured experience is one way "facilitators manage our own anxiety" (p. 65). If people are naturally anxious, then it follows that a large-group intervention will be fraught with anxiety, which can only be managed with no hope of allaying it completely.

A Search Conference is part of an intensive planning process, beginning with preconference preparation activities and extending beyond into postconference implementation. Participants are briefed on, if not involved in, every aspect of the purpose and method. Each stage of the Search Conference itself is clearly defined, work proceeds until clarity is achieved, and agreements are made before moving on to the next stage. The work of the entire conference builds cumulatively upon the agreements made in each of the previous stages. Once a conference is under way, people display high energy and interest, and rarely reveal any sign of anxiety.

On the other hand, Weisbord observes: "Transformative change, I believe, always means a journey through denial and chaos. It seems to me inevitable that we make the journey into confusion—even anger, frustration, despair . . . [People] tend to become agitated by external data—the world, the environment, history, complexity" (1992, pp. 53–68). Weisbord and Janoff (1995, p. 3) have observed that in their conferences, "Some feel a strong urge to run away." As another observer notes, "The process is calculated to throw participants into a form of chaos through data overload" (Bailey and Dupres, 1992, p. 513). Future Search proponents regard these reactions as essential to the success of their process.

However, it is possible to observe the same phenomena and draw different conclusions. The behavior described in the previous paragraph bears a very strong resemblance to that of a group operating under Bion's (1952) basic group assumption of flight. It can be argued that Future Search groups have a tendency to fall into the flight mode not because of any deep-seated psychological factors, but because something is preventing them from developing into creative working groups. We believe that some aspects of the process may well provide an alternative to human nature as an explanation of the observed behavior.

As Asch (1952) points out, increases in working group size increase members' need to orient themselves to their surroundings and to perceive that they are relating to a task that has significance and meaning for them. In a Future Search, participants are asked to perform skits and develop idealistic futures without reference to real-world goals. Other tasks involve attempting to analyze their system and its environment at the same time. These activities seem to us to run counter to the participants' need for enhanced orientation and significance, and thus to be very likely to trigger the basic group assumption of flight.

Weisbord and Janoff base much of their theory on Claes Janssen's "four-room apartment model" of psychological change (Janssen, 1982; Weisbord, 1992, pp. 101–103; Weisbord and Janoff, 1995, p. 63). They maintain that people must move through four emotional phases before they are motivated to change: contentment, denial, confusion, and renewal. "Understanding how we move through all four rooms together in our conference helps us accept feelings of anxiety, fear, powerlessness, without which we could not know certainty, security, and empowerment" (1995, p. 64).

However, our own observations—from twenty-five years of search conferencing with a wide variety of participants—suggest that the Janssen model falls short of explaining universal attributes of human behavior. In our experience, people rarely get stuck in negative and dysfunctional emotional states: on the contrary, they are usually delighted to be participants, and ready and willing to engage in task-oriented discussions.

These differences in observations undoubtedly reflect real differences in behavior among participants in the two types of large-group intervention under discussion. If anxiety and tension are regarded as essential, there is no reason—and indeed, no practical way—to eliminate these reactions. However, if they are seen as potential byproducts of conference design and participant orientation, then it is equally natural to seek a way around them. We view participants in the Search Conference as our fellow citizens, not as our clients, and we believe that the absence of anxiety and tension from the Search Conference environment establishes the soundness of our basic assumptions about human capacity.

Design Principle 2 and the Mixed Mode

Group interventions also embody some form of design principle, and the chosen principle and its application have a material effect on the outcome. In our view, Design Principle 1 and Design Principle 2 are mutually exclusive; one can set up a structure either to make decisions for people or to support the decisions they make for themselves. Search conferencing relies wholly on DP2. Future Searches employ elements from both. We believe that this alternation between design principles explains much of the behavior observed in Future Search conferences, as mixing the modes in this fashion carries a high risk of activating basic group assumptions, as discussed in Chapter Six.

Common Ground and Avoiding Conflict

In a large-group intervention designed to make practical plans for the future, people inevitably encounter areas of disagreement. The treatment of disagreement is thus a major feature of an intervention method. Search Conferences and Future Searches appear similar in that both set aside areas of disagreement and attempt to concentrate on the participants' common ground. However, they differ in the point at which conflict is set aside. A Search Conference rationalizes conflict; that is, the conference managers encourage participants to discuss things long enough to make sure that the disagreement is substantive rather than semantic, and that there is no obvious way to get both sides what they want on the issue. Only then is the matter moved to a formal disagree list and removed from the work of the community. This process draws a sharp line between areas of agreement—real common ground, which is normally much larger than expected—and areas of disagreement. We regard this process as an essential component of the search for common ground.

A Future Search moves away from areas of disagreement after much less discussion:

> We neither avoid nor confront the extremes. Rather, we put our energy into staking out the widest common ground all can stand on without forcing or compromise. This stance toward conflict is the most radical aspect of these conferences and a major break with the recent past. When we invite the right people, we will nearly always find unresolved conflicts and disagreements. *Yet we discourage conferees from "working" their differences.* Instead, we create a figure/ground reversal. We put the dysfunctional "shadow" dynamics *in the background.* People . . . tune in on different aspects of themselves— the more constructive and cooperative impulses [Weisbord, 1992, p. 7, emphasis added].

In our view, discouraging conferees from working their differences prevents them from clearly identifying their areas of agreement. As Asch noted, "The possibility for joint action rests equally upon the grasp of similarities and differences among participants" (1952, p. 131). The rationalization process treats conflict as one of the natural by-products of creative group activity. Disagreements allow participants to do a reality check on their ideas. "A dispute about a fact or an action, or even a quarrel, is basically an appeal to a deeper-lying unity . . . We do not argue about colors with the color blind" (Asch, 1952, p. 132).

The Future Search process builds in procedures designed to promote the avoidance of conflict by shortening the discussion of individual items. In most cases, small groups in Future Search conferences prepare lists of items similar to those prepared in Search Conferences, but they do not take the time to analyze them. These lists are then reported out to the large group and acknowledged, and groups move quickly on to their next task. This way conferees are, indeed, discouraged from "'working' their differences," but they do not work on their areas of agreement, either. Thus the apparent common ground that emerges includes an undifferentiated and unexamined array of data. Discussion flows smoothly over areas of potential disagreement, but the disagreements are still there, and are apt to resurface when the group gets to the action planning phase of the conference.

This is unfortunate. Disagreements about fundamental directions or goals seriously disrupt the sense of community when a group is at the action planning stage. For example, toward the end of one Future Search, observers noted a "lack of patience with other participants and the process" (Bailey and Dupre, 1992). In our view, this describes an outbreak of fight-flight group dynamics, but the observers interpreted it as a simple case of fatigue.

More recent Future Searches have included a session designed to develop "common future scenarios," which do provide a form of integration. In the course of these scenarios, "Sometimes, disagreements are raised. The ground rule is that we report the lists AS IS. . . . Anything that stirs up disagreement is reported as a potential future wished for by some" (Weisbord and Janoff, 1994, p. 5). This is a step in the right direction, but in our opinion it still tends to marginalize those who disagree with the majority opinion. The basic group assumptions—dependency, fight-flight and pairing—are easily activated when people in work groups feel that their ideas and dissenting opinions cannot be aired and fully examined in an open and honest manner. Thus the search for common ground and group harmony can backfire if it depends on avoiding or suppressing conflict.

Effective Communications

Large-group interventions by definition involve a great deal of intense communication among the participants and between the participants and the managers. The way in which a method deals with this transfer of factual and emotional information tends to set the tone—and to a large degree the content—of the resulting interventions. Asch's (1952) specifications—openness, shared field, psychological similarity, and trust—provide a useful yardstick for analyzing communications.

Openness

In a Search Conference, participants have a clear view of the purpose and process of the meeting, and all the data and conclusions the group generates appear on flip-chart paper posted on the walls. In a Future Search, by contrast, small groups are often preassigned and set to particular tasks with no discussion of group makeup. Openness and community-building are curtailed when people are designated to work as stakeholder representatives of special interest groups. Rather than emphasizing large-group community discussions, the Future Search entails having individuals privately complete worksheets. In fact, the first thirty to forty-five minutes of the Future Search begin in silence as individuals are absorbed in the task of filling out worksheets, then rewriting their private responses on flip charts for all to see. This is a variation on the nominal group technique. While this technique provides time for thoughtful individual reflection, it is not conducive to establishing a spirit of openness or community and democratic dialogue right from the start.

Shared Field

By conducting a community scan of the external environment, participants in the Search Conference learn to pool their perceptions of changes in the external environment, which results in a rich mosaic image of a shared field and a sense that they are all living in the same world. What affects one affects all. A shared field contextualizes the system in its environment. The common enemy is our major competitor, not the department down the hall. In a Future Search, participants are given the opportunity to share their collective concerns and to map environmental trends, but these tasks are mixed together with analyzing data about personal history and internal system issues. Having to keep different foci in mind at the same time makes it difficult to develop a vivid image of the system in its environment, thus significantly reducing the chances of establishing Acsh's condition of a shared field.

Psychological Similarity

Although participants at a Search Conference are selected to reflect the whole range of knowledge and interests involved in a system, they attend as individuals, speaking only for themselves. The conference process focuses their attention on their overall similarity to each other by highlighting their shared aspirations for the world and for their system before entering into discussion of specific problems. In a Future Search, participants are specifically regarded as stakeholders. They are segmented and identified by colored dots, and assigned to sit at designated and separate stakeholder tables. In addition, some of the stakeholder groups have no direct responsibility for the system in question, which further underlines the differences among them. This stakeholder identification tends to mask rather than enhance psychological similarity among participants, and makes it difficult for them to assume a nonrepresentative and collaborative stance.

Trust

In Asch's theory, the first three conditions are essential to produce the fourth, and the fourth spirals back to enhance the first three. Openness in communication leads to perceptions of a shared field and thus to knowledge of psychological similarity, and trust springing from psychological similarity allows openness to increase. Eventually, people learn to trust each other to take responsibility for actions on behalf of and in the interest of the whole community. In our view, the Search Conference mobilizes this process more effectively than the Future Search.

Community Building

Because the first session of the Search Conference is the launching pad for building community—which sets the tone for the entire event—it is important that this session gets off on the right foot. A Search Conference comes into being in the first session. People form a large group and engage in a face-to-face process of puzzle learning. This first session serves three major purposes: it generates data about significant trends and changes in the environment relevant to the formulation of future plans and strategies; it provides an experience for a shared context of the environment to emerge; and, by searching for desirable trends into the future, it elicits shared human ideals.

This is far more than an icebreaking exercise. Indeed, it is essential to avoid using that term for the opening session, so as to avoid misleading participants into saying (the next morning), "Well, that was good fun last night, now let's get on with the real work." Such a reaction would trivialize the central role of the contextual environment in long-term, active adaptive planning.

The first session also puts the stamp on manager-participant relations. No matter what the manager says, the participants will absorb their main message from what the manager does by way of acting out the egalitarian principles the Search Conference is designed to support. Thus the first session is critical both for setting the right tone and for establishing the right conditions for the creative working mode. Let's now take a look at some of the essential tasks for kicking off the first session.

Introductions and Briefings

During the introductory briefing, Search Conference managers should present an overview of the objectives, roles, structure, process, timetables, and essential details of the meeting. In most cases, the sponsor will introduce the overall purpose of the Search Conference. Apart from the normal formalities, managers must explain the plan and rationale for the design and process, as well as their role as managers. The plan, usually corresponding to the funnel design, illustrates the various phases and approximate starting and stopping times. It is drawn up on flip-chart paper and remains in full view throughout the conference. This serves to anchor time management and the responsibility of both managers and participants to honor the commitment to complete the event within the time allotted.

The duration of the introductory briefing will vary. However, this presentation should be simple and clear. It is important for Search Conference managers to be genuine and approachable. During the briefing, their demeanor should not give an impression of superior status or intellectual smugness. As noted, participants will learn more from what managers do than from what they say. No matter what the verbiage—even if the aims declared are democratic ones—people still tend to gauge the second-level messages sent by managers as the most valid. Briefings that sound like formal school-teacherly lectures convey an unspoken message that the Search Conference manager is above the audience, that he or she is the leader and they are the unknowing followers. People who are unable to let go of their lofty professional personas do not fare well as Search Conference managers. Delivering instructions in a condescending manner diminishes the conditions for effective communication.

As part of our briefing, we provide a quick overview of the Search Conference approach to planning. As a matter of practice, we emphasize to participants the importance of learning about the changes that are happening in the turbulent environment, and the need to plan in ways that are actively adaptive. We inform the large group that they will be invited to contribute their knowledge in the course of the conference.

Before we move directly into the first task, we conduct an expectations session. The process is relatively simple and straightforward. Participants are seated in groups of five to eight. We ask the groups to report their responses on flip-chart paper. Their task is to come up with answers to the question, "What are your expectations for the Search Conference?" We allocate no more than fifteen to twenty minutes for this task. When finished, a spokesperson from each small group provides a summary of his or her group's expectations to the whole community. For groups of strangers coming together, this task also provides an easy and structured way for them to get to know each other.

The briefing and expectations session create an open atmosphere. One word of caution: We advise against setting up a pre-designated seating arrangement. To promote Asch's condition of openness, it is very important for participants to feel that they are not walking into a setup. However, because we do want a heterogeneous mix of people at each table, after the expectations session but before the beginning of the first main task we informally ask people to sit together with people from different functions, or we ask them to count off by the number of tables in the room for random seating.

Setting the Ground Rules

As a preface to the first task, managers must make the ground rules for this session absolutely clear. The basic ground rule is a simple and nonnegotiable fact: *all perceptions are valid*. Managers must clearly state that all observations will be recorded and considered worthy of public examination. Once the session is in full swing, participants brainstorm and contribute their ideas and observations. The introduction should make clear that the Search Conference is focusing on the future and that participants will be examining all possibilities associated with the future. Hence, nobody can claim to have a privileged or superior view. During this phase, there should be no arguments about another person's statement, whether a contribution is right or wrong, probable or improbable, and so on.

Large-Group Brainstorming Sessions

The first task is conducted as a large-group activity. The Search Conference manager refers again to the open systems diagram and explains the importance of developing an appreciation of trends and changes in the contextual environment. Note that while jargon—specialized terminology—helps one grasp concepts and work at a theoretical level, it is extremely important to avoid using jargon with Search Conference participants, who need to focus on an immediate task. Thus in this briefing, the conference manager should use a phrase like "the world around us" for "contextual environment" and make similar substitutions for other terms not in common use. The manager reminds the participants that they are brainstorming for actual perceptions of changes that have been taking place in the world at large, and that they should observe the basic ground rule—that all perceptions are valid during the brainstorming session.

Participants are invited to contribute any significant changes that they have seen happen in the last five to seven years. During this session, Search Conference managers stand in front of the room and simply record on flip charts each person's perceptions and observations in phrases as close to the actual words spoken as possible. We do not paraphrase, interpret, or process other people's statements. If a person offers a contrary observation to one already made by someone else, that perception too is recorded. If someone challenges a person's statement, the manager should firmly but politely enforce the ground rule, allowing questions for clarification only. Again, as managers, we do no more than record these perceptions, and if necessary ask questions like: What have you seen happen in the world of work? . . . the family? or whatever major areas appear to be lacking.

As managers introduce and explain the task in everyday language and record perceptions as stated by participants, they set an example for the entire community. The brainstorming session reinforced by the ground rule brings into play the epistemological paradigm of direct perception, giving credence and value to it. Participants immediately come to experience the Search Conference meeting as participative and democratic as it was avowed to be. The session thus contributes to openness and begins the process of building trust.

The time frame of five to seven years for participants' perceptions elicits "embryos of social change," events that may herald significant changes to come or other major value shifts and social movements (Emery, 1977). As participants add to the list of perceptions and the data base grows, they become aware that they are all living in the same world. The mass of data produced is taped up on the walls where it stays for the duration of the Search Conference. The flip-chart pages continuously remind participants that the contextual environment is still out there, shaping their future and their plans. This is important because, in the later stages of the conference, it is easy for participants to become so immersed in the details of their own operations that they forget the influence of the environment. It is also useful to tell the community that if they find an important piece of data missing from the list after their group work is done, they may add it to the list provided they tell the community when they do so.

The first session serves the purpose of community building; individuals realize their interdependence as they develop their perception of a shared context. The success of this first session can be gauged by whether the community has moved into a creative working mode. This can be judged by the levels of energy and positive affect, as well as the quality of the group products. The success of this first phase is as an incentive to further creative work and community learning.

Key Management Skills

The functional skills of the Search Conference manager consist mainly of managing the context in which work groups accomplish their tasks. Managing the context means managing the boundaries of group work. This includes providing clear definitions of tasks, determining the forum in which work gets done (large versus small groups), setting and negotiating time constraints in harmony with the rhythms of groups, integrating small-group reports, and of course rationalizing conflict. Defining and regulating boundaries is a key management responsibility.

Providing Clear Task Instructions

Managing the context of a Search Conference hinges upon the ability to provide clear task instructions. Clear tasks set the boundaries for self-management. Therefore it is critically important for the Search Conference manager to clearly describe task instructions to groups, giving explicit requirements for the format of reports, amount of time for a given task, and so on. In other words, task instructions must clearly state the objective, the expected output requirements, and the amount of time available for completing the task. For example, the task instructions given to the Most Desirable Future groups might be as follows: "Based on your analysis of what is going on in the environment, come up with five statements on your flip chart that describe the most desirable future for the world in the year 2000. You will have forty-five minutes to complete this group task, and then a member from each group will report the group's list in a five-minute presentation to the community." If clear specifications like this are not provided, a group may bring back a long list of statements, making the task of integration difficult. Therefore, clearly specify and emphasize that reports should be limited to the stated number of key statements; however, always remember to convey the task instructions in a collaborative manner.

Exhibit 9.1 contains a sampling of instructions for each of major conference tasks. Since each Search Conference design and circumstance will have its own unique features and conditions, these are at best generic instructions.

Exhibit 9.1. Sample Task Instructions.

Environmental Scan (large-group brainstorming session)

"What changes have you seen happening in the world over the last five to seven years that strike you as significant or novel?"

Desirable Future for the World (small groups)

"Based on your analysis of desirable trends in the environment, come up with five statements on your flip chart that describe the most desirable future for the world in the year 2000. You will have forty-five minutes to complete this group task, and then a member from each group will report the group lists in a brief five-minute presentation to the community."

Probable Future for the World (small groups)

"Construct a list of five statements on your flip charts that are descriptive of what the probable future of the world will look like if current trends continue. In other words, if we do nothing and current trends continue, what will the probable state of the world be in the year 2000? You will have forty-five minutes to complete this group task, and then a member from each group will report the group lists in a brief five-minute presentation to the community."

History Session (large group)

"What are the milestones and turning points that have shaped your system? What major events or historical developments over the years are significant to making your system what it is today? What is unique about the history and evolution of your system?"

Present System Analysis (large-group brainstorming session)

"What aspects of your current system do you want to keep? Drop? Create?"

Desirable Future for the System (small groups)

"Describe the most desirable future for your system in the year 2000 in five or six key statements. Consider these statements to be your strategic goals. Your group will have ninety minutes to complete this task and we will begin taking reports at 3:00 P.M."

Dealing with Constraints (small groups)

"Identify a list of the most serious constraints, together with strategies for dealing with or getting around them. You have forty-five minutes to complete this task."

Action Planning (small groups)

"Develop a set of action plans for implementing your strategic goals. Your plans for action should specify exactly what activities need to occur by a given date, stating who will be responsible and provide support. What other people not currently in attendance need to be involved in the implementation of your plans?"

While it is important to provide clear and specific task instructions, these should be limited to the minimal critical specifications for group work. In other words, the Search Conference provides whole tasks, with clearly defined outputs; the group itself has control over how it will manage and complete its tasks.

Integration of Group Reports

The Search Conference is designed to strengthen and build upon natural human interdependencies by producing an integrated community product. This community product is a strategic plan or vision of the future that everybody is in agreement with and is committed to making happen. Therefore integration of the group reports is a crucially important management task—this is how important community decisions are made. Integrating group reports is a deliberation that requires the community to make judgments and decisions about those points members share in common (their common ground) and that they can agree to separate from those points that are the cause of disagreement. For example, the Search Conference manager helps the community to integrate group reports on the desirable and probable futures of the world, their most desirable future for their system (deciding upon key strategic goals), and the priorities they place on their strategic goals and action plans.

One method for integrating group reports is to assign a number to each of the statements on a given report. Then the community is asked to look for statements from the other reports that are identical or similar enough to be combined. These items are assigned the same number. Items that stand alone are assigned a different number after the commonalities are determined. Two kinds of questions are then raised. First, questions of clarification regarding items on the report are surfaced and discussed. After everyone is clear about the meaning of the items in question, the Search Conference manager then raises the critical question: "Are there any items on the report that anyone cannot live with or is unwilling to endorse as a community product?" If no disagreements are raised, this report becomes an integrated community product. However, strong disagreements often do surface, and the Search Conference manager must skillfully rationalize the conflict.

Another method for integrating group report is what is called the cut-and-paste technique. With this method, items on each of the group reports are cut apart in strips of paper that can easily be moved around on the wall. The process works like this. Each small group first reports their strategic goal items for a desirable future system, and the Search Conference manager follows up by testing to see whether each item is understood by the whole community. Once clarification checks have been made, each small group is instructed to cut apart their strategic goal items on separate strips of flip-chart paper. Then they are asked to come up to the front of the room and to post their strips on the wall alongside other strips that have essentially the same meaning or common elements. At this point, the Search Conference should step back and allow participants to self-manage their way through this task. Once strips have been posted, the Search Conference manager can engage the large group in a discussion around which strips should stay together and which ones should be moved, or stand alone. This activity usually takes several iterations until everyone is in agreement with the item clusters.

Conflict Rationalization Skills

When there is conflict over an item, the issue is first debated in the large group. If the parties still dispute the item or statement, the Search Conference manager can ask the people who are in conflict to immediately form a negotiating team, leave the large group, and see if they can come to some resolution. In the meantime, the integration session continues. If the negotiating team comes back empty-handed, the disputed item goes on the disagree list.

In this process, all of the richness of the different reports is retained and nothing gets lost. By precisely sorting out items the community agrees to and supports from those that are points of serious contention, the area of common ground is clarified. Once an item is placed on the disagree list, it ceases to get further attention; the community continues to move forward on those tasks for which there is agreement, mutual support, and positive energy. The integrated reports, as well as the disagree lists, are considered community products, which are taped on the wall in a prominent place. From that point, the integrated reports serve as benchmarks and guides for the direction of future work. They also serve to remind the community of the extent of its common ground and ideals.

When the Search Conference manager uses this rational approach to dealing with conflict, basic group assumptions are managed and kept in check. Work groups do not feel threats to their security or identity since the focus of activity is always directed toward matters they accept and support. When the Search Conference manager introduces and uses the rationalization of conflict model, work groups know there is a way to deal with conflict and strong emotions in a nondestructive manner. This method counterbalances the fear of aggression, so work groups do not fall prey to the dependency group assumption (Sullivan, 1995). Similarly, the fight-fight dynamic does not arise in its negative form, because work groups remain focused on tasks they have energy for. In addition, the integration of data from different work groups during each phase of the conference builds toward a community product, neutralizing any tendencies toward an us-versus-them atmosphere. When basic group assumption activity has been managed in this way, work groups in the Search Conference operate in a task-oriented mode, transmuting the energy of unconscious group forces into their conscious dimensions. When work groups are in the flow of the creative working mode, participants make sophisticated use of the basic assumptions (Rioch, 1975). Instead of being dependent, participants become dependable to each other. Instead of succumbing to fight-flight group dynamics and becoming hostile or withdrawn, participants are courageous and assertive. And instead of building castles in the air and resorting to wishful thinking or blind optimism, participants are pragmatic and creative.

Managing Group Rhythms

The management of a Search Conference is both a science and an art. The artistic dimension comes into play when managing the pace of large- and small-group work. Because the Search Conference is not a rigidly programmed event, the community must be allowed to work at its own pace and in its own style. This means that the managers will need to attune themselves to group rhythms, which often vary considerably through the course of a conference. In some phases, there may be exciting spurts of group creativity— the noise level in the room is high as animated discussions permeate the atmosphere and things just seem to be falling into place. At other times, groups may reach a plateau when nothing much appears to be happening. There are phases when direction seems to be lost—matters are half-raised, half-explored or apparently agreed, only to be set aside to be returned to later. This rhythmic progression is not like the linear step-by-step sequence through a prepared classroom lesson, or the sequential program of a traditional training workshop. Instead, learning in Search Conference groups goes around in circles.

When the community or the small groups appear to have reached a plateau, Search Conference managers can sometimes help if they provide a clear and acceptable summary of what the conference has already accomplished. Such a summary can be reassuring to the community insofar that it shows them that they are making real progress. It may also aid them to digest what they have done. However, summaries should be offered very sparingly and sometimes not at all; by exercising too much control—or even being perceived as wanting to do so—a conference manager runs the risk of evoking basic group assumptions. Search Conference managers should not be preoccupied with details of the group's tasks; such meddling will surely lead to an erosion of confidence in the group's ability to work and learn.

Sometimes when groups reach a plateau they are merely in a resting phase. If Search Conference managers begin to show too much anxiety when the community is in a resting phase, they inadvertently communicate a negative and harmful message. Similarly, managers may communicate a negative message if they show agitation about whether there is enough time to complete a task. Given enough of these messages, a community will drop out of the learning mode by becoming defensive, withdrawing from the task, or saying, in effect, "Well, you show us how to do it!" If this occurs and is not corrected, the community will show a lack of ownership and commitment to the end product.

These difficulties and subtleties emphasize the need for two Search Conference managers. A manager who works solo, no matter how highly skilled or experienced, is at risk of missing cues or misinterpreting behaviors. By working in tandem, managers can more readily stay abreast of the group rhythm. While one manager can attend to the content of what is being said by the group, recording statements on flip charts, the other manager can devote more attention to listening to the music of the group and its underlying dynamics. Thus, two managers can easily stay attuned to both the content and process of the group, improving the chance that one or the other will spot something that needs to be done and take independent action while there is still time to do it smoothly, and intervene in ways that sustain the creative working mode.

After the Search Conference

No two processes of implementation are the same, but the design principle adopted for this phase can make or break it. In our early experiences, we occasionally saw that when the community met for the first time following the Search Conference, it organized itself into a traditional committee structure. And frequently supervisors or managers put the brakes on the implementation process by second-guessing and meddling in the work of action teams. The consequences of this mode of organizing the implementation phase are quite predictable: rapid decline in energy and enthusiasm, territorial bickering, refusal to address difficult issues, foot-dragging, and a general dissipation of the gains made in the Search Conference.

To avoid slippage and regression back to business as usual, the Search Conference manager can play a valuable role by educating the conference community, and particularly the sponsors, on how to organize for successful implementation. At minimum, the conference community will need to come to grips with the question of organizing itself to ensure the implementation of its action plans. The major challenge after the Search Conference is to maintain continuity of organization so that participants retain responsibility and authority for implementation of action plans. Unfortunately, most existing organizations are structured according to Design Principle 1. Organizational reentry of action planning teams should be such that they are granted the authority and legitimacy to carry their plans forward. Action planning teams need sanctioning from sponsors; they need access to resources, information, and time to meet. Parallel learning structures can be set up that allow action planning teams to continue their work unimpeded by bureaucratic constraints (Bushe and Shani, 1990). In addition, action planning teams can establish *link-up groups*—co-opting other people in the organization who need to be either directly involved, informed, or consulted as the process of implementation unfolds.

Therefore, if sponsors and participants wish to maintain the momentum of the work and creative energy as experienced and generated in the Search Conference, they will need to find ways of circumventing structural impediments to communication and action. In some cases, sponsors have elected to completely redesign their organizations after the Search Conference into a self-managing Design Principle 2 structure. In these cases, the Search Conference will be followed up by a *Participative Design Workshop*—a meeting that employs specialized methodology for designing organizations so that they meet human as well as economic and technical requirements. To learn more about the method and its effects in organizations that have adopted it, see *Participative Design for Participative Democracy* (M. Emery, 1993).

SOME RULES OF THUMB FOR SEARCH CONFERENCE MANAGERS

Be sure that you fully understand the theoretical framework and concepts underlying the Search Conference. Try to acquire some experience in applying and utilizing these concepts by helping an experienced person run a conference before striking out on your own.

Explain the overall plan and provide clear, well-defined tasks for each phase.

Manage time wisely, but not mechanically. Provide clear markers for the timing of tasks. For example, "We need to be action planning by midmorning of the third day." Let participants know the game plan and timing of all activities so they can share the responsibility for time management. Time management is one of the most skilled managerial tasks as it involves fine judgments about how to juggle and sequence tasks, balancing large- and small-group discussions, allowing time for integration of data, managing group dynamics, and still finishing within the allotted time.

Keep the funnel design and plan of the Search Conference in a prominent place throughout the meeting. This way the whole community can see where they are at any point relative to the amount of time available. Experienced managers constantly refer participants to the agenda, reinforcing and increasing their responsibility for self-management. Participants are inclined to become engrossed in intermediate stages when the plan is not constantly before them, but they are very disappointed if they run out of time for action planning.

Avoid identifying people as representing stakeholder interests. If small groups have been deliberately composed for diversity, explain the rationale for this up front so as to preserve the condition of openness.

Monitor but do not intervene in small-group work.

Make sure to change small-group composition every couple of sessions. We have learned that small cohesive groups can form quickly, and tend to reinforce themselves through competition with other small groups. This interferes with the process of building a cooperative community. When group composition needs to change, use a totally open and randomized selection process right in front of the group. Explain to the participants that they need the chance of working together with as many different people as possible during the course of the conference.

If participants want to ask extensive questions about the Search Conference process, tell them you will answer such questions during breaks. This serves to keep attention focused on the conference purpose.

Ask participants to refrain from using individual notepads or working out responses in writing before transferring them to flip-chart paper. Private notes contradict the condition of openness. Also, any process that depends on individual writing will disadvantage people who are illiterate. One of the great advantages of the Search Conference is its universality through the medium of spoken language and its ability to use this oral social cement to heighten community.

Stay within the limits of your role as designer and manager, leaving the responsibility for content and outcome to participants.

Manage all plenary sessions toward the integration of work into a community product, using the rationalization of conflict model.

Be task oriented, but with a light-hearted and positive attitude.

Chapter Ten

The Search Conference
Step-by-Step

This chapter provides an in-depth look at a real Search Conference project. We describe the events that occurred in considerable detail, from the initial planning to the dialogue among participants in the conference and all the way through to the follow-up activities in the implementation phase. This story provides a concrete example of what a Search Conference in action is all about, illustrating how it differs from conventional top-down and expert-driven approaches, and also highlights some of the typical dilemmas and decisions that Search Conference managers and sponsors face when attempting to put theory into practice.

Ron Purser and Linzy Waters conducted the Search Conference described here for the purpose of developing a community-based economic development plan for impoverished neighborhoods on the West Side of Chicago. Planning for a community or issue-based Search Conference often requires a great deal of activism and community organizing skills on the part of the Search Conference manager, and this case provides a good example of the types of activities and challenges involved when working with underorganized systems. When we get into the account of the conference, Ron often writes in the first person, as he was there and can tell the story directly.

Background

In January 1994, President Clinton announced the introduction of the Empowerment Zone and Enterprise Community (EZ/EC) Program. The stated goal of the program, which is administered by the U.S. Department of Housing and Urban Development (HUD), was to start the process of rebuilding blighted inner-city communities. A comprehensive community-based strategic planning process would be used as a process for linking economic, physical, and human development to build viable communities, create true economic opportunities, and foster a vibrant civic culture in the nation's distressed urban areas.

HUD designation as an Empowerment Zone would bring with it $100 million in Social Service Block Grant funds over a two-year period, as well as tax credits, waivers, and other financial incentives. Chicago was one of many cities that immediately began working for such designation.

In June 1994, West Side activists—working closely in a partnership formed of community representatives, the City of Chicago Department of Planning and Development, and a variety of other city agencies and financial institutions—developed a community-driven application and submitted it to HUD. This application also contained input from two other Chicago communities interested in acquiring Empowerment Zone designation. Together, these three groups (or clusters) applied to HUD for designation as the Chicago Empowerment Zone. The empowerment zone application included a broad range of community development concepts organized around seven initiative areas: human and organizational capacity, health and human services, youth futures, economic empowerment, affordable and accessible housing, public safety, and cultural diversity. HUD received seventy-eight applications, coming from just about every blighted city in the country, from New York and Los Angeles to Gary, Indiana and Newark, New Jersey.

On December 21, 1994, Chicago was designated one of six federal urban empowerment zones. The West Cluster Collaborative (WCC) is the key institution responsible for the West Side of Chicago's Empowerment Zone designation. The mission of the WCC organization is to coordinate the implementation and fulfillment of long-term strategic plans within the empowerment zone. The formation of the WCC resulted in six committees focused on economic development, health and human services, education, housing, public relations (which produces the newsletter), and public information (which coordinates membership and distributes information).

Empowerment Zone Principles

The framework for the Empowerment Zone program was developed around four key principles:

- *Economic opportunity.* The establishment of situations that promote economic opportunity is considered the first priority. Developing economic environments that stimulate the creation of jobs for local residents, job training for upwardly mobile careers, entrepreneurial initiatives, and small business expansion are the key elements of this principle.

- *Sustainable community development.* This initiative supports a holistic approach to community economic development. Its goal is the coordination of development initiatives affecting economic life, physical well-being, environmental health, and personal development into a unified strategic plan. Economic revitalization must be built around neighborhoods, not governments; focus on the development of human scale services and buildings rather than massive projects and bureaucracies; design balanced communities instead of unresponsive and isolated government programs; and promote restoration of human and natural resources.

- *Community-based partnerships.* One of the most interesting parts of this program is its concept of developing new partnerships. This means that community residents, small business owners, government agencies, community-based organizations, health care providers, educators, and all those considered stakeholders in the community take part in the planning and implementing of this program. The HUD guidelines specify two underlying requirements. One is that community residents must play a decisive role in planning how their communities are developed. The other is that community empowerment cannot take place solely through the use of public resources. It takes the added involvement of both private and nonprofit support to revitalize the community.

- *Strategic vision for change.* Creation of this community-driven vision forms the basis for the development of a revitalization strategic plan. It focuses all of a community's concern into a single, holistic document, the road map for the community's future.

Searching for a Sponsor

Given the collaborative thrust of the empowerment zone initiative, the Search Conference method seemed to be an ideal approach for ensuring the grassroots participation of zone residents in a community-based strategic planning process. We received a call from Abu Bakr Nurruddin, a West Side community organizer, who was seeking help in developing a strategic planning process for the West Cluster Empowerment Zone based on broad participation from diverse coalitions within the community. In June 1994, before Chicago officially received its designation as an empowerment zone, we met with Abu and several other West Side community organizers to assess their readiness to sponsor a Search Conference, as well as to educate them on the method. While interest and enthusiasm for sponsoring a Search Conference for the West Side was high, at this time most people were preoccupied with completing the federal application for HUD.

Over the course of the summer, we made several more informational presentations to West Side organizers, and Abu became an advocate of the method. Again, despite the interest in the Search Conference method itself, no group, committee chair, or political figure seemed willing to step forward to take the risk of sponsoring one. The idea of sponsoring and conducting Search Conferences on the West Side as a means for empowering local and community residents in the strategic planning process was put on hold.

Once Chicago did receive its official designation as an Empowerment Zone, discussions resumed. Because economic development was the center of community revitalization efforts, Abu advised us to contact Mary Nelson, director of the economic development committee for the West Cluster Collaborative. In our initial meeting, Mary instantly saw the usefulness of the Search Conference as a method for developing a common vision of economic development among diverse coalitions, agencies, financial institutions, and city officials, and as a means for building new collaborative relationships, strategic alliances, and networks. She also recognized how the democratic process of the Search Conference method was congruent with the Empowerment Zone's philosophy of active citizen involvement and participation. Seeing the fit between the method and the need for community-based planning, Mary proposed that the economic development committee sponsor the first Search Conference for the West Cluster Empowerment Zone.

Planning the Conference

The planning team for the conference met five times over the course of three and a half months, from mid February through late May 1995. Here is a brief synopsis of the activities that were addressed at each of the meetings, to give you a sense of how the planning of the conference evolved over time.

February 15: We met with Mary Nelson, Abu Bakr Nurruddin, and two other community organizers to outline the work of the planning team. We also gave the two new planning team volunteers some background on the Search Conference method. We advised the group that the planning team needed to include a broader representation of people from the West Cluster community. The group decided to send a letter to members of the economic development committee, inviting them to join the newly formed planning team.

March 9: In this second meeting, four new people from the community showed up, ready and willing to volunteer their time to the planning team. The composition of the planning team now consisted of the chair of the economic development committee and one other member of that committee, two community organizers, three nonprofit agency directors, and a banking officer. We saw the key tasks for this meeting as reintroducing the Search Conference concept, defining the purpose of the conference, and beginning work on participant selection by introducing the community reference system process.

After informal introductions, we explained the features of the Search Conference event and provided a jargon-free overview of the open systems approach to planning. We then engaged the planning team in a discussion to clarify the overall purpose of the conference. The planning team agreed that the conference task would be to build a common vision of economic development for the West Cluster Empowerment Zone, and that other issues, such as public safety, housing, and education—while extremely important—were not the focus of the conference. This discussion led to some fairly cogent statements about the main purpose of the conference. All during this process, one of us used a flip chart to capture the main assertions that people were making. We agreed to condense and wordsmith the ideas the group generated into a purpose statement that we would present at the next planning meeting.

Following this, we moved on to explain the community reference system. All twenty members of the economic development committee were considered to be a core group that would be invited. In addition to this core group, we had the planning team brainstorm the key institutions, constituencies, and sectors that had an interest in helping to achieve the conference purpose, or whose participation would be critical to the success of the conference. Seven sectorial groups were identified: city government, state agencies, the Chicago Transit Authority (CTA), financial institutions, nonprofit community development organizations, industrial and manufacturing training centers, and other major institutions (hospitals, research facilities, and universities in the area). We asked each member of the planning team to take one of the seven sectors and generate a list of names of people likely to contribute to the goals of the Search Conference. We instructed them to bring their lists of names with them to the next planning meeting, where we would begin to develop more stringent selection criteria. We also volunteered to write a draft of an invitation letter.

March 15: At this meeting, we presented to the planning team the revised statement of purpose and goals for the conference: "To develop a shared vision of economic revitalization for the Westside, with a plan for achieving the vision, that identifies existing and potential resources, which enhances our capacity to work together, making it a national model." The team ratified and approved this statement. Next, we asked the planning team to develop a set of criteria for the selection of participants. The key criterion for participation centered around determining whether individuals had knowledge of existing or potential resources for economic development. From there, the team discussed their lists of potential participants name by name, attempting to gauge how well each individual met the selection criteria. After a final tally, several sectorial areas were still underrepresented in terms of potential participants. Several planning team members volunteered to track down and identify additional individuals in those underrepresented sectors before the next planning meeting. We also reviewed the draft of the invitation letter, and Mary Nelson took on the responsibility of revising it.

The planning team also set the date for the Search Conference as June 2–3, 1995, deciding to hold it at one of the nearby corporate conference centers. We proposed that the Search Conference be held for a full two and a half days, but the planning team as a whole regarded that as an unrealistic expectation. Knowing their own system and the potential participants better than we did, the planning team felt that people from these sectors simply would not commit to more than a day and a half. There were also budgetary constraints to contend with. We trusted their judgment, but informed them that a condensed Search Conference design always carries with it the risk of diluting the outcomes. Given the amount of time we had already invested in making this Search Conference happen on the West Side, we all decided that we would have to work within the constraints.

April 6: By this meeting, the planning team had identified and selected participants for the conference. The final list was reviewed and approved. Invitation letters and registration forms were sent a few days after the planning meeting. A sample copy of the invitation letter appears in Exhibit 10.1. The planning team discussed the need to create a preconference information packet, along with a West Side Economic Development resource directory. Several members of the planning team volunteered to take on this task. We decided to send preconference materials to participants as soon as their completed registration forms came in. Mary Nelson's administrative assistant provided us information on the accommodations of The Lodge, a conference center at Hamburger University. We made our needs known with regard to the room setup, number of flip charts, meal times, and so forth. Mary Nelson also gave us an update on her fundraising efforts, reporting that five local financial institutions, along with the MacArthur Foundation (whose liaison personnel were also invited as participants), pledged to make contributions to cover the costs of the event.

May 11: This planning meeting attended to final preparations for the conference. We presented a rough sketch of the Search Conference design, outlining start and stop times for each of the major phases. We made some minor but important adjustments to the schedule, such as changing the knock-off time on the first night from ten to nine o'clock. The planning team wanted to ensure that there was plenty of time for informal gatherings and

Exhibit 10.1. Invitation Letter for
West Cluster EZ/ED Search Conference.

WEST CLUSTER EZ/ED COMMITTEE
c/o Bethel New Life, Inc.
367 N. Karlov
Chicago, Illinois 60624
(312) 826–5540 826–5728 FAX

April 10, 1995

Robert Wharton, Director
Program Operations & Development
224 N. Des Plaines
Chicago, Illinois 60606

Dear Bob,
The Economic Development Committee of the West Cluster of the
Chicago Empowerment Zone cordially invites you to participate in a
major planning event to develop key strategies for economic development with the West Cluster Zone area which will be held Friday-
Saturday, June 2–3rd at McDonald's "Lodge." Because space is limited,
this is a by-invitation-only effort.
    The overall purpose of this Search Conference is to develop a
shared vision of economic revitalization for the West Side:

- with a plan for achieving the vision
- that identifies existing and potential resources
- which enhances our capacity to work together
- making it a national model of community economic development.

The West Cluster EZ Economic Development Committee, with
approval and commendation from the Cluster, has chosen to use the
Search Conference approach as it is a highly participative method of
strategic planning. This approach is designed to build community,
foster collaborative group interactions, and provide a mechanism in
which we can forge creative and long-lasting partnerships critical to the
West Side economic revitalization. The expected outcome of this
conference (limited to a total of 40 people) will be a set of strategic
vision goals for economic development along with a concrete plan for
implementation. The Search Conference will be managed by Ron
Purser from Loyola University and his graduate student, Linzy Waters.

**Exhibit 10.1. Invitation Letter for
West Cluster EZ/ED Search Conference, Cont'd.**

This is a working conference. Everyone will have the opportunity to put their knowledge and ideas to work. There will be no lectures, no speeches, no sales pitches, only honest and lively discussions, creative thinking and downright hard work focusing on producing plans that can be implemented and actualized by people on the West Side.

This is a demanding conference. It will require your full partici-pation. Because of the intensity and seriousness of this effort, we are holding it off-site with the expectation that you stay overnight at the conference center, Hamburger University, starting at 1 P.M. on Friday, June 2nd and ending on Saturday (June 3rd) at 5 P.M. Enclosed is a registration form which you will need to return with your payment at the latest by May 10th to EZ/ED, 367 N. Karlov, Chicago, Illinois 60624. To ensure the success of this conference, it is critical that you plan to stay for the whole event. To make it affordable, we are asking not-for-profit/ community participants to pay $25 and corporate/government to pay for the full costs of $125 each. This covers both the costs of the meals and the overnight lodging. We are seeking corporate sponsors to contribute $1,000 to help defray the costs of the community participants.

Approximately 40 people will participate in this event and hopefully you will accept our invitation to be one of them. We believe you have an important contribution to make, that your knowledge and perspective of the issues related to economic revitalization are a key piece of the planning puzzle. Your participation, along with others who will attend, represent a microcosm of the planning community.

It is our hope to pull together a Resource Directory on economic development for the West Side. There is a lot of great information available, and the Center for Neighborhood Technology is working with us to assemble the information. Enclosed is some beginning information to "tickle your interest."

If you have any questions about the arrangements at the conference center or your registration, please contact Lea Davis (312) 826–5540. If you have any questions regarding the Conference itself or participa-tion, contact Mary Nelson, Chair, at (313) 826–5540.

Sincerely,

Mary Nelson, Chair
West Cluster EZ/ED Committee

socializing after hours. At this point, only twenty-six people had sent in registration forms. We had invited nearly sixty participants, predicting that at least twenty to twenty-five people would be unable to accept the invitation due to scheduling conflicts or other personal commitments. Many of those invited had indicated interest in attending the conference, but had not made a final commitment. Each member of the planning team volunteered to make personal phone calls to those who were still pending.

The conference managers made plans to meet one week before the event to make final adjustments to the design, as well as to coordinate their roles and responsibilities for each of the conference tasks. Exhibit 10.2 shows the final design for the conference.

At the Conference

We reached the Lodge at Hamburger University several hours before kick-off time. Lea Davis (the administrative assistant to the planning team) was already there and had set up a registration table upon which lay all the name badges for participants. There appeared to be quite a few badges on the table! Lea informed us that registration had grown to forty-five people, and that they had to begin turning away a number of people at the last minute. We immediately had to make last-minute design adjustments in terms of gauging proper table and seating arrangements, as well as estimating the time that reports would take for each of the tasks.

The beauty and quiet of the natural surroundings, as well as the amenities of this conference center, provided ideal social-island conditions. One of the intentions for convening this conference was to provide the atmosphere in which people could get to know each other informally.

After checking into our rooms and touring the conference facility, we set out to get the meeting room in order. We arranged tables and chairs, set up flip chart easels, and prepared our initial briefing presentation on a flip chart in front of the room. Also, in preparation for the first large-group brainstorming task, we brought two more flip charts to the front of the room. It is essential that these small details be taken care of well before the official starting time.

Exhibit 10.2. Final Design: West Cluster Search Conference on Economic Development (June 2–3, 1995).

Friday, June 2

1:00 P.M. INTRODUCTORY PLENARY SESSION
- sponsor's welcome and statement of purpose
- briefing on Search Conference
- overview of agenda
- expectations session

1:45 INTRODUCTION TO GROUND RULES

2:00 PLENARY: ENVIRONMENTAL SCAN

(Changes in the World brainstorming session)

2:45 SMALL GROUP SESSION: DESIRABLE & PROBABLE FUTURES OF THE WORLD IN THE YEAR 2005
- 6 groups with 7–8 persons
- 3 groups work on Desirable Futures, the other 3 groups work on Probable Futures
- Each group will report out 4 scenarios

3:15 PLENARY: REPORTS AND INTEGRATION SESSION

4:00 SMALL GROUP SESSION: IMPLICATIONS AND IMMEDIATE OPPORTUNITIES
- Each group selects 2–3 scenarios/trends and identifies implications of what these trends mean to our strategic future for economic development
- Each group will report their findings

4:30 PLENARY: REPORTING SESSION

5:00 FREE TIME

6:15 DINNER

7:00 PLENARY: HISTORY OF THE WEST SIDE

8:00 PLENARY: PRESENT SYSTEM ANALYSIS (start)
- Brainstorm Lists of What to Keep, Drop, Create

9:00 P.M. CLOSING COMMENTS

Saturday, June 3

8:30 A.M. PLENARY: REVIEW AGENDA

8:45 PLENARY: PRESENT SYSTEM ANALYSIS (continued)

9:30 SMALL GROUP SESSION: DESIRABLE FUTURE OF ECONOMIC DEVELOPMENT FOR THE WEST CLUSTER
- Group Task: Develop shared/common visions for what the WCEZ will look like in the year 2005 with good economic development

Exhibit 10.2. Final Design: West Cluster Search Conference on Economic Development (June 2–3, 1995), Cont'd.

10:00	SMALL GROUP SESSION: STRATEGIC GOALS FOR THE NEXT 3–5 YEARS

- how do we get to the future?
- strategic goals should be seen as the means for accomplishing the shared visions generated in previous task.
- major goal statements should:
  - be long-term and strategic in nature
  - capitalize on existing and potential opportunities, build on strengths
  - overcome and deal with "issues" and "constraints"
  - each small group should pursue and develop 3–4 Strategic Goals which are linked to the shared vision

11:30	PLENARY REPORTING SESSION

- take two group reports before lunch

12:00	FREE TIME
12:30	LUNCH
1:00 P.M.	PLENARY REPORTING SESSION (continued)
1:45	PLENARY INTEGRATION SESSION

- agreement on key strategic goal clusters

2:15	PLENARY: FORMATION OF ACTION PLANNING GROUPS

- self-selection of action planning groups around strategic goal clusters

2:30	SMALL GROUPS: ACTION PLANNING SESSION

- go over criteria for developing good action plans

4:00	PLENARY REPORTING SESSION
4:45	CLOSING CEREMONY
5:00	ADJOURN

Afternoon Kick-off

Mary began by welcoming participants and restating the purpose for convening the conference. Ron proceeded by introducing the concept of open systems planning, emphasizing the importance of building a community able to learn and plan together. Linzy reviewed the plan for the conference, referring to the funnel design diagram. He then started the informal task of asking participants at each of the tables to take twenty minutes to introduce themselves, and to discuss their expectations for the conference.

Twenty minutes later, Linzy said, "We like to have the reports from the respective groups by having the spokesperson summarize the hopes and expectations, keeping your comments very brief. Then we would like for each person at the table to stand up and introduce themselves to the whole community." A woman from a table near the front of the room volunteered to go first. She began by stating, "My name is Betty Boston and I am the West Side Small Business executive director. Also, I am the secretary to the board of directors of the West Cluster. I wear several different hats in the community. As far as expectations for this conference, our group wants to influence the politics of economic development that is happening on the West Side. We also want to really work toward having true economic development by, for, and with the people for the good of the whole." The expectations session set the stage for the first Search Conference task.

Ron spoke next, introducing the ground rules for the conference:

What I would like to do now is to talk about the ground rules for the conference. The number one ground rule is that *all perceptions are valid.* At least
during the generation of ideas, we have to honor everyone's perceptions. They
go up on the flip charts, if you have an opinion and someone else has a contrary opinion, that's fine. That will go up on the flip chart as well. We will have
time to discuss these, and battle it out if we need to; it doesn't mean that we
can't disagree. But in the initial phase, in the idea generation phase, all perceptions are valid. The second ground rule is that what we're aiming to accomplish here is a community product. And what I mean by that is everything
that we do as far as data generation has to be public. It has to be in open view,
and that is why we have the easels and flip charts. Each table will post its work
on the flip charts. The whole idea is that we are trying to build a common data
base as a community. Everything is going to be discussed publicly, so that there
will be no room for hidden agendas.

After introducing the ground rules, Ron proceeded to move the conference directly into the first brainstorming task:

This now sets the stage for our first task. We are going to do a scan, brainstorm
as a group to see what is going on out there in the world. That is our first task.
Now, we want to ask you to think about what types of change that have been
going on out there in the world in the past five to ten years that are significant.

Trends that we need to be aware of and pay attention to as we plan for the future. All perceptions are valid. This is going to be very informal. What types of changes have been influencing the West Cluster? What is happening outside the boundaries of the West Cluster? People are simply going to shout out their ideas and perceptions. Everything will go up on the flip chart. This is how we will build our data base. It is simple as that. So let's start!

In less than thirty minutes, the group generated over twenty flip-chart pages of data. Exhibit 10.3 provides a brief sampling of some of the aspects of the changing environment that participants perceived as significant to their planning system.

Exhibit 10.3. Sample of Data from Environmental Scan.

Crippling federal debt	Permanent underclass
Lack of civility	The dumbing of America
Increase in mental illness	Angry white men, black men
Impact of foreigners	Demise of affirmative action
Dysfunctional citizenry	Growth of information technology
Racism, racial polarization	Export of American jobs
Sexual harassment in workplace	Loss of respect for life
Increase in gang activity	Negative impact of media
Perseverance of community organization movement	Saturation of suburban retail and housing markets
Record breaking homicide	Inadequate health care system
Environmental pollutants in the community	Unique school reform in Chicago
Decrease in community banks	Growth in prison industry
Declining of voter turnouts	Urban sprawl
Sexual abuse of children	Suburbanization of wealth
Increase in right wing groups	Downsizing continuing
Tenacity of Chicago industry	Proposition 187
Increase in homelessness	Anti-immigration
Isolation of elderly	Increase in teen violence

Gloom and Doom or Potential for Opportunity?

In the majority of cases, the environmental scan of changes in the world often produces a great deal of data easily interpreted in negative terms. The initial reaction is one of gloom and doom. This is because people are reacting emotionally to the effects of turbulence, and the perception of a world that appears to be spinning out of control. The next task helps people to come to terms with the realities of the environment and social forces that are impinging on their system. It is both sobering and uplifting. The sobering aspect is revealed as people develop probable future scenarios of the changing environment, that is, what might come to pass in the future if social trends continue on their present course. The uplifting aspect is evoked as people search for their most desirable future. Here, people begin to share their hopes, dreams, and ideals for a better world. In this sense, the changes happening in the wider environment can be seen as potential opportunities for transformation.

Linzy introduced the basic group format for this task as follows:

> The next task that we are going to this afternoon is to reflect on this world that we live in. The trends we've identified represent the changes that have taken place. With that thought in mind, what will the probable future will be if these changes continue on their present course? The other side of the coin is the desirable future. What would we like to have happen, if the best possible things happen instead of the worst ones. Now, we'd like this half of the room to concentrate on the most probable future, and the other side of the room to address the most desirable future for the world. What we will need out of each group, and this is where you will be using your flip charts, is to come up with four to five points that describe your future—probable or desirable, depending on where your group is sitting. What are four or five likely scenarios for the probable and desirable future in the year 2005? Report outs will be taken from each of the groups in thirty minutes.

Desirable Future Reports

Four groups reported out their desirable future scenarios. For our purposes here, we will provide a snippet of the first group's report. The Reverend Vercena Stuart stood up and spoke for her group:

"Our desirable future was inclusive of these four points. One, an economy that allows fair participation and reduces the disparity between the haves and have-nots. Secondly, a holistic community where families flourish and a community that fosters spirituality, morality, and human values (which includes education, health, public safety). Thirdly, a society that operates in harmony with the environment. And fourth, a true participative democracy, everyone has real voting privileges and influence in public affairs."

A participant responded by asking, "How did you come up with such an eloquent report?" The Reverend Vercena Stuart replied, "When we talked about our desirable future, we tried to be inclusive. These are things that we want and need to strive for. We need the hope that society can look like this. We need to envision this and collectively work toward this desirable future."

Mary chimed in from the other side of the room, "This reminds me of a Jamaican song, 'The time to be happy is now, the place to be happy is here, the way to be happy is to make others happy, and we will have a little heaven down here.'" (Applause and laughter from the audience.)

Probable Future Reports

Tom Worthy made a dramatic report to the large group on the scenarios likely to come to pass if disintegration of society continues. Here are his statements verbatim:

Classism and economic segregation. We are going to see more concentration of wealth. We have areas in the city right now where this is happening.

Massive homelessness and decreased ownership. Homeless people are being pushed aside.

The poverty mentality. Some people around here want to be victims all the time. There is a lot of poverty mentality running rampant even through this organization.

Social service bureaucracy. Poverty creates a deficiency of hope. Hope is lacking in our neighborhoods. You can go to other countries around the world, and they may be poor, but the people have hope. We don't have hope.

Violence and increase in crime. We have to worry about crime. Right now one of the major industries is security.

The break-up of families. Taking families and putting them in jail. You know, my dad is in jail, my mama is in the drug program, my kids are in Department of Child and Social Services.

Building of more prisons. There is a new juvenile hall right down on Odgen Avenue, have you seen it? What an unbelievable facility. It looks like a big business.

The police state. Yes, before you know it we will be giving up our rights and let the police raise our kids.

Increase in churches. Well, we were trying to figure out whether that was good or bad (laughter from audience).

Social civil war. We have a civil war going on right now in our neighborhoods. We have drug dealers that are fighting us. That's civil war! If we don't get our tools and weapons together, we will be taken over. We have old people that won't come out of their house.

Disintegration of democracy. When I call City Hall to clean up the dirt in my backyard that the Street Department left, I'm ignored. That is not democracy. When you call City Hall, they hate you.

Media control. We have people that are controlling what and how we think. Most of what the media puts out is garbage.

Health issues. Suicide is on the rise. We are becoming a reservoir for more and more diseases. Who gets health care? More people are going to be kicked to the curb when they're sick.

Education. This is the foundation of our problems. We have to fix the school system.

Doc McClelland followed by summarizing his group's analysis of the data. Doc began, "Our group took a look at probable outcomes should the situation remain the same. We came up with four bullets and a summary." Here are Doc's comments:

- Increased polarization between the haves and the have nots. If you take the way things used to be with the rich, if you imagine a bell curve with the rich at one end occupying a small space, and the poor occupying another small space and the majority of people falling in the middle, calling that the middle class. We noted that the middle class has shrunk and the two ends are getting bigger, and we expect that might come to a head in the future.

- Rebellion. This includes a possible revolution. That is another thing that might come to be as a byproduct of all the negative changes that we identified earlier.

- RoboCop or Lockdown State. This is an increased police state. The police themselves are fearful of entering certain areas. ["They already are," one participant remarks.] Police might have to send in "mechanized" units to keep order.

- Endangerment of democratic society as we know it today. The people will be saying the heck with democracy because the people will be saying democracy is not of the people, by the people, and for the people.

Our summary is that although we have all these resources coming into our area, and revenues, and people are starting to get together, it might be enough to win a few skirmishes, but as far as the overall war is concerned, we are going to continue to be victims if these trends continue and if these probable scenarios do come to pass.

Where Were You When Martin Luther King Was Assassinated?

The history session in this Search Conference occurred after dinner on the first evening. It was a pivotal session for the conference community. It is in this session that participants are asked to review their past, to look for those elements that have shaped the character of their system. And it is here that participants are drawn into what Asch (1952) would call "a relation of mutual relevance," as they perceive that similar events have happened to others as well, where they have a chance to confirm their thoughts and feelings with others, and where they seek sympathy and support from others.

Linzy kicked off the history session. He began by informing the group:

What we would like to do now for the next hour is to point out one of the differences between traditional strategic planning sessions and the Search

Conference. One of the things that you will find that is different is that we are going to take into consideration "our culture." We are going to focus in on that right now. To help us do that, we are going to look at the history of the West Side. So that everyone in here will be able to gain a shared appreciation for the history, a very rich history, of the West Side. You will notice the line running across the flip charts that we have up here in the front of the room. And what we would like to do now, is starting with the elders, to ask you to come up here and tell a story about the significant events or milestones that you recall and that you consider to be important to the history of the West Side. As you describe the event, place a mark on the time line, whether the event occurred in 1920, 1930, or whatever.

Immediately, Tom Brown volunteered to start the history session. He walked up to the front of the room where the flip charts were and began to recollect what life used to be like on the West Side forty-five years ago. Here is an excerpt from Tom Brown's remembrances:

In 1950, I was fourteen years of age and I had just entered high school. What was significant was the interaction of the religious community with a variety of young people. There was a tremendous interest on the part of the Catholic community to embrace the black people in the area. And there was a tremendous interest on the part of young students from Wheaton College to help the black people. At that time, what was really significant and has had a lasting impression on me is that people began to lose their racial identity due to assimilation. In the high school, in the various stores up and down Madison Avenue, and in some of the churches, there was integration without even talking about integration.

One of my best friends was a little white fellow. And what was highly significant, when we were looking for a job, he was discriminated against. And I felt sorry for him. [Laughter] But, after I became a young adult, the laugh was on me. Because the job he was discriminated against was a dishwasher's job that they gave to me but wouldn't allow him to have.

Isn't it interesting that things have changed that where now we have the same area, totally black, but we still have the Christians or we have the Catholic element that are trying to embrace people who have separated. What I am trying to convey here, I am not trying to apologize, I am just trying to say that our culture and identity, the people and their interactions have changed, possibly because we have allowed it to. We have started looking at people as "whites" and as "blacks." In 1950, through 1955 or 1960, people were interacting on the West Side. There was not a big problem. . . . Sometimes in our enthusiasm to become apart, we become separated.

And, looking at the many faces here, there are white people here, it is interesting that we are coming together here and we are talking about things that affect us. Not as individual ethnic or racial groups, but as human beings. We are human beings suffering a similar problem, and whatever the illness that affects one racial group here is going to affect the other one. And if we do not acknowledge where the problem is we are going to suffer from the effects of the problem. . . . Now in 1995, we are facing a completely different element of social and racial interaction. But let us not forget our history. History should teach us from the mistakes and things that have happened in the past how to better interact and socialize in the future. If we do not learn from history, I use a term and I apologize for it, we are damn fools. History should teach us how to be human and how to interact with one another.

Amen! [Applause]

Mary Nelson, a long-time West Side community organizer and activist, told her own story:

I remember 1965. I moved into West Garfield park to help my brother get settled at Bethel Lutheran Church on a hot August afternoon. Three days after we moved in, we were coming back from a concert and we had a little Volkswagen with a hole in the top. We were getting off Independence on the expressway and there was a big bus in front of us, and people were shouting at us, "Close your top! Close your top!" All of a sudden bottles, and bricks and stones came crashing at our car. That was the beginning of the riots.

The other thing that I remember is 1968 when the second set of riots took place. We had been marching out in the streets. Martin Luther King had moved out to the West Side. I remember the marches when we when out to Marquette Park. Mahalia Jackson was there that night before singing "The battle of Jericho and walls come tumbling down" at the temple on Warren Boulevard.

We started marching through Marquette Park, arm and arm, while Martin Luther King was up in front with a group of pastors and they were throwing fire crackers at us and you couldn't tell if they were gunshots. But King never flinched once in that whole time. Some women with hate in their faces, even housewives, were shouting obscenities at us. One women was so incensed that she had this big blob of spit that landed right on Mahalia Jackson's face. And I remember Mahalia taking her hand and wiping that spit off her face and looking at that lady in the eye and saying, "God bless you my child." That lady shriveled up and walked away. At that moment, I knew what power was all about. [Applause]

Several more people shared their recollections and memories of events that were significant to the history of the West Side. Robert Steele, the Director of the West Cluster Empowerment Zone Collaborative, also remembered the events that made a lasting impression on him when he was a youth. Looking back on these events, Steele said:

I will start in 1968. I was in second grade. The whole school just hushed when our principal announced that Martin Luther King got killed. Everybody walked home, *quiet*. Not a word was said. Nobody had anything to say to anybody. You just looked to each other in astonishment. Even for a kid in second grade not really knowing the significance of this event, and then the next day just watching your neighborhood turn into a war zone.

I lived on Ogden Avenue. Where the most prominent car dealerships set. Every corner was a dealership, a Cadillac dealership, Oldsmobile, Chevrolet . . . that's where I played, in between the cars. And the next day I saw these cars totally demolished, I mean windshields were broken, the cars were overturned. The salesmen wouldn't even go to work because they were so afraid of the fear of being hurt. You weren't even allowed to go out and play during that time. We couldn't even go to see my grandmother at her house. The National Guard were in our neighborhoods! I mean these were like the army men I played with right in our neighborhood. We were on house arrest so to speak because we had a curfew. I had never experienced anything like this or even seen anything like this in watching some of the stories of war.

I guess the significance for me is having lived right in the neighborhood where Martin Luther King began to walk and helped to desegregate housing. He lived and slept four blocks from my home. My dad and mom were the first black family on our block. We still live on the same block. That is forty-some years later. Our house only cost $13,000 when we bought it. One Italian family is still there, fifty-seven years later. It's a three-flat building. A black family has never lived there. Nobody else lives in the building because of what her dad taught. They have more cats than they have visitors. [Laughter] But she lives on the third-floor apartment and the rest of the building is empty. The building is kept in perfect shape. Just watching my neighborhood change, you know the shopping district that it used to be, we played in between cars, we would ride our bikes around Kostner and Cicero.

The biggest thing that I really remember is not being able to curse around adults. [Laughter and applause] If I said a bad word in front of adults you would be whipped for the next six years! I mean your neighbors would whip you if you cursed in front of them, your aunt would whip you, your mother would whip you, and then your daddy would come home, and oh no, now I am going to get a whipping by you! [Laughter]. . . . Those kind of things show how kids have changed. I mean we were happy just to wear Levis. "Jeepers" and "Allstars" were the biggest gym shoes.

But our values have changed. Things are so materialistic now. When it was a family value, if I got something it was shared with everybody in the family. If one family had a sofa, the whole family would sleep on that sofa if someone came to visit. The value system and how it has changed over the years is what I think is significant.

My biggest time frame, up until the time before the riots tore up Ogden Avenue where I played, was watching Western Electric leave us, it was the biggest company on Ogden Avenue. Sunbeam, General Electric, and Westinghouse and then Sears left. Sears, where everybody in my family worked. I worked at Sears after high school. My father, my mother and sisters worked at Sears on Homan Avenue. We watched the flight of all these major companies take all these jobs with them. And they said to us "You guys will be OK, we'll see you later."

But now it suddenly seems that it's time for all these companies to come back because there is no more space out in the suburbs—in Elk Grove Village and Hoffman Estates—they can't move out there anymore. Well . . . our arms aren't open that wide right now, so, you know, I just think we should make them pay a little bit more before they get back in.

Robert Steele went on to point out:

I just wanted to make one last comment. I notice that 1968 was a major change period. Women became major leaders. Women started to taking leadership positions in nontraditional ways, in communities, in families, but mostly in politics. They started to save men at this time as the jobs left. Just listening to women talk here in this room shows this. And I would just like to point out four key women that were leaders in our neighborhood over the years, Mabel Manning, Bell Waitey of North Lawndale—helping senior citizens. These are people who died in the saddle of their jobs. Also, Nancy Jefferson. She changed the West Side politically. She lived in the Governor's office. Another woman is still with us—Erling Linzy. She was the cause of having the University of Illinois campus being built on the West Side.

Another participant related his story of where he was when Martin Luther King was assassinated.

I will use the same starting point. I was also in second grade when Martin Luther King was killed. But I went to St. Francis Cabrini on California and Lexington, and all our teachers were white nuns, the janitors were white. My father and I never have got along for some reason. You know, you are just born and the father and son have bad blood, or the mother and daughter have bad blood. But no matter how much I disliked him, my best memory was when we were all under our desk because everybody came into our school beating up nuns and setting the school on fire. My father and his boys—they were all conservative vice lords at that time—came through the window, and I remember that, got me out of that school. And I remember vividly holding my father all the way home, second grade, not knowing what the hell was happening! They were trying to explain to me that Martin Luther King was killed.

I remember driving through the streets, coming down California, and seeing just plums of people lined up throwing rocks and bottles at white people in cars. Now remember, from preschool to second grade I was in Catholic school, with white teachers. So it was all right with me, you know, I didn't understand why people were throwing things at white people. I had a child's rationale, and they were telling me, well white people killed Martin Luther King. But I've always been burdened, I have always asked questions since then. That's probably why my father and I didn't get along. But they could not make me understand why did they want to kill Martin Luther King who was a man of peace and nonviolence.

That was a turning point in my life. Now I have seen a plan to rebuild my community that I was born and raised in. I have always said that once I had enough resources, clout and power I want to redevelop that neighborhood. I hope my son doesn't stand and tell a story like this about where he used to live and what it used to be like, knowing that he didn't have anything to do with the rebuilding of this neighborhood.

A minister who grew up on the West Side told his story, which touched everyone in the room:

Back in 1918, my father was born at St. Anthony's in Douglas Park. For me, being back on the West Side has meant getting back to my roots. South Lawndale used to be a Bohemian neighborhood. Back in 1918 my grandmother used to teach English as a second language to Bohemian immigrants. When Martin Luther King was assassinated, I was a junior at Proviso East High School. I can remember one of my black friends from the football team telling me in English class, "At 3 o'clock stay away from this part of the school, because all hell is going to break loose." And it did.

I remember at the same time, my father, he also worked at Sears Roebucks for twenty-five years. Shortly after Martin Luther King's death, he drove a truck and someone up on a third floor had a rifle aimed at him. It's funny after that, he took out his old World War II helmet. [Laughter] Personally, this created a sense of fear in me that I needed to be careful when going through black neighborhoods.

Then skipping ahead to 1992, I used to be a missionary in Spain. There weren't too many people of color there. But when I came back to Chicago, it was a shock. What hit me was this spirit of fear, everywhere. Even in the churches, there is this fear of people going out into the streets. The other experience was, just as a white person, walking through South Lawndale an all-Latino neighborhood and then North Lawndale, an all-black neighborhood and being the only white person there. This is the first time that really impressed me how racist our country is, how divided we are, and seeing how the church might help to break some of the curses of this country. As men and women of faith, how can we break this curse? It is a curse over all of us. We're all bound by this plague of racism.

I worked for eight years with drug addicts. Every day you could see the power of evil. You would get new heroin addicts whose bodies were destroyed by drugs. And I had this anger that grew up inside me. I was always a pacifist type, I came out of the Mennonite church. Many people died and never recovered from drugs. There is a real hurt inside. I think we all are getting in touch with this real pain and seeing the condition that we are all in, and it doesn't make any sense. It's a blessing for me for the last two years being able to meet Hispanic pastors and black pastors. Despite all this darkness behind us [He points to the probable future data], I know there is greater strength within us

as we come together. And I am excited about this Search Conference, of what
we can do if we are united as one community. [Applause]

We allowed the history session to go on until 9:30 P.M., ex-
ceeding the time we had allotted for it by ninety minutes. This is
the kind of judgment call that Search Conference managers have
to make. Linzy and I could sense that this history session was bringing the community together, deepening Asch's conditions for effective dialogue. We were sitting on opposite sides of the room, so
we acknowledged that this was the right thing to do by gesturing
to each other.

The history session came to a close with these comments from
another long-time West Side activist:

I was born in St. Ann's hospital. I graduated from St. Angela's in 1962. I was
an altar boy for Senior Egan. Ten years later I met another West Side woman,
Gail Seehada. I want to come back to a couple other historical events. Tom
Brown was talking over dinner about different government policies that are
supposed to be beneficial. But when all is said and done you find out that they
were written to be screwing people, as was the Federal Housing FHA loans in
the 1970s. Cities destroyed for cash. The program was set up to give the American dream to African-Americans to buy a home, but the whole time it was
written as a scam to rip people off while the mortgage companies walked away
with the bucks. I saw Gail, I saw African-American residents from Roseland,
also one of the heaviest hit zip codes in the country, take on federal bureaucrats and say, "You screwed us, you owe us money, you owe us big time." That
stuff was happening in the late seventies.

At our table earlier this afternoon, we were talking about "windows" in
history. The community reinvestment act came out of one window during the
Carter administration. Now the community reinvestment act is fighting for its
life. Senator Mosely Braun is one of the few voices in the Democratic Party that
is threatening a filibuster in the Senate on this piece of legislation. Many of the
banks that are here today grew out of the West Side. So as we make a transition
to our agenda tomorrow, I would just like to add up here, August 1996. The
whole world will be watching Chicago again. The Democratic National Convention. We are in another window in history. And it's all coming back here on
the West Side.

All of your collective work that you have been doing and that we will be
doing, is not just about the rebuilding of the West Side, it's about rebuilding

communities throughout this country. I just wanted as we make this transition, to leave you not only with your vision for the West Side, but a mission that you all are carrying out for colleagues, brothers and sisters and communities, whether they be urban or rural that are struggling with the same community development issues that you are on the West Side. This is a challenge and an opportunity. So all this gloom and doom up here, yeah this is only probable without your actions, without your dedication. So while there may seem to be major obstacles, I think just from the stories that we told this evening, the perseverance, the tenacity, the dedication, and the commitment, all different ways in our own individual lives that brought us here can all come forward in not only rebuilding the West Side, but making a difference in history. [Applause]

Reflection on the History Session

After this session came to a close, the energy in the room was different. Linzy and I both sensed that people were more at ease and intimate with each other. Looking back on the conference, Tom Williams remarked, "This history session was the turning point for me. It was very special because we all suddenly began to recognize that we all had been struggling and fighting for the same cause. I had the feeling that everyone simply spoke from their heart, and that opened things up." Clearly Asch's condition of psychological similarity had been established: People were now seeing each other simply as human beings, providing the conditions for trust to develop.

The Present System of Economic Development

The following morning, we began the conference by having participants analyze the present system of economic development, in terms of what the community wanted to keep, drop, and create. This task was conducted as a large-group brainstorming session that lasted about forty-five minutes. The session generated a tremendous amount of data. This took form in numerous suggestions for enhancing current economic development, as well a host of ideas for creating new development opportunities and initiatives. These ideas were made use of later in the conference, when groups worked on developing strategic goals and action plans. Exhibit 10.4 shows a small sample of the data:

Exhibit 10.4. Sample of Data from Present System Analysis.

Keep	Drop	Create
Community Reinvestment Act	Competition between groups	Common focus for all groups
Existing ownership of land	Vacant lots	Venture Capital Fund
Existing businesses	Cheap recovery homes	Legislation to access United Center
Schoolhouses as community centers	Organizations that are not led by the people	Independence from government financing
Renewed Lake St. line	Red lining	Opportunities for home ownership
Manufacturing base	Hopelessness	Insurance pool that is resident controlled
Street vendors—utilize	Crime	Franchise fund
Community hospitals		Citizen proxy system
		Infrastructure projects
		Consumer education mechanisms
		Community capital trust fund
		Creative financing mechanisms
		Arts community

We Have a Dream!

By midmorning the conference task shifted to a focus on the future. Now the community was engaged in envisioning their most desirable future for the West Side. This session was structured into two parts. First, groups were asked to generate a compelling image of their desirable future, that is, what their community would look ten years from now as a result of successful economic development. Second, small groups were also asked to articulate a set of strategic goals to aim for, goals that if achieved would bring them closer to realizing their desirable future.

There was a great deal of common ground among group presentations when they reported their most desirable future for the West Side. The community settled upon three key desirable future statements:

Desirable Future 1

The community must be economically sustainable through the creation of living-wage jobs. It must be culturally sustainable by reinforcing our own cultural values. It must be politically sustainable by enforcing accountability. It must be environmentally sustainable by enforcing standards for the air and quality of the material used to build our community.

Desirable Future 2

There is true participative democracy where people plan and manage the development of their neighborhoods. We have an economy in harmony with the environment that maximizes the productive capacity of the individual while providing employment for all with an adequate income to enjoy the nation's bounty and wealth. We have a holistic community where families flourish and that fosters spirituality, morality, human values, toleration of other lifestyles, and ensures the safety of the residents. We have an educational system that prepares people to sustain all of the above and is equal in accessibility and quality for everyone.

Desirable Future 3

There is a comprehensive collaboration of community residents, local businesses, churches, public and private sector that provides economic sustainability and safe, beautiful, and spiritually fulfilling environments where individual and collective needs are met.

To achieve this future state, the community agreed upon ten key strategic goals for economic development:

- Community mobilization and involvement in economic development
- Increased ownership of businesses and residences
- Increased private investment in the community
- Increased infrastructure of investment in the area
- Recirculation of purchasing dollars in the community from one hour to seven days
- Within five years, develop 50 percent of current vacant land
- Unemployment rate dropping from current level to parity with state level
- Increase household income average to 80 percent of median income of Chicago area for current residents
- Increase number of businesses in zone by 20 percent over five years
- Double annual sales of existing companies and businesses within five years

Integration of Goals

Due to the compressed time format of this conference, we attempted to speed up the process by offering a framework for integrating the various strategic goals that had been developed into a manageable set of action initiatives. We suggested that the integration of this list of strategic goals could be categorized into different logical groupings. We presented our process for conducting the integration task, recognizing that our categories might not resonate with the perceptions and orientations of what people had generated in their groups. The participants rebelled immediately. Our logic and framework sounded much too abstract for their purposes. Why go through such an exercise of rearranging items into our categories when they already knew what the major strategic thrusts were? When would the data generation process stop and the real action planning begin? We should have known better. The community had taken full responsibility for generating, analyzing, and interpreting their own data from the beginning of the conference. Why should they forgo such responsibility at the most crucial juncture of the planning process? At first, we were somewhat at a loss of what to do when the community nullified our suggestion.

When we realized that the community needed to own this process, we posed the problem of integration back to them. Immediately, several informal leaders stepped forward and cut to the chase. They proposed that the strategies for achieving their desirable future could easily be consolidated and collapsed into four community-based economic development initiatives:

- Comprehensive community planning process
- Creative financing fund for capital development
- People development
- Industrial education partnerships

The community agreed unanimously to the decision and the conference immediately shifted into the action planning phase.

If Not Us, Who? If Not Now, When? A Unified Action Plan

Participants were more than eager to turn their attention to the task of action planning. Action plans address the work and activities required for achieving strategic goals and making their desirable future a reality. A high level of trust, energy, and creativity had been building among participants and seemed to peak during this phase of the conference. Also, by this point in the conference, small groups had developed a great deal of confidence in their ability to work together and self-manage their own affairs.

The strategic goals generated from the previous phase became the focus of the four action initiatives. Individuals were then asked to choose one of the action initiatives and commit to making it happen. This self-selection process resulted in the four action planning groups.

We introduced a simple set of guidelines for the action planning task. We asked each group to develop their action plans in precise and concrete language, specifying what each person was actually going to do after the conference. We instructed them to specify in their action plans a time sequence, with milestones, subgoals, review points, and deadlines. Each group also needed to figure out how they were going to get other people from the community involved in the implementation effort. Below is an example of an action plan developed by one of the groups.

Action Plan—Community Participation

1. By June 20, we will take part in Alderman's briefings and request that part of the City's $2 million be used to fund a comprehensive plan and marketing of the West Cluster Collaborative (WCC).
2. By June 24, we will initiate a community development forum to begin community planning at the neighborhood level.
3. By June 24, the marketing committee will make a presentation at the Corporate Breakfast. We will present the three Small Neighborhood Action Plans (SNAPS), plans for WCC participation in the Chicago Transit Authority's renewal of the Greenline, and an overview of our plans for the commercial and industrial areas within the West Cluster.
4. From June through August, we will help other areas develop their comprehensive plans. All of the SNAPS activities will be implemented by this time. In addition, by the end of July, we will have our input and proposals finished for the city's capital improvement plans.
5. By mid August, we will have finished a draft of the comprehensive community plan. Later that month, we will communicate the plan at a Community Congress meeting for the WCC. We will share this draft with the Department of Planning and elected officials. This comprehensive plan will represent a consolidation of the seven neighborhood plans.
6. By September, we will hold the Community Congress to seek ratification of the comprehensive plan.
7. By October, we will submit the ratified plan to the Chicago Planning Commission.

The conference ended on a high note with many thanks to Mary Nelson and Abu Bakr Nurruddin, the lead organizers.

Postscript

The four action planning groups have maintained their self-managing structures for organizing the implementation of their strategic initiatives. As Mary Nelson reported several months after the conference, "We now have the focus, commitment, and cooperation to work together on these initiatives, because the people who are working on them are the people who created them." One of the action planning groups developed a collaborative process for issuing and reviewing Requests for Proposals. The Economic Development committee now reviews and evaluates proposals, and endorses only the ones that are consistent with the strategic goals and ideals for a desirable future developed at the Search Conference. Each proposal for economic development is evaluated according to the criteria agreed upon at the Search Conference, such as whether a project has sufficient community involvement, increases ownership of businesses and residences, develops vacant land, and so forth.

The Economic Development committee has endorsed eighteen proposals to date, three of which originated from within the West Cluster. The first proposal, called Joblink, will result in two thousand new job placements by linking existing training and job placement agencies to a computerized network connected to firms in the industrial corridor and other Empowerment Zone businesses. The Finance Initiative on Economic Development will provide community residents technical assistance in business planning and financing. The third proposal, Employer Assisted Housing, will assist employers to stabilize their workforce by providing tax credits to promote home ownership for employees of West Side businesses. In addition, the Economic Development committee has formed a joint partnership with several local banks to develop a community loan fund for business development. The sponsor of the West Cluster Empowerment Zone Search Conference, Mary Nelson, was appointed by Mayor Richard Daley to the Chicago Empowerment Zone's Coordinating Council.

Beyond Stagnation and Stalemate

According to Robert Goodman (1971), "Any form of politics will ultimately fail if it is not consistent with people's most fundamental needs for cooperation, and a sense of love and joy in human experience—in essence, a humane existence." Robert Reich (1987) goes so far as to say that cooperation is the next frontier. Several questions come to mind. How will we embark upon this new frontier? What new directions of hope will guide our journey? How will we overcome the current culture of mistrust that is eroding the social fabric of communities and organizations? What role does the Search Conference have to play in the cultural transformation of society?

In this chapter, we address these questions by examining the constraints and opportunities to cultural transformation. We point out that the Search Conference is part of a larger communitarian movement in North American society. This movement can strengthen the role of mediating institutions in the *middle space* of society, that is, between individual organizations and the nation state. It is here that one may find new directions of hope, and new possibilities for creating a more desirable future for society.

False Starts, False Promises

The rebellion of the 1960s seriously challenged the values of the establishment and authoritarian institutions. At the time, there was a great deal of idealism and hope that a more humane, democratic, and socially responsible society was on the horizon. However,

267

while the activists of the movement challenged authoritarian values, they lacked the tools and practices for effecting fundamental structural change. The aftermath of the 1960s led to a cultural vacuum, the "me generation," and a general sense that the social fabric of society was slowly unraveling. As Amitai Etzioni points out, "The problem is that the waning of traditional values was not followed by a solid affirmation of new values; often nothing filled the empty spaces that were left when we razed existing institutions" (1993, p. 24).

Competition took up the slack. Competitiveness in all its various forms reigns now, and is even held up as a behavioral trait necessary for survival in a social Darwinian world. Especially during the 1980s, we witnessed a glamorization of the dark side of human behavior, in effect, turning private vices into public virtues. "Greed is good" chanted thousands of newly minted MBAs—until they fell victim to their own financial medicine. Many of them found themselves riffed or downsized and thrown out of the corporate jungle. The jungle-fighter attitude—what Macoby (1976) referred to as a "gamesman" orientation—is the product of radical individualism taken to its extreme.

Radical individualism would seem to be a healthy response to the stifling forces of bureaucratic organization. After years of struggle, however, it has become apparent that radical individualism alone will not overthrow bureaucracy, nor will bureaucracy completely succeed in controlling the will of the individual. We are at a stalemate. On either side of this war zone, cooperation is nowhere to be found. Alasdair MacIntyre summarizes this face-off:

> On the one side there appear the self-defined protagonists of individual liberty, on the other the self-defined protagonists of planning and regulation, of the goods available through bureaucratic organization. But in fact what is crucial is that on which the contending parties agree, namely, that there are only two alternative modes of social life open to us, one in which the free and arbitrary choices of individuals are sovereign and one in which the bureaucracy is sovereign, precisely so that it may limit the free and arbitrary choices of the individual. Given this deep cultural agreement, it is unsurprising that the politics of modern societies oscillate between a freedom that is nothing but a lack of regulation of individual behavior and forms of collectivist control designed only to limit the anarchy of self-interest [1984, p. 34].

In the oscillation of debate between unrestrained individualism and stifling bureaucracy that MacIntyre refers to, public discourse has become caught in the quagmire of this dichotomy, growing ever more shrill and less civil.

Radical Individualism Gone Wild

We contend that radical individualism—which has run rampant in modern culture—now needs to be balanced by a concern for the common good. This is difficult to do, given our cultural heritage. Our very notion of self is one of a free-standing, self-sufficient, sovereign, and autonomous individual. A strong legacy grounded in the classical doctrine of liberalism claims that only individuals are in a position to make choices of their aims and interests, or to define conceptions of a higher good. This political doctrine values the primacy of the individual, and it is a vision of society governed by the protection of individual rights. Both private and public institutions have become a battleground in the war of rights-based individualism (Glendon, 1992). The fight for the protection of individual rights and freedoms has become the sole guiding principle for organizing society. It has become, in the words of Jean Bethke Elshtain (1995), the "ultra-liberal social contract."

The heavy price paid for this imbalance of attention can be seen in the erosion of civil society, what some now refer to as a growing "culture of mistrust" and a "crisis in social capital formation," that is, the decline of social bonds necessary for public engagement. There is strong empirical support for this trend. In 1960, the civic culture study reported that 60 percent of the public said that "people can be trusted." In 1993, that figure dropped to an all-time low; only 37 percent of the public felt that they trusted people (Elshtain, 1995).

It appears that in a society bent only upon attending to the needs and rights of the individual, civic virtues are brutalized. We are finding it more difficult to enter into a rational public dialogue with others, settle our differences without resorting to litigation or violence, or work to find areas of common ground that could lead to cooperative outcomes.

Whether one leans toward the conservative right or the liberal left, one encounters the belief that the individual is the fundamental social unit of analysis; that ends, purposes, interests, aims, and conceptions of the good are distinctly matters of individual choice. But what happens when my good conflicts with your good? The answer is, nothing happens—so long as your lifestyle preferences or values do not invade upon or conflict with mine. To ensure some measure of protection from such conflicts, more people are choosing to avoid public life by taking refuge in lifestyle enclaves. Many people have elected to shut out the wider world around them. This is a dangerous trend, for the capacity to enter into rational dialogue with others diminishes as social bonds dissolve. This trend is related to the privatization of values in a society of atomized individuals. We avoid conflict by trying to be politically correct, and we refrain from speaking of our values and ideals for fear that they may make others uncomfortable. The superficiality of public discourse makes it difficult to develop deep bonds and lasting ties to others in the community.

In more serious matters, a common reaction has been to settle differences in court, or by calling in professional third parties—arbitrators, mediators, consultants, and so forth. This is a juridical model of conflict resolution, or what Sandel (1984) has called a "procedural republic" where resolution of conflict is dependent on a judicial process for weighing and upholding individual rights. In even worse cases, violence has been seen as the answer; bombs strike abortion clinics, guns blaze in Postal Service offices, race riots tear up neighborhoods.

In the battle to protect individual rights, we have underestimated the need for protecting civic spaces. As de Tocqueville ([1840] 1969) noted, the integrity of democratic social life is dependent upon the existence of mediating institutions, informal organizations, and voluntary associations. It is in these civic spaces that individuals come to know a good in common that they cannot come to know alone. These mediating institutions provide both the context and the opportunity for the development of democratic dispositions.

With the decline of civic spaces, the burden of solving social problems has shifted to the government and to institutional experts. The government has taken responsibility for issues it is ill-equipped to handle; the government cannot legislate mutual trust among the population. Alternatively, we call in experts, expecting them to solve large-scale problems—and when they don't, we lose trust in them and become even more cynical. As more of the burden for solving large-scale problems is shifted to large-scale bureaucracies, more failures and disappointments can be expected. The result is a spiral of delegitimation.

Radical individualism gone wild is leading to a social ecology where competitiveness, self-interest, and aggression are becoming the way of the world. Radical individualism has made it difficult for groups of people to take joint responsibility for their actions. This is due in part to the conception that only individuals, in their own separate ways and unencumbered by outside influences, can decide what ends or ideals should be pursued. As we pointed out earlier, in such an atomistic society values are viewed as private, personal possessions of the individual. According to this framework, there is no such thing as a common good—only the sum total of individual desires and an aggregate of private goods. The free market is a euphemism for this, based on the maximization of individual wants and preferences. Political theorist Michael Walzner observed:

> We are perhaps the most individualist society that ever existed in human history. Compared certainly to earlier, and Old World societies, we are radically liberated, all of us. Free to plot our own course. To plan our own lives. To choose a career. To choose a partner or a succession of partners. To choose a religion or no religion. To choose politics or an anti-politics. To choose a lifestyle—any style. Free to do our own thing, and this freedom, energizing and exciting as it is, is also profoundly disintegrative, making it very difficult for individuals to find any stable communal support, very difficult for any community to count on the responsible participation of its members. It opens solitary men and women to the impact of the lowest common denominator, commercial culture. It works against commitment to larger democratic union and also against the solidarity of all cultural groups that constitute our multi-culturalism [1992, pp. 11–12].

The state of affairs that Walzner describes is what can be expected from possessive individualism, where individuals are considered purely as "owners of one's own person." This unencumbered self takes on a wholly instrumental relationship to society, dominated by a what's-in-it-for-me mentality.

In Search of New Social Covenants

Our ability to restore social structures that serve the common welfare and public interest will be blocked until we acknowledge communal values, and work to rebuild healthy, sustainable communities. This requires the capacity to identify shared ideals in the search for new social covenants. Search conferencing aims to do just this. It is, in MacIntyre's terms, a new social practice that can transform the texture of public discourse, where language is taken out of the realm of private values and placed into the communal space where shared ideals can emerge.

Participation in a Search Conference offers individuals an opportunity to rediscover their shared ideals for a common good. We do not hear the language of individualism, with its emphasis on "me and my rights," in a Search Conference. Rather, we hear communal voices regarding shared concerns and affirmations of ideal statements based on shared images of a desirable future. We hear people articulating, staking out, and building upon common ground. We hear a community language, inspired by future possibilities, not past problems. What we hear is the unified voice of the *demos,* "We the People."

While the pursuit of shared ideals as guidelines for long-term planning decisions is rooted in the reality of people coming together in groups, this is not a move toward collectivism. Search conferencing is not an outlet or vehicle for group tyranny. And the type of community building that occurs in Search Conferences does not suppress the individuality of persons. The learning-planning community that develops in a Search Conference is neither individualistic or collectivistic in orientation. Rather, search conferencing is a practice that integrates the rights and responsibilities of "I" and "We." It establishes a "responsive community" (Etzioni, 1993).

The Divisiveness of Bureaucracy

Radical individualism gone wild is only one half of the problem. The other half is the antidemocratic nature of bureaucratic institutions. Bureaucracies have also run amok, systematically inhibiting cooperation. The stifling effects of bureaucracy that MacIntyre speaks of are insidious and pervasive. Bureaucratic structures, whether they be industrial, commercial, governmental, or educational, tend to foster competition and a competitive mentality. In bureaucracies, the creative energies of people are absorbed in internal struggles and constant fights for self-preservation. These in turn are more likely to induce basic group assumptions and negative emotions—anger, contempt, and shame—rather than creative group work and positive emotions of excitement and joy.

The bureaucratic organization denies people the responsibility of controlling and coordinating their own affairs. Bureaucracies are also designed to suppress lateral forms of communication. A bureaucracy prohibits the individuals who are doing the job, even the job of supervising and managing others, from deciding how best to coordinate their own efforts or from offering each other help, advice, or information (Emery, 1989). And exceptions or ideas that fall outside one's job description have to be referred to the supervisor or manager, who then takes credit for any successes that arise from such suggestions.

Similarly, when pursuing a promotion, an individual needs not just to look good in the eyes of the supervisor, but to look better than co-workers competing for the same job. This task amounts to inviting invidious comparison; quite simply, putting down co-workers as a means of self-promotion. Thus, communication is dominated by concerns for self-advancement. In many cases, all communication is distorted by individuals' efforts to advance themselves and protect themselves from criticism.

In addition, communications up and down the organization do not have the give and take of normal discussion between equals. Orders passed down are expected to be obeyed by whoever is occupying the relevant subordinate post. A them-and-us orientation develops, creating a culture of mistrust. This could, in turn, lead to a lack of communications, suppression of information, feeding of misinformation, and even outright lying. The them-and-us syndrome encompasses warring internal factions, as well as antagonistic interactions between organizations and their stakeholders. Both sides see advantages in keeping others in the dark with respect to what they are doing or what they intend to do.

Bureaucratic organizations also do not allow their members to have a voice in shaping and determining the ends that should be pursued. A democratic society, however, depends on this form of direct member participation. As long as this bureaucratic principle dominates organizations, it will be difficult to have widespread cooperation in society.

No Limits to Cooperation

The path to this new frontier is very different from the one traversed by those rugged individualists who ventured out into the hinterland of the Western Frontier. Neither radical individualism nor any form of coercive collectivism will lead us where we need to go. If we are to realize our full cooperative potential, we cannot keep clinging to individualistic behaviors. Nor can we simply resort to coercive methods that attempt to force or persuade people to be good team players in an environment built on bureaucratic command and control.

In the heat of the battle, the middle ground that exists between the extremist positions of radical individualism and stifling bureaucracy has been lost. What we need now are new social practices that can help us to reclaim the lost middle space, find common ground, rediscover community, and revitalize civil society. Search conferencing is such a social practice. By working with community groups, organizations, and domains, the Search Conference is one vehicle by which we can begin to build a pluralistic society based on cooperation. But to do so, we believe people must renew their commitment to public and community life. This implies that we must search for a common good with others in a community, and as a community.

Have we lost this capacity? Why has it been so difficult for people to do this? As we stated earlier, the atomistic conception of the individual in society does not recognize the community as a constitutive element of the self. Yet our identity is partly defined by the communities we inhabit, the institutions we rely upon, and the organizations we work in. In fact, one could argue that we come to know ourselves through relationships; who we are is always defined in a social context. Human identity is socially constructed through the common bonds that we develop with parents, family, friends, co-workers, neighbors, and so forth. As a result, our identity as persons is in turn also shaped by the purposes and ends that govern our social institutions.

For these reasons, the search for a desirable future for our communities, organizations, and world cannot be a lonely, individual pursuit. Contrary to classical liberal doctrine, individuals are not autonomous actors who can simply choose their own good. As Etzioni (1993) points out, individuals can only find a common good as members of distinct social systems.

For this to happen on a widespread basis, bureaucratic institutions have to change at a fundamental level. The change must be toward more democratic forms that foster local participation and self-management. Most efforts at planned change have attempted to transform organizations by working at the top, and cascading programs down through the bureaucratic hierarchy (Beckhard and Harris, 1977; Beer, Eisenstat, and Spector, 1990). Other change efforts have occurred on the periphery with limited success, introducing workplace innovations that are rarely understood by those in the corporate centers (Ketchum and Trist, 1992). These change efforts have been limited to the humanization rather than the democratization of work (Elden, 1986).

Rather than keeping citizens apart, which is what representative structures were designed to do, we now need forums for participative democracy that pull citizens together. Many scholars and civic activists are working on the problem; the title of this section (No Limits to Cooperation) was the subtheme of a recent Academy of Management conference, "Organizational Dimensions of Global Change," held at Case Western Reserve University, May, 1995.

The Search Conference is such a forum. Individual rights are upheld and protected in this forum because all perceptions are valid. The Search Conference process prevents any one group from dominating the agenda or restricting access to alternative views. All members of the Search Conference community have the ability to deliberate with regard to the ends they wish to seek, and, if necessary, to engage in rational conflicts of alternative views. It is a forum for community politics, where ordinary citizens can discuss contentious issues face-to-face, differentiating for themselves between issues that can be reconciled and those that should remain unresolved.

These deliberations are not merely procedural bickerings or zero-sum game arguments. The vigorous debates and airing of alternative views occurs in the context of shared understanding and against the backdrop of common ground. This form of community politics is concerned with creating a desirable future for all the groups who share a common interest in ensuring the long-term survival of their system (organization, community, region, and so on). This is quite different from interest group politics, which tends to be based on the promotion of independent objectives and aimed at achieving a winner-take-all outcome.

The Search Conference, as participants often describe it, is an environment for discovering new ways of relating, leading to an unexpected capacity to get things done—not through third parties, legal battles, experts, bureaucratic procedures, or instruments of government, but through the power of cooperative action. We view search conferencing as part of the larger communitarian movement that is concerned with fighting the forces of disintegration through a revival of civic culture, restoration of democratic virtues, and activation of citizenship. It is a step toward building an "S-type" (symbiotic) society (Perlmutter and Trist, 1986), where cooperation and negotiated order strategies help to counterbalance the destructiveness of zero-sum competition for domination (Pasquero, 1991).

The promise of an untapped frontier of cooperation offers new directions of hope. Trist envisioned the path to this frontier:

> As a more participative, more self-reliant yet more collaborative society begins to emerge—and this will be our doing, it won't happen automatically—the individual will resocialize in step with it. We will discover we have more shared values with others than we thought and that we do desire many of the same ends. As we experience this we will be using our personal networks much more extensively than we do at present in order to bring these common ends about, finding opportunities we had never thought of before. As we do this . . . we will feel more empowered and become more socially responsible, not in a begrudging and duty-driven way, but because we feel more personally fulfilled through acknowledging our interdependence. We will begin to find we can make some difference, that our efforts are contributing in a way we can see concretely to making a better society for ourselves and others [1979, p. 450].

For Trist (1979), new directions of hope are to be found not in the centers where power, resources, and wealth have traditionally been concentrated, but on the periphery, in bottom-up change, in the middle space between single organizations and the nation state, and across voluntary networks. Vitality is not in the centers, but on the periphery, in local councils, small-scale civic and community groups, and entrepreneurial firms, and among the avant garde. While Search Conferences conducted for corporations must often be sanctioned by the top and center, the effect of such a bottom-up approach is to redistribute and equalize power relations in the organization. Similarly, the leverage for change is not in top-down, centralized programs, but in grassroots social movements and bottom-up, self-managed initiatives. And political spaces between the single organization and of the nation state need to be developed, strengthened, and kept vibrant.

Organizing within this middle level, in what Trist referred to as a domain, is relatively weak in Western societies. Too much power has become concentrated, or is exercised at a level beyond that which permits and encourages direct participation. The formation of voluntary networks and associations also offers the possibility for diffusion of learning across formal boundaries. Further, people participate in networks as themselves, free from the constraints imposed upon them by their organizational roles.

These new directions of hope offer the possibility of responding actively and adaptively to the pressures of widespread social change. While a small community or organization acting alone may not be able to change significantly the social environment at large, the process of search conferencing can have a powerful diffusion effect. When powerful change takes place within single organizations and communities, it spreads as individuals promote the new values and talk excitedly about their hopes, achievements, and future direction. Indeed, individuals can literally make all the difference in the world. Innovations are adopted by individuals. As individuals in systems change and cooperate, new alliances are formed, and these in turn spread innovation to more and more systems. When this occurs, we refer to it as a social movement. Complex and large-scale social problems—such as those having to do with dwindling natural resources and increasing environmental degradation, the effects of technological change, poverty and diminishing quality of life, and global issues at the transnational level—are "meta-problems" (Chevalier, 1968). Now the range of issues associated with meta-problems is too extensive and complex to be tackled by any single organization (Trist, 1983). As Morley (1989) points out, single organizational responses to meta-problems "at any scale suffer from lack of frameworks for the collective framing of issues, opportunity to realign interests (and power) through re-framing of problems, space to develop shared perspectives, and to search for opportunities that challenge constraints on concerted global action" (p. 187).

To deal effectively with meta-problems, the unit of analysis needs to shift from the level of the single organization to the pop-ulation of organizations that share a concern for the meta-prob-lem. This "organizational ecology" perspective (Trist, 1977) aims at making it possible for a range of social organizations to be drawn together around meta-problem issues in order to develop a multi-organizational response capability. Search conferencing is a potent vehicle for developing the formation of *collaborative alliances,* which Gray and Wood (1991) define as "interorganizational efforts to ad-dress problems too complex and too protracted to be resolved by unilateral organizational action" (p. 4).

Such concerted action among previously competing organiza-tions and interest groups requires institution building at the level of interorganizational domains. This occurs through a learning process that leads members from an interorganizational domain to develop shared appreciations (Vickers, 1965) of the meta-prob-lem. As attention is shifted to the domain level and shared appre-ciations of the meta-problem are developed, the domain acquires an identity that transcends the boundaries of any singular organi-zation or interest group.

Collaboration at the level of interorganizational domains can result in an emergent network that bridges the boundaries of ex-isting organizations within the domain (Trist, 1983). This form of multipartite collaboration can facilitate a process whereby learn-ing can occur at the individual, group, organization, and interor-ganizational levels. Search conferencing has been used extensively for domain formation and development, bringing together multi-ple interest groups and organizations for the purpose of develop-ing shared definitions of the meta-problem, setting agreed-upon directions, and creating new structures or infrastructural support for coordinating activities and managing interdependencies (Baburoglu, 1992; Morley and Wright, 1989). As Pasquero points out, "These types of social partnerships share some common characteristics: Their role is to foster social problem solving across organizations, through the multipartite collaboration of otherwise conflicting interests, while retaining their autonomy and relying on influence more than authority" (1991, p. 41). The majority of these applications for domain development have occurred at local, regional, and national levels. New directions of hope also lie in extending the application of Search Conferences into the domains of international organizations and for organizing collaborative action in response to global issues (Brown, 1991).

Toward a Desirable Future

We believe that one of the central tasks for socially engaged theoreticians and practitioners is to help citizens in different sectors of society to search for their most desirable future. We might even argue that this is the social responsibility of social science. As we look to the future, we also find ourselves returning to our roots in the work of Kurt Lewin, who pioneered the idea of an action-oriented social science. For Lewin (1946), a socially responsible social science would not be found in a passive, detached, value-free, form of inquiry. Instead, Lewin's vision called for a socially engaged social science, one that would involve "pioneer work in action research that hopefully might . . . revolutionize certain aspects of our social life" (Lewin, as quoted in Marrow, 1969, p. 163). For social science to genuinely serve the needs of humanity, social theory must take as axiomatic an image of people as active, co-creators of their world (Chein, 1972; Cooperrider and Pasmore, 1991b). Moreover, a humanistic social science needs to "put idealism on empirical footing and to construct a science whose constructive mandate is to become a generative-theoretical partner with evolution itself, in the service of promoting the widest good and, ultimately, in the service of life" (Cooperrider and Pasmore, 1991a, p. 780). This is a tall order for action researchers. Yet, we agree with Cooperrider and Pasmore that social science must move toward becoming an "*appreciative science,* a science that is no longer tranquilized by the trivial but is instead inspired by the 'reverence for life'" (1991b, p. 1051).

The desirable future for the world as it has been envisioned by people from hundreds of Search Conferences expresses a set of common human ideals. The world people wish to bring into being is a world in which they can work together, be joyful in their daily lives, and make wise decisions. It is a new world order that can be characterized as associative, joyful, and wise. This most desirable future for our world is in every way different from what we fear may come to pass, a probable future world where people are dissociated, miserable, and ignorant.

Regardless of the exact words people use or the language they speak, their desirable future always includes components that state that we all belong to the same human race, and that we will live together in peace, respect our differences, and cooperate to better our world. This includes the belief that we will extend care for others regardless of their differences. That we will care for the thing that most binds us, our physical home, the planet Earth—in all its dimensions. People know that there cannot be a desirable future for us as a species if there is no home, literally no common ground, no common unity or "community" (Kemmis, 1990) to sustain us and future generations.

People also see themselves as belonging to and working for the future at multiple levels from national to local, as well as in various groupings. But all of these levels and groups are seen as having permeable boundaries such that they may come together in different configurations at different times to cooperate and work toward solving common problems. There are statements about learning and the ways in which our uniquely human gifts and propensities are used to nurture both children and adults so that they can realize all their potentials and exercise them in the interests of the whole. Our ways of learning must again be holistic and capture the challenges that people need if they are to grow and to develop. The learning envisaged will include the expert knowledge we acquire from the pursuit of science, as well as the common sense and wisdom we inherit from our elders.

These different ways of knowing will inform each other and will be available to all. There will be no need for a technocratic elite. Everyone will also have the opportunity to contribute to this collectively held knowledge through a lifelong process of action learning. As everyone is born with the capacity to learn, so everyone will be respected as equal in the learning process. The way in which we structure our institutions will mean that they will function as environments for learning, as does the Search Conference. People will understand the concepts behind these structures and know how to design and redesign them for continuous learning.

In this desirable future there is work that has dignity and is based on "the human use of human beings" (Wiener, 1967). There will no longer be exploitation, slavery, or an abuse of human rights. Work as a challenging and productive activity will meet human needs, and replace drudgery in dehumanized organizations under poor working conditions. Productive activity will cross work and leisure boundaries, contributing to individual growth and a social identity. There will be a choice of lifestyles that meet individual needs, yet contribute in their own way to a pluralistic society. And decisions about technology and economics will recognize that people really matter and the planet really matters.

There is the notion that we are related by our common humanity, that what affects one ultimately affects all. People desire happiness and a world without daily misery, suffering, and depression, one in which people greet their new day rejoicing and with hope because they know they have a significant part to play in making it better. In this world, people are taking responsibility for their affairs rather than delegating them to remote representatives, and they are confident in their ability to make wise decisions.

The desirable future is also beautiful in all its aspects. Natural, social, and built environments will be aesthetically pleasing and attractive. There will be wilderness areas. Recreation will be a positive part of our lives, not a way to kill time or a euphemism for unemployment. In fact, leisure and recreation will be as fulfilling as productive activity. The scenario of people living, working, and celebrating together as equals, creating their own desirable future, is inherently attractive and motivates people toward greater heights.

This picture may sound like a utopian dream, but it is an expression of the highest human ideals. It is the kind of world that we collectively desire and would create if our institutions were aligned with our hopes and dreams. Search conferencing is a potent way of awakening people to new possibilities for the future. Pockets of this dream can be found in progressive companies that have truly empowered their employees, where work has become meaningful and business is thriving. Glimpses of this desirable future can be found in communities where people have banded together to solve social problems, inspiring a revival of civic culture that is spirited, healthy, and responsive. For individuals, the diffusive power of searching has helped them not only to adapt and survive in a rapidly changing world, it has also fostered the development of their human virtues and competence as democratic citizens.

Epilogue

Fred Emery

It is true that when you give a little boy a hammer he tends to see everything around him as affording, nay, demanding a hammering. Unfortunately, this characteristic seems to be true of the applied behavioral sciences. The history of the applied behavioral sciences, and organization development in particular, has been marked by an intense and faddish devotion to techniques. No sooner do they have a new tool in their hand than, like the little boy with the hammer, they start seeing the solution of every sort of problem as requiring this tool. Like the little boy, they do not stop to wonder about what objective requirements the tool was invented to meet. Increased technical sophistication, no matter how baroque, is much admired and rewarded without questions being raised about the theory specifying the function of the tool. Applied behavioral scientists and organization development practitioners are, in fact, very intolerant and impatient with attempts to wonder about such things as the theory behind the tool; they want to see the latest results that have been achieved with the tool.

These should not be confused with "practical results." Most applied behavioral scientists are academics; the most important result for them, the result that increases their professional standing and increases their prospects of promotion, is publication in a peer-reviewed journal for their specialty. I am describing the mainstream social sciences. The social sciences have outstanding renegades, but the mainstream is the reference group when it comes to adopting a new practice. For organization development practitioners, results are often evaluated in terms of whether an intervention served the needs of the client, but programmatic evaluation of such results is more the exception than the rule. Results for the organization development practitioner often are measured in consultant-centered terms: a tool is considered to deliver results if it increases consulting income, leads to economies of scale, and increases professional popularity.

This is not the place to wonder why the applied behavioral sciences remain fixated at such an immature level. It is enough to know that Search Conferences, as a new tool, might well become a professional fad and suffer the fate of the other fads. That fate is destined to occur when a tool is used far beyond the circumstances for which it was designed, and then it is judged by its inevitable failures.

Not unnaturally, I think that Search Conferences should be more widely used, but I am concerned that the Search Conference might become yet another one of the social science and organization development fads.

What are the prospects?

The social pressure toward using Search Conferences is very considerable. In the workplace, and increasingly in community affairs, the expectation is of greater participation. Social scientists, unless tenured, are not immune from those expectations. And organization development practitioners, unless they are well established, are hungry for the next consulting contract. Certainly the Search Conference is a great tool for increasing participation in areas of strategic planning traditionally dominated by experts. One can expect that it will be seized on as such by the soft social scientists. This tool will not, of course, be welcomed by the hard-nosed social scientists, those who are dedicated to statistical and experimental tools. The latter happen to be numbered among the experts, if they appear on the social scene or enter the field setting at all.

This is only one side of the forecast. The other side is that the theoretical assumptions underlying the Search Conference are contrary to the dominant assumptions of social science, even the soft versions. One can expect them to adapt the tool to their assumptions till little is left but the name.

As successful products of the educational system, having made it through to the tertiary level, social scientists will tend to disbelieve that people can have direct knowledge of even part of the world out there. They will believe that that knowledge is only attainable indirectly by logical inference and hence only available to university-trained specialists. That is, without any personal experience of search conferencing, they will dismiss the very first phase of the conference as some sort of psychological trickery; necessary, perhaps, but trickery nevertheless. Rigorously speaking, they would say, one cannot speak of people establishing that they are acting in the same world. Berkeley and Hume proved that individuals can only know for sure the world bounded by their own sensations. Less rigorously, one might allow that a gathering of people could be led to the collective delusion that they live in the same world. The traditional experimental studies of perception and social conformity have appeared to confirm these views—but only by assuming beforehand conditions created by the experimental designs. Heider (1959) and subsequently Gibson (1966, 1979) and his colleagues, proved that these studies were grossly misleading. They proved, with new experiments, that people are capable of direct perception, and therefore knowledge of the part of the world that they live in. Collectively, people can put their partial knowledge together to provide a broader validated picture, because of their overlapping experiences. They are also well aware from their collective experience that some people are so concerned with the uniqueness of their world that no genuine search conferencing is possible with them. Quite literally, if the participants are not able to assure themselves that they are living in and talking about the same world, then they have not reached first base for a joint Search Conference. Contrary to the assumptions of the educated sophisticates, the first stage of reality testing whether the participants live in the same world is for real; it is in no way a trick to create a collective delusion. In fact, there is no point in proceeding to the next stage of considering probable and desirable futures if the participants believe that they live in and talk about different worlds. If the product of this first phase is treated as some sort of induced collective delusion, instead of being a real picture, even if partial, the subsequent phases of the Search Conference will be impoverished.

Second, those who have graduated with degrees in the social sciences tend to have difficulty with the next phase of the search process. The psychologists tend to have difficulty with the assumption of the basic psychological similarity of people because they have been impressed with the scientific nature of IQ studies; the sociologists because of the ubiquity of dominating hierarchies and the circulation of elites; and organization development practitioners because of their propensity to assume that people are born with a social handicap that requires remedial human relations training. The product of this phase is important as participants search out the probable and desirable futures implied by the data generated from the product of previous product—the scan of the wider environment. Together these products define the agreed context within which participants can confront their existing differences about where the community can or should go. More critical to the process itself is the way this entire phase enables participants to see, and test out, whether they are accepted by the others as equally human. People are well aware that they are not equally quick-witted, intelligent, learned, and so on, but they take deep umbrage at any suggestion that they are less human. If they feel that other participants are putting on superior airs, pulling rank, or otherwise treating them as less than equals, then the conference will eviscerate itself in fight-flight group assumptions. No matter how good or promising the products might be coming out of this initial phase, people will not be willing to accept or work in a context that excludes a genuinely democratic dialogue. They will deny ownership of the products and attribute them to the manipulations of the allegedly superior parties.

These are the two preconditions that I think are at most risk if search conferencing is adopted unthinkingly by applied behavioral scientists and organization development practitioners as the next hammer for enhancing participation. Normally, one would check beforehand to ensure that these preconditions can reasonably be expected to be met. If not, one should advise against search conferencing. If after a conference starts it appears that either condition is not achievable after all, then the conference manager should confront participants with the problem and recommend that they stop or, at best, go back to the beginning and try again. Unfortunately, many people will feel locked into a gathering even when they believe these preconditions have been violated. This is particularly so when the participants are all employees of the same organization, but it will also happen when people are so deprived of opportunities to speak up that they feel they might as well make the best of a bad situation. If the faddists have such a captive conference, the next point of control is with the final stage of the conference report. Occasionally, the Search Conference managers will have the individual participants fill out a questionnaire that the managers take away for analysis. This is a crude but underhanded way of taking over ownership of the conference. Whatever the conference concludes, collectively, the conference managers are able to say that individuals really believed this, that, or the other. Less crudely, the conference managers will offer to prepare a final report from the flip-chart sheets generated by the conference with the help of a few representatives from among the participants. If the participants have been less than convinced of the genuineness of the process, they will welcome the excuse to wash their hands of the whole thing. This might be an efficient way to generate a printed report for the sponsors. However, it cuts across the buildup of trust among the participants.

Some trust must exist among the participants for them to take the penultimate step of appointing specialist groups to work on the practical steps of implementing their plans. The final report should be a statement of the respondents' own commitments. The postconference follow-up is the test of how much they can trust each other to honor those commitments. That is the true test of the success of search conferencing.

So far, I have dealt with how far search conferencing fits the assumptions that have dominated the social sciences for the past seventy years, or more. Obviously, I do not think that they fit together, even for many of the soft social scientists and organizational development practitioners—that is, those with a more clinical and humanistic approach. They will, I suggest, be sorely tempted to turn the Search Conference into another manipulative tool, while preserving the appearance of participation. I have suggested some of the likely ways in which this transformation (corruption) has been attempted. A degreed level of training in the applied behavioral sciences is not required for the management of Search Conferences, but it is difficult to envisage a social science that does not seek to encompass search conferencing.

There is the much broader question of what kind of social groupings will allow, let alone encourage, search conferencing?

In the first place, the Search Conference did not emerge from any breakthrough in social science. It was an idea whose time had come. More precisely, the time had come in the 1960s and 1970s to recover an idea that had a long prehistory. All that is genuinely new are the steps that have had to be designed in order to break through a centuries-old layer of dominant institutions and a century of rapidly multiplying bureaucracies with their cohorts of certified

meritocrats. Those new design features can only influence the selection of participants and protection of the process once it is
under way. They cannot bring about a willingness to engage in
search conferencing. However, if we reflect on the assumptions of
search conferencing, we will not find it too difficult to predict
where demand for this tool is most likely to arise.

Before the counter-cultural movement of the 1960s, the very
notion of search conferencing was inconceivable. Before then,
some restricted circles of elites might have found the technique of
value for themselves, but it probably would not have occurred to
them that it might be of wider social use. Whatever else the
counter-culture achieved in Western societies, it certainly stripped
away faith in the wisdom of the established institutions and the ex-
pert-rich bureaucracies, public or private. The 1960s have long
gone, but the social demand for participation and empowerment
has continued to grow. That social demand can be expected to
show itself in increasing use of search conferencing in these areas
where people have most control over their affairs, that is, in voluntary associations and local community government.

However unpalatable it might be to some readers, I suggest that
a critical social demand will arise from private enterprise. The job
of private enterprises is to ensure the growth of capital with which
they are entrusted. So long as that seemed to require autocratic control of a recalcitrant workforce, managers in private enterprises were
autocrats to the hilt. Nowadays the leading edge of private enterprises realize that return on capital, and hence growth, can only be
achieved with the cooperation of their managers and workforces.
They no longer talk in Tayloristic terms of minimal training in
skills, narrowing individual job specifications, and close supervision but instead of multi-skilling, teams, and self-management. It
is no distance from there to search conferencing with middle management, workers, suppliers, and customers. I rate that as a critical
development because it outflanks those socially powerful people
who have a vested interest in representative democracy. They, and
their advisors and consultants, will not see themselves as further
empowered by search conferencing.

I do not think that in this epilogue I have added anything to
what the authors have said. It is simply that at the end you have to
count your friends and enemies. They may not be the ones you
started with.

Resources

This section includes a sample slide presentation that we have used to introduce the Search Conference to senior managers and administrators. In addition, we provide the names of institutes that offer courses and training seminars on Search Conference methodology as described in this text. There are also competent Search Conference practitioners located throughout the United States and Canada, but it would be impossible to list them all here.

1. Slide Presentation for Prospective Sponsors

What is a Search Conference?

- Participative, strategic planning method
- Planning for the people, by the people
- Experience in participative democracy
- A 24–28 hour event (2 days) that establishes a learning-planning community

Search Conference Applications

- Community development
- Regional issues
- School system planning and development
- Organizational strategic planning
- Industry or professional association issues
- Public sector planning
- Economic development

What Happens in a Search Conference?

- 20–35 people from system participate
- Knowledge of the system, diverse perspectives, and potential for implementing the plan
- SC is usually 2–2.5 days and two nights, preferably off-site
- People work together in large conference community, people simultaneously learn and plan the future of the system together

Principles at Work in Search Conferences

- Open Systems Thinking
- Democratic Design Principle
- Conditions for Open Dialogue
- Conditions for Ideal Seeking, Seeking Common Ground
- Rationalization of Conflict

Search Conference Ground Rules

- All perceptions are valid
- Participation is equal and open, regardless of status or position
- People's perceptions are spoken and recorded on flip-chart paper
- No presenters, no lectures, no speeches, keynote addresses, games, icebreakers, or training sessions
- People are self-managing and responsible for tasks and outcomes

Role of Search Conference Managers

- Design structure and plan of SC
- Manage and ensure optimum learning environment
- Stay out of content
- Time management
- Manage large group dynamics
- Consult with planning group in SC preparation

Search Conference Preparation

- Formation of a planning group
- Decide on specific focus and time-line of SC
- Identify "the system" and its boundaries
- Devise criteria and process for participant selection
- Provide pre-briefings and education on the SC
- Handle logistics, facilities set-up, etc.

2. Education and Training in the Search Conference

Center for Organization Development
Ronald E. Purser, Ph.D., Associate Professor
Loyola University
25 East Pearson
Chicago, IL 60611
Phone: 312–915–7518

The Center for Organization Development (CORD) at Loyola University was founded in 1981 and is nationally recognized as one of the few stand-alone graduate programs in Organization Development. Students and professors often are engaged in action research projects focused on a broad range of concerns: large systems change, quality of working life, health care management, reinventing government, technological change, labor and trade union revitalization, school reform, urban renewal, and economic development. CORD offers academic courses on both the Search Conference method and Participative Design, which can be taken toward either a Certificate or a Masters of Science degree in Organization Development. In addition to formal academic courses, CORD offers special professional development workshops for practitioners wishing to learn more about the Search Conference method. CORD is at the hub of a growing network of professionals, managers, community activists, academics, and consultants who are interested in the advancement and diffusion of the Search Conference and other participative methods in workplaces, communities, and public-sector agencies.

International Institute for Natural, Environmental,
and Cultural Resources Management (IIRM)
Joel Diemer, Ph.D., Director
New Mexico State University
Box 30003
Dept. 3169
Las Cruces, NM 88003
Phone: 505–646–1044

Since 1993, IIRM has been the Western Hemisphere sponsor and coordinator for Merrelyn Emery's training program, Designing and Managing Search Conferences and Participative Design Workshops. IIRM's goal is to assume a leading role and to work with collaborators both within and external to NMSU to provide assistance and support that fosters informed, participative, democratic, and sustainable management of natural, environmental, and cultural resources throughout the Americas. Implementation of the IIRM agenda also involves the development of international networks of collaborators (agencies, academic institutions, nongovernmental organizations, and so on), and trained, technically proficient professionals to assist at the community level. These networks cover North, Central, and South America, the Caribbean, and Australia, with capabilities in French, Spanish, and English.

To enhance communications among IIRM collaborators, the Institute maintains dp2logos@nmsu.edu, an international e-mail listserver.

Appendix: History of the Search Conference

For a vivid look at the beginning of the Search Conference concept, this Appendix opens with an excerpt based on an interview between Ron Purser and Fred Emery. It goes on to discuss other milestones in the development of search conferencing.

Barford: The First Search Conference (1960)

Ron Purser: Fred, could you tell us about the situation that led up to the design of the first Search Conference?

Fred Emery: In 1959, the Tavistock Institute of Human Relations was posed the problem of designing a conference that would enable the senior executives of the Bristol and Siddeley Aero-engine companies to create a single operating entity, Bristol-Siddeley Aero-engines. The merger was forced upon them by their major customer, the Royal Air Force (RAF). The two companies had shared a mutual contempt since World War I. Siddeley was production-centered and aimed at producing noninnovative but sound, inexpensive, and reliable workhorse engines for training aircraft and the like. Bristol was dominated by its design engineers, who saw themselves as competing at the front end of the world's aero-engine industry: "the blue ribbon market" for the highest-powered jet engine. It was common knowledge that their products did not always match their advanced designs. Bristol had the upper hand and their Managing Director was the Managing Director-elect for the joint enterprise. He was a Fellow of the Royal Society (FRS) known for his creative work on the jet engine and other such engineering innovations.

Purser: So what was your thinking at that time in terms of designing this conference?

Emery: On behalf of the Tavistock, Eric Trist and I laid down the criteria for the conference. First, I knew that we had to meet the Asch (1952) criteria for effective discourse. Second, this conference needed to produce a high level of emotional engagement but be safeguarded from moving into the group emotions of fight-flight or dependency (Bion, 1952). It was theoretically inconceivable at the time that we could have set the positive goal of sustaining the creative work mode. Third, the conference had to produce a mission statement that would be valid into the seventies and a corporate plan for the embodiment of the values appropriate to that mission (Selznick, 1957). Some six months went into designing this six-day conference for twelve participants. Cost was not a constraint because of what was at stake.

Purser: Were there other issues or considerations that influenced how you designed the conference?

Emery: We were under pressure by a) slotting the distinguished guests into the after-dinner role; and b) selecting and briefing those guests so that there would be a resonance between what they spoke of and the problems that we planned for the participants to be engaged in at that time. We were concerned that the participants not be diverted from the task and were not at all sure that the task, which was very much an intellectual task, would engage them strongly enough.

Purser: What was your experience? How did the Barford Conference turn out?

Emery: As it turns out, we were being too cautious in our assumptions. The participants, with one exception, became so involved with their problems that they would have distorted anything the guest speakers said into answers for their problems. The level of energy in the group was such that they all reported having difficulties shutting off their minds after the six days were over and returning to their normal duties. This group had worked on a number of challenging intellectual tasks. They developed a better understanding of the complexities and uncertainties associated with the aircraft engine industry; they devised new, joint business strategies in a declining military market; they overcame the problem of capital requirements for research and development; they developed organizational forms more appropriate to the emerging enterprise; they considered the prospects for developing a small, gas turbine engine; and they dealt with the shortage and need for attracting and developing well-trained managers and top-caliber talent. Clearly, the conference design achieved its planned objectives: an effective dialogue was achieved and sustained for most of the time; there was but one brief period in which fight-flight dynamics dominated, and only one in which dependency threatened to dominate; a mission statement emerged that can be traced through to the present day, despite the subsequent merger with Rolls-Royce. As predicted, the learned addresses were, at least, negligible, and at most a potential disruption to effective dialogue. This was a surprising finding given that the expert lecture or learned address is the cornerstone of the traditional conference.

Purser: What else did you learn from working with groups in this way?

Emery: The serendipitous finding for me was the great strength of emotional involvement that the intellectual task created. We wrote in our original report (Trist and Emery, 1960, p. 1), that one of the key features of the conference was "that of *the great psychological intensity . . .* which was due to the *very high level of personal involvement in the overriding demand for intellectual integrity.*" The immense energy and enthusiasm on the part of participants during a Search Conference has been a common observation. The unchallenged assumption of the day (Tavistock at that time had a very psychoanalytical orientation) had been that only matters of love and hate could sustain the intensity of dialogue that was to be found in Bion-type groups. Yet this experiment suggested that love and hate might in fact be defensive mechanisms to offset the catastrophic impact of intellectual overload.

The overload problem was readily resolved at the practical level. After one more experience of that problem, we resolved that conferences of this nature should not be extended beyond two days and two nights. The powerfully motivating force of effective, democratic, task-oriented work was a welcome finding. It made it unnecessary for us to design for a long conference and we were absolutely certain that providing external stimuli in the form of powerful speakers or audio-visual aids were also completely unnecessary. A very considerable body of experience has accumulated since 1960, thus enabling more precise specification of the design requirements and deeper theoretical understanding of the dynamics of such conferences.

Purser: Everyone asks us why you labeled this process the "Search Conference" . . .

Emery: We called this new form of conference the "Search Conference" because its primary function was to allow "mere possibilities" to surface. In searching for meaning in these emerging possibilities, the participants are usually confronted with unexpected new directions and new ways of approaching old issues. This is very different from simply examining significant probabilities, which are usually under the control of a good chairperson in traditional committee meetings. In other words, when uncertainty is high, the primary task shifts from means to searching for new strategic goals or end points. I want to end by saying that while it appears that Trist and I discovered the Search Conference in the early sixties, it would be more accurate to say that we went through the wasteful process of rediscovering it. Certainly anthropologists have many examples of tribal gatherings and rituals that involve a form of searching. And even the Society of Friends might claim ownership to the idea. If you look at the historical writings of Herodotus, his description of the council meetings of the ancient Persian tribes reads like a Search Conference. And among the Pathan tribes, there is this institution of the *jirca,* which also very much resembles what we do in Search Conferences.

Looking Back on Barford

The term "searching" first appeared in Emery and Trist's research report on this novel conference (Trist and Emery, 1960). Fred Emery designed and managed the Barford conference, while Eric Trist was there mainly to observe, specifically for Bion's group assumptions. Trist served as backup in case the group dynamics got of hand (as it turned out, they did not). Both Emery and Trist learned that Bion's group assumptions could be minimized by designing conferences to meet Asch's criteria for effective and influential communications.

At that time, Asch's condition for openness was achieved mainly by encouraging genuine participation of all group members. Unlike the way flip charts are used in Search Conferences today, group discussions and outcomes were not continuously recorded for each task. Instead, flip charts were used mainly to keep track of the agreed agenda for each session. Emery recalls that he occasionally took notes on the content discussed during each session. Participants were not disturbed by this because they understood his motives. However, when they noticed that one of the sponsor's close associates also resorted to taking notes, they became suspicious. Several participants managed to sneak a peek at this person's notes when he left the room during morning tea.

Apparently the notes were of a highly personal nature regarding certain individuals present at the meeting. Participants assumed that this person was collecting data for the sponsor to use in evaluating key personnel decisions. This incident initiated an episode of fight-flight.

Fred Emery clearly remembers one other brief incident that led to an outbreak of fight-flight. He claims that this was caused by another participant, a marketing manager who, in his opinion, never should have been invited. Discussions at Barford were focused mostly on technological issues; the marketing manager, apparently feeling out of place, left one day and didn't return.

Barford still achieved great emotional intensity despite a number of design flaws. Most serious was the conference's mixed-mode design. The mixed mode occurs when a large-group meeting shifts back and forth between bureaucratic and democratic structures. Mixing guest speakers and outside experts with work performed by participants created personal strain for all involved. There were other design faults built into this first attempt. The roles of experts, managers, and observers, and the nature of the external and internal structure of the conference, were far from optimum. It also turned out that six days was far too long to keep people in the creative working mode—some participants suffered overload.

Since its invention at Barford, every aspect of the Search Conference has been subjected to intensive conceptual and action research. Nobody today would run a Search Conference by copying the design of the 1960 Barford version.

Experimental Period (1960–1970)

Fred Emery ran another eleven Search Conferences before returning to Australia in 1969—one of them the first to be successfully applied to an international conflict. None of these Search Conferences exceeded three days, although there was experimentation with varying the number of participants. Emery conducted a Search Conference for the National Farmers Association with fifty participants, and the process suffered as a result. He found that the quality and depth of dialogue in Search Conferences is diminished when the number of participants exceeds thirty-five. In

1965, Emery was approached by John Burton, an Australian diplomat from the United Nations, to intervene in an international dispute between Singapore, Malaysia, and Indonesia. At this time, Singapore and Malaysia were still part of the British Empire. The conflict involved a territorial dispute, and Emery was brought in after all mediation had failed. During this intervention, Emery discovered the rationalization of conflict approach (F. Emery, 1966). He found that the resolution of conflict occurred once the parties stopped trying to tackle key conflict areas and shifted their attention to areas of common ground.

Diffusion of Innovation in Australia (1970–1982)

During this period, Fred and Merrelyn Emery were calling this innovative approach to participative strategic planning and community development the "Search Conference" or "Future Search" (F. Emery and M. Emery, 1976). Between 300 and 400 Search Conferences were conducted in Australia during the 1970s.

Merrelyn Emery's first Search Conference opportunity arose in 1972 with the proposal for planning the town of Gungahlin near the national capital of Canberra. After long and intensive discussions with the National Capital Development Commission, Merrelyn Emery convinced the Commission that social planning needed to incorporate the perspectives of those who were the seeds of the town's future—young people in the region. Angela Sands and Merrelyn Emery were awarded a contract to design a Search Conference on the "Future of Gungahlin" with participants sixteen to twenty-five years old. There was a great deal of skepticism about the ability of this age group to plan efficiently on their own. The Commission insisted that these young people could not work without the supervision of adults. Subsequently, leaders were assigned to each of the three subgroups of young people in the conference. The Commission also sent several professional urban planners to attend as a resource. If this wasn't enough to dampen the creative spirit, the Commission also insisted on an orientation day, during which the participants were lectured about town planning and future studies.

None of the Commission's worst fears and dire predictions came to pass. Rather, the kids took to the task like ducks to water.

We could hardly keep up with them. In line with the usual protective and paternalistic concerns, no work in the evening had been scheduled. However, we soon found that we couldn't stop them, and on some evenings we couldn't get them to bed! The urban planners were never called upon (M. Emery, 1974). News of the Search Conference planning for Gungahlin diffused rapidly.

In 1974, Merrelyn and Fred Emery were invited to help a major contractor involve the community in the planning of a new transportation system in Geelong. While planning the Geelong conference, they ran into a great deal of resistance from the professionals involved. "Let the community make decisions! How can ordinary townspeople know what is good for them!" was the sort of elitism the Emerys encountered. The preconference meetings for Geelong were heated and intense. This led to the creation of ground rules for the Search Conference: "all perceptions are valid," professionals are not allowed to dominate the conference, and condescension will not be tolerated. Fred and Merrelyn Emery learned another means for enhancing Asch's conditions. Geelong also turned out to be a success (Schwartzkoff, 1974).

Many organizational, community, industry, issue-based, and national Search Conferences were held across the country. Some of their titles may be illustrative: "The Future of Nursing Education," "The Future of Industrial Relations in Australia," "Creating the New Maximum Security Prison of the Future," "Telecommunications 2000," and "Policies for the Department of the Environment." During this period there was wide diffusion of the method, precipitating a rash of so-called Search Conferences conducted by practitioners with no formal training. Many of them used techniques that had little resemblance to the Search Conference method. With deep regret, Merrelyn and Fred Emery witnessed how a lack of practitioner competence can quickly damage the reputation and credibility of a reliable method.

Meanwhile, a national network of well-trained Search Conference practitioners in Australia had grown. Network meetings were exciting, as practitioners discussed variations and innovations in their practice and analyzed the theoretical bases for successes and failures. Experimentation continued apace, as did the conceptual work. This period clarified the essential components of Search Conference theory and practices (M. Emery and F. Emery, 1978).

Particularly important during this time was the increasing use of local community Search Conferences, which contributed to the concept of the searching community. Previously there had been a distinction between social planning and community development. Planning was the province of trained experts (urban planners), and community development was also beginning to become a professionalized domain (social workers, community psychologists). Men and women who lived in the community were perceived as lacking the means and responsibility to manage their own local, regional, and community affairs. The result was a proliferation of social engineers and professional planners who found jobs in welfare agencies, government offices, and other social service bureaucracies. Citizens in the community became their clients. These professionals perceived community Search Conferences as threats to their status and expert-based authority. Narrowing the distance between planners and the planned for—which is the basis for involvement and participation—is an emotional phenomenon that often looks irrational to a rational planner. Creative ideas, emotionality, and the joy of participation cannot be easily encompassed within mechanistic equations. Community search conferencing overturned planners' assumptions about the capabilities of local residents and demonstrated that the distinction between social planning and community development was an artificial one. The search community at Geelong was quite explicit in seeing itself as a group of planners.

The Search Conference was also adapted as a method for creating and planning new structures, learning processes, and curricula in education (Williams, 1982). Innovation in the education field was booming, and search conferencing followed a typical diffusion curve. By 1977, so many Search Conferences had been conducted in Australia that it was impossible to keep track of them.

This enthusiastic diffusion by individuals required further investigation. Search Conferences appeared to offer individual participants some ability or quality of experience that had an empowering effect, motivating them to diffuse the innovation. Individual, community, and organization development seemed to be rooted in this same process. The Search Conference appeared to integrate individual creativity with an inspired sense of communal responsibility. In 1976, the Centre for Continuing Education at the Australian

National University published a research monograph (M. Emery, 1976) describing the work conducted on Search Conferences up to this point.

In 1976, the group at the Centre for Continuing Education held an international conference for social scientists on "The Future of the Search Conference." We later came to refer to this event as the "Search Search." The purpose of this event was to bring interested social scientists together to experience a Search Conference and use its processes to learn about the theory and practice of Search Conferences. In short, it was Merrelyn and Fred Emery's first attempt to deliberately design a training course for Search Conference managers. Merrelyn and Fred realized that firsthand exposure to the method as a participant at a Search Conference was insufficient. A training course was needed, one that provided an integrated conceptual and experiential understanding of the theory and dynamics of the search methodology. Merrelyn and Fred were also concerned about the diffusion of the method by untrained practitioners. One of the aims of a Search Conference is to enable those with no privileged access to social science knowledge to learn how to learn about the totality of their everyday affairs. Those that had participated in Search Conferences were indeed learning, and had increased control over their own affairs, but they did not know how they were doing it.

The final program sent to prospective participants in the "Search Search" read as follows (M. Emery, 1978):

> The Search Conference is being used more and more in Australia in a variety of planning and policy-making contexts. In our review of this area we see two main needs emerging. The first could be generally stated as a need to assess the state of the art, to evaluate the effectiveness of the search conference as a new planning methodology. The second is a need for an opportunity to learn systematically about the structures and processes which are intrinsic to a search conference. Both these needs are related to the problems of a diffusion of this new methodology. To be able to replicate a search conference one needs not only previous experience with the method, but also a conceptual understanding of the elements which go together to make the search conference a potentially powerful tool in the current social environment.
>
> There is in existence a body of social science knowledge and skills in this field. In the particular area of search conferences I

have attempted to put together and edit the available writing and some search conference reports. While this is a start to solving the problem, it does not take us far enough in the direction of turning social science into the sort of common sense that can be picked up by the man in the street. We are concerned here particularly with the social responsibilities, not only of social scientists, but all those in executive positions in organizations and community structures, to disseminate the best of social science experience to the wider community. At the moment there is only a small group of practitioners and interested people looking at this problem. Many of them are working in fairly isolated circumstances. Our task as we see it at the moment is to attempt to bring together these people in such a way and with such a programme that the dimensions of the problem can be explored and practical plans arrived at.

The plan for the meeting is our attempt to design in all the various components that we see as necessary to fulfilling the task. The meeting needs to be a genuine experience of a search conference which takes as its central problem the diffusion of appropriate social science knowledge to an increasingly participative and democratic society. There also needs to be opportunities to reflect, analyze this experience, and compare it with what stands as the academic literature. This will perhaps lead to the production of a more concise and refined manual for others interested in search conferences, or it may lead to the basic redefinition of the parameters of a search. As with any search activity the plan is open-ended, and the conclusions are intended to constitute guidelines for future action. [pp.4–5]

The design of this event followed a classical Search Conference format, except that an extra day was added to explore the difference between search conferencing and modes such as committees and conventional scientific conferences. This also allowed time for discussion around particular areas of interest, such as applications in education, industry, or government, while also leaving ample time for outlining unanswered questions and for follow-up activities. Twenty-five participants attended the conference.

The conference was generally agreed to be a disaster, but it ended on a high note. In the first session, there was a great deal of sniping and argument. Fred Emery had started off the session without mentioning the ground rule that all contributions were valid. Many participants were critical that the list of trends were so negative. Others criticized the methodology. Contributions became sporadic and were more speculative than factual. The point was raised that this task could be better performed in small groups. It wasn't until the morning of the last day that a cohesive conference community emerged.

The task of searching how to make social science accessible to the person on the street evoked a great deal of resistance on the part of social scientists. Moreover, the methodology of searching based on a paradigm of ecological learning and direct perception seemed to be directly at odds with the mainstream scientific paradigm of many of the participating social scientists. Much of the hesitation and conflict in the groups was directed toward the methodology, describing it as unscientific, ideological, superficial, and subjective. Shortly after the conference, the Emerys received a letter of reflection from one of the participants in the "Search Search." A portion of it appears below (M. Emery, 1982):

> You had taken on one of the most difficult and perhaps impossible of tasks. A group of so-called Social Scientists . . . with all that means of stress and frustration. Each person has an image about his own professional competence; any threat concerning changes of that image will produce a mild or severe identity crisis.
>
> I belonged to "the pro's" group and we very quickly developed a culture with norms like how to behave expertly, to be competent experts. No learning could take place because it was a closed system. It was a socio-emotional collusion. . . . With this it was impossible by definition to do the task properly, that is to spell out a desirable future for Social Science . . . that was threatening and could not be expressed. Therefore the depressive scenarios. Any other form of perspective on the future would include designing yourself out of the system. . . . There was no trust whatsoever. People were so locked into their social scientific roles that they couldn't afford to lose their face—a status feeling. [p.43]

After subsequent work and learning, it is easy to see in hindsight that the state of the art at that point still had a long way to go. However, the problems inspired Merrelyn Emery to develop a systemic theory explaining such diverse phenomena as diffusion, the mixture of hostility and apathy from social scientists, and the power of the Search Conference method itself. She also found that the emotional (affective) system played a major role in the learning and diffusion process. These subsequent findings were published in an updated report called *Searching: For New Directions, in New Ways, for New Times* (M. Emery, 1982).

Search Conferences Go International

By the late 1970s, Fred and Merrelyn Emery were conducting Search Conferences in other parts of the world. In Holland, the Emerys trained Hans and Ingrid van Beinum. The van Beinums subsequently brought the method to Canada and began diffusing it through the Ontario Centre for Quality of Working Life. The first Search Conference in Norway was held in 1977 on "The Future of North Sea Oil and Gas." From Europe, the Emerys went to India and worked with Nitish De, who also became an early adopter of the method. In 1978, the International Council for the Quality of Working Life made the Search Conference a major component of its meeting in Paris. After these projects, the Emerys were convinced that the Search Conference was a cross-cultural method, one capable of fulfilling all its early promise.

Theory and Practice in North America

Eric Trist moved from the Tavistock to the University of California, Los Angeles, in 1976. He introduced the Search Conference concept, but the method's evolution in the United States did not really begin until much later. Search Conferences had been introduced in Canada by both Hans van Beinum at the Ontario Centre for Quality of Working Life and by Eric Trist when he was on the Faculty of Environmental Studies at York University (Wright and Morley, 1989). By 1981, Morley and Trist reported having conducted some thirty Search Conferences throughout Canada (Morley and Trist, 1993).

The Search Conference method as described in this book was first introduced to the United States by the Emerys in 1982. Fred and Merrelyn taught the theory and practice of the Search Conference method in the Department of Social Systems Science in the Wharton School at the University of Pennsylvania from 1982 through 1984. Together they ran three Search Conferences during this period, one for economic development of the Seneca Nation in New York state, the second for the future of the Pennsylvania school system, and the third for the Georgia state senate on the future of juvenile offenders. In each of these, the Emerys involved interested Ph.D. students from the Wharton school so that the interdependence of theory and practice could be readily grasped.

During this brief stay in North America, the Emerys also enjoyed a close working relationship with the Ontario Centre for Quality of Working Life. Merrelyn ran a Search Conference for this group to establish an adaptive direction and set of strategic goals. These efforts contributed to the diffusion of the method in Canada.

The Seneca Nation Search Conference was followed up by two doctoral students, one of whom returned to his native country of Turkey. There he has enjoyed great success with the method, which is increasingly being used in both the private and public sectors to make effective change. In August 1995, the Emerys went to Turkey and helped design and manage a Search Conference titled "University of the 21st Century," sponsored by Sabanci Holding, a new university in Istanbul.

Despite these activities, there was little diffusion of the method in the United States itself during this period. A number of us have pondered the reason for this, and the most common answer is that the wealth, investment boom years, and international status of the United States at that time insulated the country from coming to a full realization of the impact of the turbulent environment. There simply wasn't a felt need for a different way of planning at this time. Without the impact of turbulence impinging upon organizations, the rationale for conducting Search Conferences could not effectively be made clear.

It is only of recent that the Search Conference method has firmly taken root in North America. In 1993, formal training courses for practitioners began to be offered through the International Institute for Resource Management (IIRM) at New Mexico State University. Ronald Purser invited Merrelyn Emery to conduct a Search Conference training workshop in Chicago for Loyola University graduate students in the summer of 1994. Later that year, he developed a graduate seminar course on the Search Conference method which is now part of the Center of Organization Development curriculum. He also developed a two-day seminar for training Search Conference managers.

References

Ackoff, R. *The Democratic Corporation.* New York: Oxford Books, 1994.

Ackoff, R., and Emery, F. E. *On Purposeful Systems.* London: Tavistock, 1972.

Angyal, A. *Foundations for a Science of Personality.* Boston: Harvard University Press, 1941.

Angyal, A. *Neurosis and Treatment.* New York: Wiley, 1965.

Argyris, C. *Overcoming Organizational Defenses.* Needham Heights, Mass.: Allyn & Bacon, 1990.

Argyris, C., Putnam, R., and Smith, D. *Action Science.* San Francisco: Jossey-Bass, 1985.

Arendt, H. *The Human Condition.* Chicago: University of Chicago Press, 1958.

Asch, S. *Social Psychology.* Englewood Cliffs, N.J.: Prentice-Hall, 1952.

Baburoglu, O. N. "Tracking the Emery-Trist Systems Paradigm (ETSP)." *Systems Practice,* 1992, *5*(3), 263–291.

Bailey, D., and Dupres, S. "The Future Search Conference as a Vehicle for Educational Change." *Journal of Applied Behavioral Science,* 1992, *28*(4), 510–519.

Barron, F. *No Rootless Flower.* Cresskill, N.J.: Hampton Press, 1995.

Beckhard, R., and Harris, R. *Organizational Transitions: Managing Complex Change.* Reading, Mass.: Addison-Wesley, 1977.

Beer, M., Eisenstat, R. A., and Spector, B. "Why Change Programs Don't Produce Change." *Harvard Business Review,* Nov.-Dec. 1990, pp. 158–166.

Bellah, R., and others. *Habits of the Heart.* Berkeley: University of California Press, 1985.

Bion, A. "Group Dynamics: A Review." *International Journal of Psychoanalysis,* 1952, *33,* 235–247.

Bion, A. *Experiences in Groups and Other Papers.* London: Tavistock, 1961.

Boje, D., and Dennehy, R. *Management in a Postmodern World.* Dubuque, Iowa: Kendall-Hunt, 1993.

Bradford, L., Gibbs, J., and Benne, K. *T-Group Theory and Laboratory Method.* New York: Wiley, 1964.

Brown, L. D. "Bridging Organizations and Sustainable Development." *Human Relations,* 1991, *44*(8), 807–831.

Bunker, B., and Alban, B. (eds.). "Conclusions: What Makes Large Group Interventions Effective?" *Journal of Applied Behavioral Science*, 1992, *28*(4), 579–591.

Burke, W. *Organization Development: A Normative View*. Reading, Mass.: Addison-Wesley, 1987.

Bushe, G., and Shani, A. "Parallel Learning Structure Interventions in Bureaucratic Organizations." In W. A. Pasmore and R. Woodman (eds.), *Research in Organizational Change and Development*. Vol. 4. Greenwich, Conn.: JAI Press, 1990.

Cabana, S., Emery, F. E., and Emery, M. "The Search for Effective Strategic Planning is Over." *Journal of Quality and Participation*, July-Aug. 1995, pp. 10–19.

Cabana, S., and Fiero, J. "Motorola, Strategic Planning and the Search Conference." *Journal of Quality and Participation*, July-Aug. 1995, pp. 20–31.

Caudwell, C. *Illusion and Reality: A Study of the Sources of Poetry*. London: Lawrence & Wishart, 1937.

Chein, I. *The Science of Behavior and the Image of Man*. New York: Basic Books, 1972

Chevalier, M. *A Strategy of Interest-Based Planning*. Ph.D. dissertation, University of Pennsylvania. Ann Arbor, Mich.: University Microfilms, 1968.

Cooperrider, D. L., and Pasmore, W. A. "The Organization Dimension of Global Change." *Human Relations*, 1991a, *44*(8), 763–787.

Cooperrider, D. L., and Pasmore, W. A. "Global Social Change: A New Agenda for Social Science?" *Human Relations*, 1991b, *44*(10), 1037–1055.

Cummings, T. "Transorganization Development." In B. Staw and L. Cummings (eds.), *Research in Organizational Behavior*. Vol. 6. Greenwich, Conn: JAI Press, 1984.

Cummings, T., and Huse, E. *Organization Development and Change*. St. Paul, Minn.: West, 1989.

Cummings, T., and Srivastva, S. *Management of Work: A Socio-Technical Systems Approach*. San Diego: University Associates, 1977.

Cytrynbaum, S. "The Tavistock Model: History, Status and Implications of Core Concepts and Assumptions." Paper presented at the 11th International Congress of Group Psychotherapy, Montreal, Aug. 1992.

Dahl, R. *Democracy and Its Critics*. New Haven, Conn.: Yale University Press, 1989.

de Tocqueville, A. *Democracy in America*, (H. Reeve, trans.; F. Bower, rev.; P. Bradley, ed.). New York: Vintage Books, 1969. (Originally published 1840.)

Dewey, J. *Democracy and Education.* New York: Free Press, 1966. (Originally published 1916.)

Drucker, P. F. *Managing in Turbulent Times.* New York: HarperCollins, 1980.

Elden, M. "Sociotechnical Systems Ideas as Public Policy in Norway: Empowering Participation Through Worker-Managed Change." *Journal of Applied Behavioral Science,* 1986, *22,* 239–255.

Elshtain, J. B. *Democracy on Trial.* New York: Basic Books, 1995.

Emery, F. E. *Report No. 2. The Rationalization of Conflict: A Case Study.* Tavistock Institute of Human Relations, document no. T821. London: Tavistock Publications, 1966.

Emery, F. E. (ed.). *Systems Thinking.* Vol. 1. Harmondsworth, England: Penguin Books, 1969.

Emery, F. E. *Futures We Are In.* Leiden, Netherlands: Martinus Nijhoff, 1977.

Emery, F. E. "Educational Paradigms." *Human Futures,* Spring 1980, pp. 1–7.

Emery, F. E. "The Emergence of Ideal-Seeking Systems." In F. E. Emery (ed.), *Systems Thinking,* Vol. 2. Harmondsworth, England: Penguin Books, 1981.

Emery, F. E. "New Perspectives on the World of Work: Sociotechnical Foundations for a New Order?" *Human Relations,* 1982, *35*(12), 1095–1122.

Emery, F. E. *Toward Real Democracy.* Toronto: Ontario Centre for Quality of Working Life, 1989.

Emery, F. E. "Educational Paradigms: An Epistemological Revolution." In M. Emery (ed.), *Participative Design for Participative Democracy.* Canberra, Australia: Australian National University, 1993.

Emery, F. E., and Emery, M. *A Choice of Futures: To Enlighten or Inform?* Leiden, Netherlands: Martinus Nijhoff, 1976.

Emery, F. E., and Trist, E. L. "The Causal Texture of Organizational Environments." *Human Relations,* 1965, *18,* 21–32.

Emery, F. E., and Trist, E. L. *Towards a Social Ecology: Contextual Appreciation of the Future in the Present.* New York: Plenum, 1973.

Emery, M. *Planning Our Town.* Canberra, Australia: Australian National University, 1974.

Emery, M. *Searching: For New Directions, in New Ways, for New Times.* Canberra, Australia: Australian National University, 1976.

Emery, M. *Searching: For New Directions, in New Ways, for New Times.* (rev. ed.) Canberra, Australia: Australian National University, 1982.

Emery, M. "Towards an Heuristic Theory of Diffusion." *Human Relations,* 1986, *39*(2), 411–432.

Emery, M. "Workplace Australia: Lessons for the Planning and Design of Multisearches." *Journal of Applied Behavioral Science,* 1992, *28*(4) 520–533.

Emery, M. (ed.). *Participative Design for Participative Democracy.* Canberra, Australia: Australian National University, 1993.

Emery, M. "The Search Conference: Design and Management of Learning." In F. E. Emery (ed.), *The Social Engagement of Social Science: A Tavistock Anthology,* Vol. 3: *The Socio-Ecological Perspective.* Philadelphia: University of Pennsylvania Press, 1996.

Emery, M., and Emery, F. E. "Searching: For New Directions, in New Ways . . . for New Times." In J. W. Sutherland (ed.), *Management Handbook for Public Administrators.* New York: Van Nostrand Reinhold, 1978.

Etzioni, A. *The Spirit of Community.* New York: Touchstone, 1993.

Farb, P. *Word Play: What Happens When People Talk.* New York: Bantam Books, 1973.

Fenton, W. (ed.). *Parker on the Iroquois.* Syracuse, N.Y.: Syracuse University Press, 1968.

Fott, D. "John Dewey and the Philosophical Foundations of Democracy," *Social Science Journal,* 1991, *28,* 30–41.

Freedman, A. "The Timidity of Consulting Psychologists." Paper presented at the conference of the American Psychological Association, Division 13: Consulting Psychology, New York, Aug. 1995.

Gibson, J. *The Senses Considered as Perceptual Systems.* Boston: Houghton Mifflin, 1966.

Gibson, J. *The Ecological Approach to Visual Perception.* Boston: Houghton Mifflin, 1979.

Glendon, M. *Rights Talk.* New York: Free Press, 1992.

Global Tomorrow Coalition. *Global Ecology Handbook.* Boston: Beacon Press, 1990.

Goodman, J. "Values Clarification: A Review of Major Books." In J. W. Pfeiffer, J. E. Jones, and L. D. Goodstein (eds.), *The Annual Series in Human Resource Development.* San Diego, Calif.: University Associates, 1976.

Goodman, R. *After the Planners.* New York: Touchstone Books, 1971.

Gottlieb, A. *Do You Believe in Magic?* New York: Times Books, 1987.

Gray, B., and Wood, D. "Collaborative Alliances: Moving from Practice to Theory." *Journal of Applied Behavioral Science,* 1991, *27*(1), 3–22.

Grinde, D. A. *The Iroquois and the Founding of the American Nation.* San Francisco: Indian Historical Press, 1977.

Hamilton, A., Madison, J., and Jay, J. *The Federalist Papers.* (Introduction and commentary by Garry Wills.) New York: Bantam Books, 1982. (Originally published 1787–1788.)

Hart, L. *The Strategy of the Indirect Approach.* London: Faber & Faber, 1946.

Heider, F. *On Perception and Event Structure and the Psychological Environment.* New York: International Universities Press, 1959.

Hirschhorn, L. *Psychodynamics Within.* Reading, Mass.: Addison-Wesley, 1990.

Janis, I. *Victims of Groupthink.* Boston: Houghton Mifflin, 1982.

Janssen, C. *Personlig Dialektik* [Personal Dialectic]. Stockholm: Liber, 1982.

Kanter, D., and Mirvis, P. *The Cynical Americans: Living and Working in an Age of Discontent and Disillusion.* San Francisco: Jossey-Bass, 1989.

Kemmis, D. *Community and the Politics of Place.* Norman: University of Oklahoma Press, 1990.

Kernberg, O. A. "Leadership and Organizational Functioning: Organizational Regression." *International Journal of Group Psychotherapy,* 1978, *21,* 3–25.

Ketchum, L., and Trist, E. L. *All Teams Are Not Created Equal.* Newbury Park, Calif.: Sage, 1992.

Klein, J. "Why Supervisors Resist Employee Involvement." *Harvard Business Review,* Sept.-Oct. 1984, pp. 87–95.

Lappé, F. M., and DuBois, P. M. *The Quickening of America: Rebuilding Our Nation, Remaking Our Lives.* San Francisco: Jossey-Bass, 1994.

Lewin, K. "Action Research and Minority Problems." *Journal of Social Issues,* 1946, *2,* 34–46.

Lewin, K. *Field Theory in Social Science: Selected Papers on Group Dynamics.* New York: HarperCollins, 1951.

Likert, R. *The Human Organization: Its Management and Value.* New York: McGraw-Hill, 1967.

Lippitt, G., and Lippitt, R. *The Consulting Process in Action.* La Jolla, Calif.: University Associates, 1978.

MacIntyre, A. *After Virtue.* South Bend, Ind.: University of Notre Dame Press, 1984.

Macoby, M. *The Gamesman: The New Corporate Leader.* New York: Simon & Schuster, 1976.

Mander, J. *In the Absence of the Sacred.* San Francisco: Sierra Club Books, 1991.

Marrow, A. *The Practical Theorist.* New York: Basic Books, 1969.

McGregor, D. *The Human Side of Enterprise.* New York: McGraw-Hill, 1960.

McLuhan, M. *Understanding Media: The Extensions of Man.* New York: New American Library, 1964.

Meyer, C. *Fast Cycle Time: How to Align Purpose, Strategy, and Structure for Speed.* New York: Free Press, 1993.

Michael, D. *Planning to Learn and Learning to Plan.* San Francisco: Jossey-Bass, 1973.

Miller, E. J. *Task and Organization.* New York: Wiley, 1976.

Mintzberg, H. *The Rise and Fall of Strategic Planning.* New York: Free Press, 1994.

Mirvis, P. "Organization Development: Part I—An Evolutionary Perspective." In W. A. Pasmore and R. Woodman (eds.), *Research in Organizational Change and Development.* Vol. 2. Greenwich, Conn.: JAI Press, 1988.

Morgan, G. Images of Organization. Newbury Park, Calif.: Sage, 1986.

Morin, E. "From the Concept of System to the Paradigm of Complexity." *Journal of Social and Evolutionary Systems,* 1992, *15*(4), 371–385.

Morley, D. "Frameworks for Organizational Change: Towards Action Learning in Global Environments." In S. Wright and D. Morley (eds.), *Learning Works: Searching for Organizational Futures.* Toronto: ABL Publications, 1989.

Morley, D., and Trist, E. L. "A Brief Introduction to the Emerys' 'Search Conference.'" In E. L. Trist and H. Murray (eds.), *The Social Engagement of Social Science,* Vol. 2: *The Socio-Technical Perspective.* Philadelphia: University of Pennsylvania Press, 1993.

Morley, D., and Wright, S. "Epilogue: Organizational and Contextual Change." In S. Wright and D. Morley (eds.), *Learning Works: Searching for Organizational Futures.* Toronto: ABL Publications, 1989.

Neilsen, E. *Becoming an OD Practitioner.* Englewood Cliffs, N.J.: Prentice-Hall, 1984.

Neumann, J. E. "Why People Don't Participate in Organizational Change." In R. Woodman and W. A. Pasmore (eds.), *Research in Organizational Change and Development.* Vol. 3. Greenwich, Conn.: JAI Press, 1989.

Ong, W. *The Presence of the Word.* New Haven, Conn.: Yale University Press, 1967.

Ong, W. *Orality and Literacy: The Technologizing of the Word.* London: Methuen, 1982.

Owen, H. *Open Space Technology: A User's Guide.* Potomac, Md.: Abbott, 1992.

Pasmore, W. A. *Designing Effective Organizations: The Sociotechnical Systems Perspective.* New York: Wiley, 1988.

Pasquero, J. "Supraorganizational Collaboration: The Canadian Environmental Experiment." *Journal of Applied Behavioral Science,* 1991, *27*(1), 38–64.

Pateman, C. *Participation and Democratic Theory.* Cambridge, England: Cambridge University Press, 1970.

Pepper, S. *World Hypotheses.* Berkeley: University of California Press, 1942.

Perlmutter, H., and Trist, E. "Paradigms for Societal Transition." *Human Relations,* 1986, *39,* 1–27.

Peters, T. *Thriving on Chaos.* New York: Knopf, 1988.

Pines, M. *Bion and Group Psychotherapy.* New York: Routledge & Kegan Paul, 1985.

Purser, R. E., and Montuori, A. *Social Creativity.* Vol. 2. Cresskill, N.J.: Hampton Press, 1996.

Purser, R. E., and Pasmore, W. A. "Organizing for Learning." In R. Woodman and W. A. Pasmore (eds.), *Research in Organizational Change and Development.* Vol. 6. Greewich, Conn.: JAI Press, 1992.

Rehm, R., Schweitz, R., and Granata, E. "Water Quality in the Upper

Colorado River Basin." In M. Weisbord (ed.), *Discovering Common Ground*. San Francisco: Berrett-Koehler, 1992.

Reich, R. "Entrepreneurship Reconsidered: The Team as Hero." *Harvard Business Review*, May-June 1987, pp. 77–83.

Rioch, M. "The Work of Wilfred Bion on Groups." In A. D. Colman and W. H. Bexton (eds.), *Group Relations Reader I*. Washington, D.C.: Rice Institute, 1975.

Sampson, E. "The Debate on Individualism: Indigenous Psychologies of the Individual and Their Role in Personal and Societal Functioning." *American Psychologist*, 1988, *43*, 15–22.

Sampson, E. "The Challenge of Social Change for Psychology: Globalization and Psychology's Theory of the Person." *American Psychologist*, 1989, *46*, 914–921.

Sandel, M. "The Procedural Republic and the Unencumbered Self." *Political Theory*, 1984, *12*, 81–96.

Schein, E. *Process Consultation: Its Role in Organization Development*. Reading, Mass.: Addison-Wesley, 1969.

Schwartz, E. *Overskill: The Decline of Technology in Modern Civilization*. New York: Ballantine, 1971.

Schwartzkoff, J. "Participation in Geelong." *Community*, 1974, *2*, 1–7.

Selznick, P. *Leadership and Administration*. New York: HarperCollins, 1957.

Senge, P. *The Fifth Discipline: The Art and Practice of the Learning Organization*. New York: Doubleday-Currency, 1990.

Simmonds, W.H.C. "The Nature of Futures Problems." In H. A. Linstone and W.H.C. Simmonds (eds.), *Futures Research: New Directions*. Reading Mass.: Addison-Wesley, 1972.

Stalk, G., and Hout, T. M. *Competing Against Time*. New York: Free Press, 1990.

Sullivan, R. "Bion's Experiences in Groups: The Original Work, Its Theoretical Roots in the Ideas of Klein, and Its Practical Application in the Search Conference Methodology." Unpublished paper, Chicago: Center for Organization Development, Loyola University, 1995.

Suzuki, D., and Knudtson, P. *Wisdom of the Elders*. New York: Bantam Books, 1994.

Taylor, F. W. *Principles of Scientific Management*. New York: HarperCollins, 1911.

Toffler, A. *Future Shock*. New York: Bantam, 1970.

Trist, E. "A Concept of Organizational Ecology." *Australian Journal of Management*, 1977, *2*, 161–175.

Trist, E. "New Directions of Hope: Recent Innovations Interconnecting Organizational, Industrial, Community, and Personal Development." *Regional Studies*, 1979, *13*, 439–451.

Trist, E. "Referent Organizations and the Development of Inter-Organizational Domains." *Human Relations*, 1983, *36*, 269–284.

Trist, E. "Intervention Strategies for Interorganizational Domains." In R. Tannenbaum, N. Marguiles, F. Massarik, and Associates (eds.), *Human Systems Development: Perspectives on People and Organizations.* San Francisco: Jossey-Bass, 1985.

Trist, E., and Emery, F. E. "Report on the Barford Conference for Bristol/ Siddeley, Aero-Engine Corporation." Document no. 598. London: Tavistock, 1960.

U.S. Department of Housing and Urban Development. *A Guidebook for Community-Based Strategic Planning for Empowerment Zones and Enterprise Communities* (HUD-1443-CPD). Washington, D.C.: Government Printing Office, 1994.

Vaill, P. "The Purpose of High Performing Systems." *Organizational Dynamics,* Autumn 1982, pp. 23–39.

Vickers, G. *The Art of Judgment: A Study of Policy Making.* New York: Basic Books, 1965.

von Bertalanffy, L. "The Theory of Open Systems in Physics and Biology." *Science,* 1950, *3,* 23–29.

Walzner, M. *Citizenship and Civil Society.* Rutgers, N.J.: New Jersey Committee for the Humanities Series on the Culture of Community, 1992.

Weatherford, J. *Indian Givers.* New York: Crown, 1988.

Weisbord, M. (ed.). *Discovering Common Ground.* San Francisco: Berrett-Koehler, 1992.

Weisbord, M., and Janoff, S. *Future Search Conference Version 3.1.* Philadelphia: SearchNet Mailing, July 1994.

Weisbord, M., and Janoff, S. *Future Search.* San Francisco: Berrett-Koehler, 1995.

Wiener, N. *The Human Use of Human Beings.* Boston: Houghton Mifflin, 1967.

Williams, T. "The Search Conference in Active Adaptive Planning." *Journal of Applied Behavioral Science,* 1979, *15,* 470–483.

Williams, T. *Learning to Manage Our Futures.* New York: Wiley, 1982.

Wolin, S. *The Presence of the Past: Essays on the State and the Constitution.* Baltimore: Johns Hopkins University Press, 1989.

Wright, S., and Morley, D. (eds.). *Learning Works: Searching for Organization Futures.* Toronto: ABL Publications, 1989.

Yankelovich, D. *Coming to Public Judgment: Making Democracy Work in a Complex World.* Syracuse, N.Y.: Syracuse University Press, 1991.

Ziegarnik, B. "Über Behalten von Erledigten und Unerledigten Handlungen," *Psychologische Forschung,* 1927, *9,* 1–85.

Index